THE STATE AND THE MONETARY SYSTEM

Kevin Dowd

St. Martin's Press
New York

First published in the United States of America in 1989

Printed in Great Britain

ISBN 0–312–03509–8

Library of Congress Cataloging-in-Publication Data
Dowd, Kevin.
  The state and the monetary system / Kevin Dowd.
    p. cm.
  Bibliography: p.
  Includes indexes.
  ISBN 0–312–03509–8
  1. Banks and banking. Central. 2. Free banking. 3. Banks and
  banking—State and supervision. 4. Monetary policy. I. Title.
HG1811.D68 1989   89–34681
332.1—dc20   CIP

Contents

Preface   vii

1 The Free Banking Controversy   1
  1.1 Introduction   1
  1.2 Background to the Controversy   2
  1.3 Issues at the Centre of the Controversy   6
  1.4 How a Free Banking System Might Operate   7
  1.5 Outline of the Rest of the Book   10
  Notes   14

2 The Stability of the Banking System Under Free
  and Central Banking   16
  2.1 The Problem of Bank Panics   16
  2.2 'Bubble' Explanations   17
  2.3 Incomplete Information Explanations   18
  2.4 The Regulatory Explanation   23
  2.5 Over-Issue in Central and Free Banking Systems   43
  Notes   48

Appendices to Chapter 2   54
  Appendix 1: The Theory of Deposit Insurance   54
  Appendix 2: Free Banking and the 'Real Bills' Doctrine   60

3 The Problem of Monetary Policy   66
  3.1 Introduction   66
  3.2 The Problem Defined   67
  3.3 Monetary Policy and Welfare   68
  3.4 How Monetary Policy Affects Private Agents   69
  3.5 Are There Macroeconomic 'Externalities'?   75

iii

3.6 Monetary Policy as a Means of Taxation   78
Notes   81

4 An 'Ideal' Monetary System   **84**
4.1 Introduction   84
4.2 Externalities   85
4.3 The Natural Monopoly Argument   90
4.4 The Medium of Account (MOA)   92
4.5 The Early Evolution of the Monetary System   93
4.6 The Development of the Banking System   94
4.7 An 'Ideal' Monetary System   96
Notes   103

Appendices to Chapter 4   **108**
Appendix 1: Counterfeiting   108
Appendix 2: The 'Separation' of the MOA and the MOE   109
Appendix 3: Legal Tender   110
Appendix 4: The Future of the Monetary System   112
Appendix 5: Competition, the Rate of Return
   and the 'Optimal Quantity of Money'   113

5 The Establishment of Central Banking   **117**
5.1 Introduction   117
5.2 The Early History of the Bank of England   118
5.3 The Development of Free Banking in Scotland   120
5.4 British Controversies Over Central Banking   124
5.5 The Early History of Banking in the USA   130
5.6 The Free Banking Period   135
5.7 The National Banking System   141
5.8 Some Conclusions   146
Notes   146

Appendix to Chapter 5
The Controversy Over Scottish Free Banking   **152**

6 The Historical Experience of Central Banking   **160**
6.1 Introduction   160
6.2 The Monetary Regime at the Turn of the Century   161
6.3 The Monetary Regime After the First World War   163
6.4 The Keynesian Philosophy of Monetary Policy   166

CONTENTS

6.5 The Great Depression   168
6.6 Monetary Policy in the Postwar Period   172
6.7 The Great Inflation   174
6.8 Central Banks and Economic Instability   176
Notes   176

7 Reforming the Monetary System   179
7.1 The Problem of Political Money   179
7.2 The Free Market Versus Central Planning   184
7.3 Depoliticising the Supply of Money   185
7.4 An Agenda for Reform   187
7.5 Free Banking in an International Context   193
7.6 Establishing Free Banking   193
Notes   195

Bibliography   196

Author Index   207

Subject Index   210

Preface

This book argues that there is nothing fundamentally different about money to justify the unique kind of state intervention into its provision, represented by our current systems of central banking. Such a viewpoint implies that money and the industry that provides it, the banking system, can be understood using the same kinds of analytical tools which we apply to other commodities and the industries that produce them. This in turn implies, I believe, that many of the problems which are normally considered peculiar to the monetary system are not in fact inherent to it, but are instead the product of that intervention. Amongst the most important of these are the problems of the excessive volatility of prices and interest rates, and the vulner-ability of the banking system to major crises. If this is correct, then we should be thinking about how to dismantle the apparatus of state intervention and establish a fully competitive monetary system instead.

Whether other economists accept this conclusion or not, it is important at least to agree on what the key issues are so we can explain where and why we disagree. The supporters of central banking need to explain why money is different, and what that implies for the role of the state in the monetary system. They need to do this not only to respond to the challenge posed by free banking, but also to clarify for themselves exactly what they support about state intervention in the monetary system, and why they support it. My own experience, though, is that if one thinks about it long enough, it eventually becomes apparent that there is nothing fundamen-tally different about money at all. This comes as a shock at first, and one's initial reaction is that that can't be right. This reaction only reflects our upbringing, however, since we have all been brought up to take the 'necessity' of central banking more or less for granted. Nonetheless, that necessity really is an illusion — the emperor *does* have no clothes. Once one appreciates this, the superiority of free banking becomes intuitively obvious — if free trade is best, and money is no different from any other commodity, then free trade in money must also be best, at least in principle. One then begins to wonder what a *laisser-faire* monetary system would look like, how it could be established, and how we ended up with central banks. This is what this book is about.

It is a pleasure to acknowledge the valuable assistance I have had from many people in putting this together. I should first like to thank Philip Allan for publishing it and Kathy Wilson for a fine editing job. Thanks also to Patricia Wilson and Lyn Everest for their research assistance. I should like to thank Catherine England, Jack Gilbert, Mervyn Lewis, John Murray, Tony Sampson, Larry White and John Zube for their kindness in reading various drafts and giving me their comments. These have improved the final product very substantially. John Murray's comments, in particular, were extremely helpful and led me to overhaul the first version completely. I am also very grateful to Charles Goodhart, at the London School of Economics, for the many valuable comments which he has made to me in correspondence over the past two years, and which have helped considerably to clarify and correct my ideas on the subject. I should also like to thank Peter Brimelow, Forrest Capie, David Glasner, Gary Gorton, George Kaufman, George Selgin, Kurt Schuler, Chris Tame, Richard Timberlake and Larry White for sending me various papers and manuscripts which have helped me enormously. I am also grateful to Mark Billings, Dave Chappell, Derek Chisholm, Alec Chrystal, Brian McCormick, Tom Courchene, Jack Gilbert, David Laidler, Tony Sampson, Chris Tame and Mike Walker for various discussions or other feedback on free banking, which have done much to straighten out my thinking on the subject.

On a more personal level, I would like to thank Dave Chappell, Duncan Kitchin and Tony Sampson for much advice and encouragement since I returned to England. I should also like to acknowledge, with much gratitude, a special debt to Basil

Zafiriou at the Library of Parliament in Ottawa. Apart from his consistent support and friendship over the past eight years, he also helped me to resolve my initial doubts about free market economics and in the process taught me a great deal of my political economy.

My greatest debt, though, is to my family for everything, and to Mahjabeen Khaliq for all her support and encouragement, and for helping me to see that there is much more to life than just economics. I would therefore like to dedicate this book to her.

Kevin Dowd
University of Nottingham
October, 1988

1

The Free Banking Controversy

Might not a proper Currency be secured by leaving the business of banking wholly free from all legislative interference?
Sir Henry Parnell (1827)[1]

1.1 Introduction

The purpose of this book is to explore some of the issues raised by the idea of a *laisser-faire* monetary system. The feasibility and desirability of such a monetary system — free banking — are topical and very controversial issues. My basic theme is that free trade in money is beneficial for much the same reasons that free trade in other goods is generally beneficial, and that most of the criticisms levelled against it are either unsound or exaggerated. I suggest that free banking is not only a technically feasible system, but also an economically efficient and highly stable one with a good historical track record — features which make it superior to our current monetary regime characterised by extensive state intervention.

We also examine the history of this intervention to explain how and why it occurred and the effects it has had. We shall see how the state, at first, intervened to raise revenue, but then a 'logic of intervention' took over in which additional interventions were thought to be necessary to correct the problems caused by earlier interventions — problems which were mistakenly attributed to the 'free' market. The book then examines our

1

options for monetary reform and outlines a programme to dismantle the apparatus of state control and allow market forces to establish a sounder and more efficient monetary system.

1.2 Background to the Controversy

It has been aptly said that there is nothing new in economics. So it is with free banking. In the early and mid-19th century there were vigorous controversies about it in Britain, the USA, and France.[2] The proponents of free banking argued that there was nothing special about the business of banking to make it an exception to the general rule, that the best way to provide a product was through free competition. They therefore advocated the suppression of state restrictions to open up the banking system to free competition. In making this case they were supported by the ideological climate of the day, which was generally sympathetic to the principles of free trade and *laisser faire*. They also had the benefit of a practical example — the experience of free banking in Scotland until 1845 — the success of which seemed to vindicate their claims and confound their opponents. The latter maintained that such a banking system could not work but were never able to explain convincingly why it appeared to work so well in Scotland.[3]

Nonetheless the free bankers lost the controversy. In one country after another the machinery of state intervention in the monetary system was consolidated and strengthened, and the framework of a note monopoly and bank regulation was established which subsequently developed into our present systems of *central banking*. Controversy came to focus on what form intervention should take, not on the more fundamental question of whether there should be intervention in the first place. In the process, the old free banking controversies were pushed into the background and gradually forgotten. Free banking was driven underground and came to be regarded as one more fringe movement with unsound ideas on monetary reform.[4]

Even the strongest supporters of *laisser-faire* in other fields came to accept that a state-sponsored monopoly of the note issue was an indispensable condition for monetary stability, and it became an accepted part of the folklore of the subject that control over the note issue was necessary, because private issuers had no incentive to restrict their issues (e.g. Friedman 1960). It was argued that under competitive conditions money would be produced until its value was driven down to its marginal cost, and since the marginal cost of printing an extra dollar bill was trivial, this could only mean that producers would vie with each other in producing so much of it that it would become virtually worthless. The result of this 'literal paper standard' would therefore be a monetary explosion. It seemed to follow from this that some sort of external limit had to be placed on the note supply.[5]

Central banking was established in an environment in which the convertibility of the currency into gold was taken for granted. The need for a convertible currency was widely accepted until the First World War, but when the war came most countries went off gold, and attempts to restore convertibility afterwards ran into fierce opposition. A gold standard was restored, but there was much reluctance in some countries (e.g. the USA and Britain) to accept the constraints on domestic monetary policy which it implied. This opposition severely weakened the restored gold standard and it collapsed when the international financial crisis hit it in 1931. In the meantime, the movement to subject external policy goals like convertibility to domestic policy goals gained further ground, and there was no serious attempt to restore the gold standard in the 1930s. According to the new Keynesian philosophy, the major policy concern had to be the reduction of unemployment, and among other things, this required that the central bank have a freedom of manoeuvre that it could not have on the gold standard. The role of the central bank was now to manipulate interest rates and credit to help 'manage' the macroeconomy, not to maintain convertibility into gold.

The heyday of Keynesian 'policy activism' lasted until the early 1970s. By that time it was becoming obvious that something was wrong. Inflation had become a serious problem and the Keynesian remedy of wage and price controls did not work. It was also becoming more difficult to maintain the exchange rate parities of the postwar Bretton Woods system because each country wanted to pursue a different rate of monetary growth. The exchange rate system finally collapsed in the early 1970s when countries like Germany and Japan refused to go along with the inflationary policies of the USA. The breakdown of the Bretton Woods system gave many countries the full monetary independence they had been hankering for, and a number of them embarked on 'dashes for growth' that produced high inflation but no demonstrable gains in terms of unemployment or higher growth. It had become obvious that Keynesianism had failed, and government after government was forced to embrace the only apparent alternative — monetarism — and get inflation under control again by curtailing monetary growth. Governments had been reluctant to adopt monetarist policies because they involved temporarily higher unemployment and interest rates, but these policies did eventually succeed in bringing inflation back down.

The failure of the experiment with Keynesianism led to a reaction against policy activism and more limited views of what government could be expected to achieve. At the forefront of this reaction was Milton Friedman's (1968) analysis of the limits of monetary policy which maintained that the effects of monetary policy on 'real' variables like output or unemployment were merely temporary, and that the only long-run effect of monetary policy was on the inflation rate. This suggested that the inflation–output trade-off on which Keynesian policy had come to be based did not exist in the long run. The Keynesian claim that monetary policy helped to stabilise the economy was also undermined by the historical analysis of Friedman and Schwartz's *Monetary History of the United States* (1963) which suggested that monetary policy had actually added to monetary instability rather than reduced it. The realisation that there was no long-run inflation–output trade-off, and the historical evidence of destabilising monetary policy, led Friedman and others to advocate that the central bank should give up trying to fine tune the economy and follow instead a 'fixed rule' that would guarantee a low and stable rate of monetary growth.

The emphasis was now on minimising the scope of central bank discretion and on the fixed rules it could follow to make its actions as predictable as possible for the private sector. Then came the *rational expectations revolution* which stressed that monetary policy worked (i.e. influenced people's behaviour) by 'fooling' people into making decisions against their own best interests due to a lack of information; and this lent further support to Friedman's recommendation that monetary policy should be as predictable as possible. The rational expectations approach also directed attention to the institutional structure in which private agents operate and form their expectations, and it stressed the effects of changes in institutional structure on the expectations and actions of the public. The emphasis was now on the choice between different institutional structures rather than the choice of particular policies within a given institutional environment.

Such an emphasis was reinforced by the growth of interest in *public choice* economics in the 1970s. This was based on the premise that governmental institutions and the people who work in them have their own private interests, and that the behaviour of government could only be understood in the light of those interests. The public choice approach was intellectually attractive because it brought the government within the ambit of standard economic analysis, and it implied that one could not bring in the government as a kind of costless, disinterested *deus ex machina* to deal with problems to which one could think of no other solution. One could no longer assume that the government was interested solely in the public interest because governmental institutions had private interests of their own. The implied policy problem — if that is an appropriate way to describe it — was to design institutional structures which provided incentives for the individuals working within them to promote the broader social interest.

This, then, was the background which led to the revival of the free banking controversy. The failure of Keynesian policies provoked a reaction against activism and a shift towards fixed rules to make central bank policy predictable. Work on rational expectations and public choice then emphasised the importance of institutional structure, its effect on private agents and, most importantly of all, the extent to which it harmonised (or failed to harmonise) the private interests of the individuals within it and the social interest. The problem for prospective monetary reformers was therefore to design an institutional framework for the monetary system that most effectively harmonised the interests of the agents operating in it. The usual solution economists recommend to problems of this kind is to establish the conditions for a market to arise. It was therefore natural for people to wonder whether the problems of the monetary system had a market solution. If they had, then we might be able to dispense altogether with central banks and the systems of monetary regulation that went with them. In this way the controversy over free banking began to revive again after over a hundred years of appearing to lie dormant.

1.3 Issues at the Centre of the Controversy

It is fair to say that the free banking controversy has concentrated on four general areas:[6]

(1) *Competition in the provision of media of exchange* Among other issues in this general area, there is the question of the limits to the note issue under competitive banking, whether competitive banks of issue would guarantee price stability, the costs to the public of having competing notes (e.g. the costs of counterfeiting, or discriminating between different notes), and the question of economies to scale (and a possible natural monopoly) in the note-issuing business.

(2) *The convertibility of the currency* The main questions that arise here are whether banks under *laisser faire* would (or should) issue convertible notes and, if so, with what media they would (or should) redeem them. There is also the question of the resource costs of convertible and inconvertible currencies.

(3) *The unit (or medium) of account* Perhaps the main issue which arises here is whether competitive banks would provide the economy with a unit (or medium) of account, and what role, if any, the state should play in this. Related to this is the question of the relationship between the medium of exchange and the unit (or medium) of account, and whether they could or should be 'separated'.

(4) *Stability issues* The principal issue here is the causes of banking instability. Depending on one's answer to this,

someone must then decide:

(i)   whether there should be restrictions on bank activities;
(ii) whether the state should sponsor any liability–insurance schemes; and
(iii) whether there should be a lender of last resort, and what rules it should follow if there is.

There is also the issue of the consequences of free banking for the stability of the banking system, and whether free banking is more or less prone to cause macroeconomic instability than central banking.

1.4 How A Free Banking System Might Operate

A preliminary answer to some of these questions may be given by explaining how a free banking system might operate. This would also elucidate the principal features of the free banking system put forward in this book.

In the system presented here, banks would be allowed to issue any liabilities they wanted, subject only to the constraint that they persuade the public to accept them of their own free will. This leads directly to the first major characteristic of this free banking system, which is that *competition would force the banks to make their notes convertible*. This answers the first question about convertibility. It also implies that there is no necessity for the state to compel banks to make their notes convertible.

To see why a bank would issue convertible notes, one only has to consider how a bank would encourage someone to hold its notes. The problem is to persuade a prospective noteholder that the note would retain its value; the solution is to make him a legally binding guarantee of the future value of the note. Convertibility does just that. This being so, a bank that issued a convertible note would have a competitive advantage over one that did not. Note also that, since entry would be free, the banks collectively would be unable to form a lasting cartel and abandon convertibility all together. If they tried they would encourage new entrants into the industry who would gain a competitive edge by offering convertible notes, and the banks would lack the legal means to keep these new competitors out. Apart from this, the banks who were members of the cartel would have an incentive to undermine it by offering 'tacit' convertibility to noteholders in order to gain an edge over their competitors. (This is what the Scottish free banks did during the Restriction period, for example; we discuss this in more detail in Chapter 5.) Either way the cartel would tend to break down and convertibility would be restored. This conclusion — that competitive banks would issue convertible notes — also seems to be supported by the weight of historical evidence, and there appears to be no historical instance of privately produced inconvertible currencies that have managed to last more than relatively short periods.[7]

It should also be pointed out that we cannot tell what kind of convertibility contract the banks would offer (i.e. we cannot predict in advance the conditions under which the banks would commit themselves to redeem their notes or the goods into which the notes would be convertible). Banks might make their notes convertible on demand, but there is no obvious reason why they should be compelled to,[8] or why the law should force them to redeem their notes with particular assets. Given our ignorance of what an *ideal* convertibility contract looks like, and the lack of any compelling reason to restrict people's choices, I suggest that the matter be left to the free market. This is probably the best procedure we have, not only to tell us what the most appropriate contract is, but to ensure that we get it as well.

This leads us to the next feature of our free banking system. *Given the fact that banks will choose to commit themselves to convertibility, then it is the need to maintain convertibility which forces banks to limit their note issue.* This is so because the circulation of convertible notes is limited by the public demand to hold them. That demand will depend on factors like the kind of convertibility contract the bank offers, the familiarity of its notes, the bank's reputation, the number of branches it has, the availability of alternatives, and so on. Any notes issued beyond the demand to hold them as determined by those factors would simply be returned for redemption, since the notes would not remain in circulation for long enough to justify the expense of putting them out and taking them back again. If a bank wanted to increase the circulation of its notes it would have to do so by promoting demand — advertising more, opening more branches, and so on — but it could not do so simply by putting more notes out. It is one matter to *put* more notes into circulation, but it is quite another to *keep* them there.

Then there is the question of the unit (or medium) of account. (Strictly speaking, it is more precise to talk of the medium of account rather than the unit of account because the point at issue is not the unit — whether we should be talking of dollars rather than cents — but the commodity in terms of a unit of which prices are expressed. I shall therefore refer to the medium of account in future when the point at issue is the commodity rather than the particular unit in which it is measured.) We shall go through these issues in more detail in Chapter 4, so I will give only preliminary answers here. One question that arises is whether the free market would provide itself with a medium of account. Following White (1984a), I suggest that the market did provide itself with a commodity-medium of account (usually gold), but the state converted the original gold dollar into an intrinsically worthless fiat one by intervening first to monopolise the note supply and then to sever the convertibility link between the notes and gold. I suggest that the fiat medium of account that this created is unsatisfactory because of the price instability it has often caused in the past and might cause again in the future. At the same time, the private sector could not easily introduce an alternative because no one would have an incentive to bear the costs of persuading the public to switch over to it. In any case, there would be very substantial adjustment costs if the public did switch over. I therefore suggest that the existing medium of account — the dollar, the pound, or whatever — should be redefined in terms of an intrinsically valuable commodity-bundle. The economy would therefore work with a modified version of the medium of account it already has, but one that was chosen to make prices stable.

This completes our sketch of how a free banking system might work and my mostly preliminary answers to some of the issues raised a few pages ago. Most of the others will be dealt with in later chapters. This introductory chapter finishes with a brief outline of the rest of the book to give the reader a 'road map' to guide him through the sometimes involved discussions that follow.

1.5 Outline of the Rest of the Book

We begin in Chapter 2 by analysing the stability of the banking system under *laisser faire* and central banking. There are three schools of thought on banking instability. The first is the 'bubble' explanation, which sees instability as caused by bank runs which are essentially random phenomena triggered off by economically irrelevant events (e.g. sunspots). The second is the incomplete information explanation of Gorton (1985c, 1987) and Goodhart (1985). This view associates banking instability with bank runs, seen as rational responses by depositors who are imperfectly informed of the state of the banks' balance sheets. We shall see that both of these explanations have serious weaknesses. The third explanation attributes banking instability to state intervention which suppresses the automatic stabilising mechanisms that would otherwise evolve in the free market. These interventions take many forms: they include restrictions on the note issue, restrictions on banks' role as financial intermediaries, state-sponsored liability insurance schemes, the use of the monetary system to raise revenue for the state, and the operation of a lender of last resort.

We then discuss the over-issue of notes under conditions of *laisser-faire* banking and a monopolised note issue. There are two major checks against over-issue under *laisser faire*: the presentation of notes for redemption by the public, and the return of notes via the note-clearing system. The return of notes through the clearing system is likely to be a particularly rapid and effective check against over-issue, but it is totally absent when the note supply is monopolised, and whether or not the first check still operates depends on whether the currency is convertible or not. We therefore conclude that note issues are likely to be more stable under *laisser faire* than with a monopoly note issuer. The chapter finishes with appendices dealing with the theory of deposit insurance and the relation of free banking to the 'real bills' doctrine.

When the note supply is monopolised there arises the question of what the note issuer should do: this is the monetary policy problem which forms the subject of Chapter 3. We shall see that no monetary policy is Pareto-optimal because of the monopoly which gives rise to the problem of finding a monetary policy in the first place, and this implies that monetary policy can deliver only a 'second-best' outcome at most. We then examine what a second-best monetary policy might be. We find that it should make prices as predictable as possible and that it should be time-consistent (i.e. the monetary authority should honour its word). We go on to investigate whether there might be macroeconomic externalities that could enable one to defend the discretionary regime despite these drawbacks. I shall argue that no plausible case has been made for such externalities and that the current regime is therefore indefensible, even if one accepts the need for a monopoly bank of issue. Finally, we investigate whether monetary policy should be used as a means of taxation, and I suggest that it is not a desirable tax to use even if the alternative is to raise taxes that distort economic activity.

Chapter 4 deals with some other issues relating to state intervention in the provision of money. We start with the argument that state intervention into the provision of media of exchange can be defended because of transaction costs externalities, confidence externalities, or information externalities. We shall see that a plausible case for intervention on these grounds has yet to be made. We then examine 'natural monopoly' arguments for state intervention and suggest that they can be dismissed as well. After explaining the role of the 'medium of account' in a well-functioning monetary system, we are in a position to explain the roles of the media of exchange and the medium of account in an 'ideal' monetary system based on the principles of unrestricted competition, a convertible currency, and a commodity-definition of the medium of account. We can then outline how such a system might be established. The chapter ends with some appendices which deal with related issues not directly discussed in the main text. These are: (i) whether counterfeiting would be a problem with a multitude of different notes; (ii) whether *laisser faire* would lead to a separation of media of exchange and the medium of account as claimed recently by Greenfield and Yeager (1983); (iii) legal tender; (iv) some issues raised by the prospective future evolution of the banking system; and finally, (v) how banks compete away the excess profits from issuing notes.

We then leave the theory and turn to the history of state intervention in the banking system to explain how our present monetary systems evolved and the role of the state in that evolution. Chapter 5 deals with the establishment of central banking and begins with the early history of the Bank of England. Throughout the 18th century the Bank bought a series of legal privileges from the Government which undermined the rest of the banking system and left it prone to serious crises. By contrast, the Scottish banking system of the same period was almost totally unrestricted, and it was both very advanced and apparently highly stable. (The Scottish banking system has provoked a lot of controversy, however, and we review this in an appendix at the end of the chapter.) We then come to the British monetary controversies of the early 19th century about the role of the Bank and the attempt of the free banking school to abolish the Bank's privileges. The attempt failed, however, and the final outcome was the consolidation of the Bank's note monopoly and the suppression of Scottish free banking. These measures failed to cure the monetary instability to which the English banking system was prone, but the Bank's monopoly position seemed firmly established and the agitation for free banking faded.

We then turn to the USA. The early history of banking in the USA was characterised by repeated but abortive attempts to set up a government bank. After the third of these failures the Federal Government withdrew from the banking system and cleared the way for individual states to introduce 'free banking' laws. These were generally successful and free banking gradually spread through the Union. At this point, however, the Civil War broke out and the federal government intervened once again to establish the National Banking System. The restrictions imposed on the banking system destabilised it and caused frequent crises, and the search for a solution to these problems eventually led to the establishment of the Federal Reserve System.

It is interesting to note that British and US monetary histories show the same basic themes despite many differences of circumstance and detail. In both countries the government's desire for revenue was a major reason for intervening in the monetary system, and this created problems which appeared to require further intervention to deal with them. This set in train a vicious circle of ever-increasing intervention fed by the unintended side effects of earlier interventions. The British and US monetary experiences are also similar in that both countries witnessed successful experiments with relatively unrestricted banking; these were eventually suppressed for essentially political reasons.

Chapter 6 deals with the historical record of central banking. When central banking was first established, it was at a time when central banks' freedom of manoeuvre was severely restricted by the need to maintain convertibility into gold. We discuss how the commitment to gold was badly shaken by the First World War and the experience of the restored gold standard of the 1920s, and how the discipline of the gold standard was seen increasingly as an unnecessary hindrance to the successful pursuit of domestic policy goals. Inappropriate monetary policies then led to the Great Depression of the 1930s, which in turn led to a further bout of monetary regulation and encouraged the acceptance of Keynesian ideas of economic interventionism. After the Second World War the major central banks established a cartel to manage the world economy. This eventually broke down because of the incompatible objectives of different member governments, but not before it produced a major inflation that discredited Keynesian economics and focused attention on the need for a stable monetary framework. As we mentioned earlier, the search for such a framework led, in turn, to the re-opening of the free banking controversy.

The last chapter deals with monetary reform. We review the problems caused by a politicised money supply process and the reasons why the 'monetary policy problem' is fundamentally intractable. I suggest that the choice we face is essentially that between free banking and tinkering with the present regime. If we maintain the current regime, then we would almost certainly face the eventual collapse of the anti-inflationary coalition on which it depends to work even tolerably well. We would also face the likelihood of an eventual banking crisis when luck runs out for the lender of last resort, as it probably will in the end. It seems to me that the only way to avoid these problems is to dismantle the apparatus of state intervention and allow market forces to provide us with an efficient and stable monetary system. We then suggest how that might be done.

Notes

1. Quoted in White (1984b), p. 62.
2. The British controversies are discussed in MacLeod (1896), Smith (1936), Viner (1937), Mints (1945), Fetter (1965) and White (1984b). The US controversies are covered in Smith (1936) and Selgin and White (1987), and the French controversies are dealt with by Smith (1936) and Nataf (1987).
3. The attempts of even eminent opponents of free banking to explain its success have sometimes been extremely unconvincing. Jevons (1875, p. 319), for instance, once said that 'If we were all Scotchmen, I believe the unlimited issue of one-pound notes would be an excellent measure' and proceeded to explain that the one-pound note worked in Scotland because of the superior Scottish banking system (!), while John Stuart Mill is said to have dismissed the issue 'with the somewhat curious conclusion, that free note issuing is very good north of the Tweed, but very bad south of it' (Wesslau 1887, p. xi). One is reminded of Sir Walter Scott's comments (1981) on those who wished to extend the English ban on £1 notes to Scotland in the 1820s:

> *Here* stands theory, a scroll in her hand, full of deep and mysterious combinations of figures, the least failure in any one of which may alter the result entirely, and which you must take on trust . . . *There* lies before you a practical System, successful for upwards of a century. The one allures you with promises, as the saying goes, of untold gold, — the other appeals to the miracles already wrought in your behalf. The one shows you provinces, the wealth of which has been tripled under her management, — the other a problem which has never been practically solved. Here you have a pamphlet — there a fishing town — here the long-continued prosperity of a whole nation — and there the opinion of a professor of Economics, that in such circumstances she ought not by true principles to have prospered at all. (pp. 184–5)

4. For instance, free banking continued to be widely debated in Britain, in the generation after the passage of Peel's Acts; thereafter, the free banking tradition was carried on by a group of libertarians and

anarchists which included O. E. Wesslau, A. E. Hake, B. Tucker and H. Seymour. The last in this tradition is Henry Meulen whose *Free Banking: An Outline of a Policy of Individualism* came out in 1934.
5. Other arguments for state intervention that appear to have been widely accepted at the time they were put forward were based on: '[i] the resource cost of a pure commodity currency and hence its tendency to become partly fiduciary; [ii] the peculiar difficulty of enforcing contracts involving promises to pay that serve as a medium of exchange and of preventing fraud in respect to them; . . . and finally, [iii] the pervasive character of money which means that the issuance of money has important effects on parties other than those directly involved . . .' (Friedman 1960, p. 8, my numbers). My response to these is as follows. The resource cost argument (i) ignores the value of the convertibility guarantee to the public, and as Friedman (1986) himself later pointed out, there are substantial resource costs with an inconvertible currency. Regarding (ii), Friedman fails to explain why it is more difficult to enforce bank-note contracts than it is to enforce other contracts (e.g. deposit-contracts). He seems, however, to have accepted this point subsequently (Friedman and Schwartz 1986, p. 51). And regarding (iii), he fails to explain why 'monetary third party effects' are sufficiently different from other pervasive third party effects to justify the state intervention they are supposed to justify.
6. These issues have been distilled from King (1983), Fischer (1982, 1986), Goodhart (1985), Friedman and Schwartz (1986) and Laidler (1986, 1987), each of whom gives some indication of what he considers some of the main issues to be.
7. This is also the opinion of Friedman and Schwartz (1986, p. 45).
8. In fact, I see a very strong reason why convertibility on demand should not be imposed: it would prevent banks from issuing notes with *option clauses*. Option clauses are potentially very useful because they enable banks to protect their liquidity if they are faced with a sudden large demand for redemption. They are discussed further in Chapter 2.

2

The Stability of the Banking System Under Free and Central Banking

The past instability of the market economy is the consequence of the exclusion of the most important regulator of the market mechanism, money, from itself being regulated by the market process.

(F. A. Hayek 1976b)[1]

2.1 The Problem of Bank Panics

Bank panics occur when a public rush to redeem bank liabilities threatens the solvency of the banking system. They are a cause for concern, not only because they threaten the liquidity of the banking system and cause the public to question the soundness of their exchange media but also because they disrupt the information-gathering and market-making functions of the financial system (see, for example, Bernanke 1983, Benston *et al.* 1986). A panic raises the costs of this sort of financial intermediation and makes credit expensive to obtain. This higher cost of credit is not accompanied by any corresponding increase in the inducement to save or to extend credit, however, and the resulting squeeze on credit cuts into economic activity generally. In this way, a severe panic can cause a major recession.

Now, let us investigate what causes panics and whether there should be some form of state intervention to protect the banking system against them. There are three schools of thought to be considered and we shall discuss each in turn.

2.2 'Bubble' Explanations

The first school of thought maintains that bank panics are akin to speculative bubbles. A modern version of this is by Diamond and Dybvig (1983), but the underlying idea goes back a long way. This type of explanation is superficially plausible because it seems to account for the 'mob psychology' that is often observed during panics. Its main characteristic is that prophecies are often self-fulfilling — that is, any factor which makes people anticipate a panic will cause a panic, however intrinsically irrelevant that factor might be (e.g. sunspots). Proponents of this view draw the conclusion that the state needs to stand by in the last resort to support the banking system from collapse. Explanations of this type have the following features:

(1) Banks operate on a fractional reserve so that they are unable to redeem all their liabilities at once without notice.
(2) Banks are obliged to redeem on demand, and they attempt to do so using an exogenously given 'first come, first served' rule.
(3) The public knows that the banks cannot redeem their liabilities at once, and it is concerned to avoid capital losses.

As a result 'individual depositors have an incentive to "beat" runs and [this is what distinguishes bubble explanations from others, K.D.] *anything which happens causing them to anticipate a panic causes the panic.'* (Gorton 1985c, p. 191, my italic).

There are two major problems with this type of explanation. The first is that it relies on a 'first come, first served' rule to generate the panic, but it fails to explain why banks operate such a rule in the first place. If banks have much to lose from runs, then one must wonder why they choose to operate a rule that leaves them so exposed. One needs to explain convincingly why they fail to insert 'option clauses' into their note contracts or time clauses into their deposit contracts to protect themselves by giving them time to liquidate their assets. The bubble explanation for bank runs is therefore, at best, a partial one because it leaves unexplained an important and relevant feature of bank behaviour.

An additional problem — as Gorton (1986) points out — is that the hypothesis that panics are unpredictable is untestable because it is consistent with any possible observed behaviour. If this hypothesis is correct, however, one would expect to observe something at panic dates that is absent at other times — like outbursts of sunspots. Gorton (1986) tests for this using a data set characterised by repeated bank panics (the USA during the late nineteenth century) and finds no evidence of special events at panic times. This suggests that they are not random events and undermines the plausibility of the speculative bubble explanation.

2.3 Incomplete Information Explanations

The second school of thought states that bank panics are caused by depositors' lack of knowledge of the net worth of banks. This kind of explanation has been put forward by Gorton (1985c, 1987) and Goodhart (1985). The basic idea is that bank runs occur when depositors get 'noisy' signals which suggest that banks may be insolvent. Gorton argues that because they do not observe the state of banks' investments, depositors:

> use a noisy indicator to form rational expectations of deposit return rates. A banking panic can be triggered by a movement of the indicator, causing depositors to withdraw all their deposits because of fears of capital losses. (p. 178)

The difference between this explanation and the previous one is that the indicator that causes the panic in this case is an economically relevant one, i.e. it conveys information — albeit imperfect — about the state of the bank's portfolio. In the previous case any variable at all could cause a bank run, provided only that it made depositors anticipate one. The run here is therefore 'rational' in a way that the speculative bubble one is not. This does not imply that the signal turns out to be correct after the event, of course, only that it is rational to rely on it *ex ante*. If it does give a correct signal that a bank is insolvent, then the depositors will act on it, withdraw their deposits and close it down. In that case, the bank run will have served a socially useful purpose in closing down an insolvent bank (see, for example, Kaufman 1987). It is possible, however, that the signal may indicate that a bank is insolvent when it is not, and this will lead depositors to close down a solvent bank — a situation to be avoided.

Gorton goes on to infer that this 'information externality' leads the banks to suppress the free market and regulate themselves. The gist of the argument (of Gorton 1987) can be summarised as follows:

- There exists a secondary market in notes, and the price of a bank note (in terms of specie) in that market gives an indication of the state of the bank's balance sheet.
- Because cheques are agent-specific as well as bank-specific the information costs of operating a secondary deposit market are prohibitive. Therefore no such market develops and the banks simply agree to accept cheques drawn on each other at a fixed rate of exchange between cheques and reserves.
- Over time, there is a gradual move towards deposits and away from notes as media of exchange.
- As a consequence, the secondary note market, which reveals the price of bank notes, is gradually replaced by a cheque-clearing system in which the price of deposits in terms of specie is fixed. The public is therefore deprived of a source of information — the secondary note market — and the free market provides no substitute.
- This information gap leads to the possibility that there might be a bank run when banks are sound. In order to stop this, the banks will co-operate to regulate themselves. They will, for example, form a deposit clearing system and delegate extensive regulatory powers to the clearing house. Among these will be the power to impose interest rate ceilings and minimum reserve and debt–equity ratios, and the power to suspend convertibility and issue 'emergency'

currency. A system of regulation — including a lender of last resort — will thus emerge spontaneously to counter the information deficiencies of the free market. To summarise, according to this view, *'regulation' was not something imposed on the banking system from without, but something that evolved spontaneously from within.*

There are a number of problems with this analysis. First of all, one might question Gorton's emphasis on the note and deposit markets to signal a bank's value. A more appropriate market to indicate a bank's value is surely the stock market. This is because the equity market values each bank individually, and because equity holders as residual claimants have a strong incentive to monitor the behaviour of bank managements. Knowing this, the noteholders would not need to duplicate their effort — all they would need to do is check that the stock market gave the bank a positive value. (The banks could also issue other forms of subordinated debt whose holders would have an incentive to monitor them.) In short, the stock market and perhaps, other markets as well, would provide the noteholders with the signal they needed regardless of the existence of a secondary note market.[2]

Second, it is not clear that the gradual superseding of notes by deposits would actually deprive the public of any information. There are reasons to believe that the secondary note market might also be 'internalised' within the banking system like the secondary deposit market: the marginal cost of setting up a note exchange is presumably lower than the costs of operating an 'independent' note broking industry, so we might expect that the banks would have a comparative advantage over note brokers and eventually drive them out of business. This appears to have happened, for instance, with the Scottish banking system and the relatively free Suffolk system in New England in the early 19th century. Once the note exchange is established the price of notes would be fixed at par, and the 'note market' would cease to convey any useful information to noteholders. Notes only superseded deposits after that, so it is difficult to see how that process would have deprived the public of useful information about the net worth of individual banks.[3]

A third problem is that Gorton's explanation of the cartelisation and gradual endogenous regulation of the banking system is unconvincing. Provided that there are no restrictions on entry, it is implausible to argue that a coalition of banks could arrange anything that was not in the private interests of each member. Cartels tend to be stable only when individual members have an incentive to abide by the cartel's rules. Membership of a clearing association would satisfy that condition if each bank reckoned that the demand for its own deposits would rise because of the willingness of other banks to accept cheques written against it. The same cannot be said for other measures discussed by Gorton such as reserve requirements, interest ceilings, and minimum capital ratios. To see this, consider the position of any individual bank faced with some restriction imposed on it by the clearing house association — either the restriction alters the bank's behaviour or it does not. If it does not, then the restriction is irrelevant for that bank. If it does, then it obviously constrains the bank from doing whatever it would have preferred to do. This means the restriction is not in the bank's own private interest, and the bank has an incentive to avoid it. Banks in this position could do this either by staying in the clearing house association and undermining the restriction, or by leaving the association and setting up a rival that did not make such demands. Either way, the attempts of the cartel to impose restrictions on its members would tend to fail. The weakness of Gorton's argument is that it fails to explain why member banks chose to submit to controls that were not in their individual interests.

Fourthly, and finally, Gorton's model makes predictions which are not borne out by the experience of other countries. The process of deposits superseding notes apparently occurred in all countries in the nineteenth century. If this led the US banking system to evolve into a cartel which regulated itself, then why did this process not occur in countries like Canada (for most of the nineteenth century), Scotland (up to 1845) and Sweden (1831–1902), which also saw a displacement of notes by deposits and were relatively free from state control? The answer, I suggest, is that the US banking system evolved the way it did not from any endogenous information-inadequacy problem, but because of state interference. (This argument is developed in the next section.)

I turn now to Goodhart's explanation (1985, 1987a). Like Gorton, he argues that depositors face a problem of distinguishing between 'good' and 'bad' banks under conditions of imperfect information. Nonetheless, he acknowledges that such problems:

> of informational inadequacy are not unique to banking, but occur quite commonly, notably in the provision of services . . . In particular the difficulty, and cost and effort, involved in trying to distinguish between better, and worse, purveyors of a service is a common problem. It occurs, for example, with the choice . . . of doctors, lawyers, teachers, stock brokers, sellers of insurance, etc, etc, as well as with bankers. (p. 28)

The difference between banks and other firms is that banks have a relatively larger proportion of non-marketed — or non-marketable — assets in their portfolio, but their liabilities are fixed in nominal value. He then concludes:

> So, the main criterion for determining whether Central Bank services are needed is the existence of maturity transformation, though transformation of a rather special kind. *If it is much easier and quicker to transfer the liabilities of a class of financial intermediary from one such institution to another, or to a substitute form of liability, than it is to transfer the assets held by that institution, then there is a need for a lender of last resort, providing Central Banking functions.* (p. 33, my italic)

To get this conclusion, Goodhart maintains, first, that the maturity transformation of banks leaves them open to the danger of illiquidity, and second, that the illiquidity of one bank poses a danger to others because of the possibility of 'contagion' (i.e. that when depositors see one bank fail they will run on others). He argues that these factors forced the Bank of England and other monopoly banks to adopt lender-of-last-resort functions and to regulate the banking system.

Goodhart's analysis is open to similar objections as Gorton's: he underrates the role of the equity market in signalling a bank's net worth, he fails to establish why the information asymmetry would produce instability (e.g. he fails to show why monitors could not arise to bridge the gap); and he fails to explain why banks choose not to undermine the process of 'endogenous regulation' that binds them. His argument also relies on bank runs being inherently contagious, but the reasons why they might be are not made particularly clear. Nor is it clear why the existence of this 'special kind of maturity transformation' necessitates a lender of last resort. Experience would teach banks how to handle their reserves to protect themselves, the terms on which additional reserves can be obtained at short notice, how they can discourage liability-holders from demanding redemption, and so on. There is simply no obvious need for a lender of last resort on top of that. In addition, in my opinion at least he fails to give convincing explanations for the success of the Scottish, Canadian and Swedish experiments in free banking.[4]

2.4 The Regulatory Explanation

According to the third school of thought, bank runs are caused by regulations which are imposed on the banking system by outside agencies. This is the regulatory explanation put forward by the free bankers. The gist of the explanation is that the market would protect itself from bank runs if it were unrestricted and allowed to do so, but it is prevented by outside interference. The free bankers do not deny that there are information imperfections,[5] but they differ from the previous school of thought in denying that they are the root cause of bank runs. For the free bankers the *sine qua non* of bank runs is outside (i.e. state) interference in the monetary system.

The argument to be developed has two main stages. First, we need to show that there are no particular reasons for bank runs to occur under free banking, but that a free banking system could cope with them even if they did. Second, we need to show how state interference actually destabilises the banking system and makes bank runs both more damaging and more likely.

Banks have to guard themselves against two types of risk: insolvency risk and illiquidity risk. The former is the risk that a bank's net worth becomes negative, and is a risk that banks share with all privately owned businesses. The latter is the risk that a bank might default on a legal obligation to redeem its notes or deposits. This can happen even if the bank is otherwise solvent, and is a risk more peculiar to banks.

To protect itself against the former a bank will endeavour to pool its risks — that is, to construct a diversified portfolio in which prospective fluctuations in asset values are likely to cancel each other out — to minimise fluctuations in the overall value of its portfolio. Of course, if the bank's net value was revealed to be negative then the creditors would run on the bank and close it down. The question, though, is whether an observation that one bank is insolvent or in serious difficulties would lead to runs on others or on the banking system as a whole. For that to happen, there must be some mechanism that makes a run on one bank potentially contagious.[6] *Gorton's work suggests that runs of this sort might occur if there is no market to price each bank's individual value. In that case an observation that one bank was in difficulties might lead note or deposit holders at other banks to conclude rationally but erroneously that the other banks were insolvent as well. However, this contagion mechanism depends crucially on the missing market, and disappears if a market arises that can price individual banks' values.* The work of Gorton and Haubrich (1986) suggests that a market in bank equity or a secondary market in bank loans would suffice to fill the gap. Since both types of market actually exist, and bank equity markets have existed for some time, it would seem that the information asymmetry argument is not a plausible explanation for bank runs that might occur in the near future or may have occurred in the recent past.

The relative 'unimportance' of runs as causes of bank failure seems to be confirmed by a number of other studies. For example, George Kaufman (1987, pp. 12–13) reports:

> a study for the American Bankers' Association in the late 1920s was summarized by a reviewer as relegating 'the run as a real reason for [bank] suspensions . . . to a position of minor importance. It is found to be an effect of banking difficulties rather than a cause as a general proposition which is contrary to the fixed ideas of the public and even many bankers'. The evidence also suggests that the primary direction of causation was from problems in the real sector to problems in banking and not the other way round. That is, both bank runs and bank failures were the effect and not the cause of aggregate economic contractions and hardships. . . . [He goes on to suggest that:] . . . The reasons for the failure of the runs on individual banks

or groups of banks to lead, with only infrequent if any exception, to runs on all banks, despite the absence of an FDIC, appear to be explained by the the combined effect of greater market discipline on bank management and more timely closure of individual banks when they became insolvent. . . . The very threat of a run served as a powerful source of market discipline. (loc. cit.)

Evidence to the same effect is also presented by Benston *et al.* (1986, pp. 53–60, 66). Among other instances, they note that bank failure rates in the USA in the late 19th and early 20th century were generally lower than for other firms (p. 58), and one would not have expected this had runs been contagious. They also point out (p. 60) that even in the crisis of 1907–8 — the most severe crisis in the pre-Federal Reserve period — less than 1 per cent of banks failed and this 'casts doubt on the contagiousness of the failures in this period.'[7]

We turn now to illiquidity risk. In principle, banks could always protect themselves by choosing to operate as 'warehouses' in which there was no danger of illiquidity because they operated a 100 per cent reserve ratio. But in this situation the banks would be unable to lend, and they could only make profits by charging depositors' fees for looking after their deposits. While such banks might be able to survive under free banking, historical experience suggests that most depositors seem to prefer fractional reserve banking because such banks can pay them interest on their deposits (instead of the fees that 100 per cent reserve banks would have to charge them to cover their expenses). However fractional reserve banks cannot redeem all their liabilities at once without notice, and this leaves them open to at least the danger of illiquidity. In practice, such banks would trade off the extra profits to be obtained from lending out reserves against the greater risk of being caught short of liquidity and being forced to pay some penalty, and experience over time would teach them how to deal with this. Granted, then, that we are dealing with at least some banks on fractional reserves, we have to explain, (a) how they would protect themselves against the danger of illiquidity, (b) whether or not the prospect of illiquidity can lead to a bank run, and if so, (c) how the banks could cope with it.

At this stage we need to distinguish clearly between two different types of bank run — *deposit runs*, in which the public rushes to convert deposits into notes, and *note runs*, in which they rush to redeem notes for *specie*. Historically, note runs were prominent in the early stages of banking, but virtually all runs since the mid-19th century have been deposit runs. Before we discuss these issues, however, we need first to define our terms clearly. For our purposes, a 'deposit' is simply a liability of a bank that the bank can redeem with another of its liabilities called a 'note', and a 'note' is a bank liability that has to be redeemed with an outside asset which I call 'specie'. We can think of 'specie' as an asset that can be used for non-transactions purposes outside the banking system and which cannot be produced by the banking system. A 'deposit run' is therefore a situation in which the public rush to convert one form of bank liability into another, while a 'note run' is a situation in which they rush to convert bank liabilities into an outside medium of redemption. The analysis of course applies to deposits, notes, and so on, as we understand them, but it also applies to any other assets — whatever we might call them — that fit the descriptions just given. The reader should keep these points in mind throughout the following discussions.

We will consider deposit runs first.[8] When these occur there is a sudden, but temporary demand to convert deposits into notes.[9] The shortage of liquid assets will be reflected in the very short-term ('overnight' or 'fed funds') liquidity market. The sudden demand for liquidity will temporarily drive up the overnight interest rate to a level well above normal. This means that bill prices will fall but be expected to rise again later. There are therefore capital gains to be had from buying bills (i.e. selling liquidity), and the greater the interest rise the larger the prospective gains. These gains can be made by anyone prepared to sell liquidity, but the banks have a particular advantage because they can create it at will. Provided only that the deposit run does not turn into a note run, they could temporarily create whatever extra liquidity they wanted simply by issuing more notes. (If the run does turn into a note run the analysis changes, but we will discuss the pure deposit run first.) As long as bill prices remain below normal the banks would have an incentive to issue additional notes with which to buy bills in the anticipation of their price rising. This would effectively stop bill prices from falling and force them to return to normal. Once that had happened the banks would realise their capital gains by selling the extra bills they had bought. In the process they would buy back the extra notes they had created and retire them. The banks would then revert to their normal operating rules and the run would be 'cured'.

In short, if any deposit run were to start, the banks would have an incentive to create the liquidity to correct it. The free market could therefore deal with a deposit run quite effectively. Furthermore, the knowledge that banks could create whatever liquidity was needed to restore interest rates to normal would almost certainly prevent runs from starting in the first place. Any rational speculator would realise that the banks would intervene once interest rates started to rise, and he would anticipate that this would restore interest rates to normal. The chances of making a profit by betting against the banks which could create notes at will would be considered minimal, and the risks of capital losses would be very high. A typical speculator would therefore have much to lose and little to gain from feeding a panic. He would instead try to anticipate the banks' intervention by buying bills himself. In this way the very anticipation of the banks' intervention can lead speculators to bet against the panic and thereby prevent it gaining momentum. It is therefore difficult to see why a deposit run should even arise under *laisser-faire* conditions.

We now deal with note runs. These occur when note holders rush to convert notes into specie. If the banks operate on a fractional reserve then they could not redeem all their notes at once without prior notice; nor is it possible simply to create specie at will (as it is to print notes to deal with a deposit run). This is the fundamental difference between a note run and a deposit run. Of course, an individual bank might be able to obtain specie from the free market and if it could alleviate a shortage of reserves in this way then all would be well. However, if the run is on the banking system as a whole then all the banks will be short of reserves and they might be unable to obtain sufficient reserves on the market. (Alternatively, the banks might conceivably be able to import specie from abroad, but this might be difficult to do at short notice, and it would be impossible at the level of the world economy. I shall ignore this possibility to focus on the extent to which the domestic free market could help itself.) If the banks are obliged to redeem on demand without notice, it follows that there is always the possibility that they might be unable to satisfy a sufficiently large demand for redemption, and this would expose them to the legal penalty for default. We will assume that this is sufficiently high for the banks to wish to avoid it.

The banks would avoid this possibility by relaxing the convertibility contract. Instead of binding themselves to redeem on demand without notice, they would insert an 'option clause' into the contract giving them the option to defer redemption for a pre-specified period provided that they pay a pre-specified rate of interest on those notes whose redemption was deferred. If a note run then occurred which they could not otherwise meet, the banks could avoid default by invoking their option to defer redemption. We must now explain, (a) the mechanics involved when option clauses are invoked, and (b) why the public would be willing to hold option-clause notes when other banks would be ready to provide them with fully convertible notes if they wanted.

Let us assume, for the sake of argument, that option clause notes are being held by the public and try to answer the first question. For the sake of simplicity, let us also assume that all the note-issuing banks issue notes with identical deferment periods and compensatory interest rates.[10] Now, suppose that there is a note run (i.e. the public rush to convert notes into gold): the sudden demand for gold will be reflected by a rise in the overnight gold interest rate, that is, the interest rate on bills promising to pay gold in the immediate future. The price of these 'gold bills' will therefore fall. The choice facing the banks is whether to satisfy the demands for redemption and, if necessary, to borrow reserves on the overnight market to do it, or whether to suspend redemption, which would relieve the immediate pressure on their reserves and enable them to use their reserves to speculate on the overnight market. We should recall that their sole aim would be to maximise their profits, and they would suspend convertibility whenever doing so furthered that aim. In order to choose the most advantageous moment to do so, they would need to look only at the overnight gold market: it would not be worthwhile for the banks to suspend while the interest rate in that market was less than the compensation rate they would have to pay by suspending. When the gold interest rate exceeds that level, however, the potential revenues from suspension would exceed the costs and it would be worthwhile to suspend. This cut-off point is when the gold interest rate has risen to the implicit interest rate the banks would have to pay if they suspended redemption.

Consider now the position of other market operators. Most would presumably expect the bill price to return eventually to 'normal' levels. They would therefore reckon that there are profits to be made in the short-to-medium term by betting against the run and buying bills cheaply to hold them until their price is restored to normal. However, they are likely to have different opinions about the precise point at which the price fall would stop and reverse itself. Some would prefer to take their medium-term profits while others — the bears — would take a chance on further price falls before the market corrected itself. As the price falls further, the potential profits to be made by taking the medium-term view increase, and those who continue to feed the run by betting on further price falls take an increasing risk of missing the turning point and suffering losses. At some point the market would break, the bear speculators would lose their nerve and bill prices would be restored to normal levels. On average, those who fed the panic by selling bills cheap would pay the price and those who bet against the panic and helped stabilise it would make capital gains.

Without the benefit of option clauses it is possible that interest rates might rise to very high levels, and the banking system might ultimately run out of reserves and default. Option clauses not only prevent this, but their prospective use, as interest rates rise, would itself encourage other market operators to take a bullish view and reverse the price fall. As the banks' intervention point approached, bear speculators would anticipate a sudden demand for bills that would steady the fall in their price, if not stop it altogether and reverse it. Furthermore, bear speculators would be nervous in any case about when the market would 'break' and correct itself and the banks' prospective intervention would encourage many of them to cut and run. The very prospect of the banks' intervention is therefore a potent force which is quite likely to break the panic. In this way option clauses can stabilise note runs even if they are never invoked.

Having suggested reasons why option clauses would protect the banking system from note runs, the question is then whether the public would be willing to accept them. Since entry to the industry is free, the banks cannot form a cartel to impose option clause notes on the public against their will. If they tried and the public did not want them, then it would be worthwhile for competitors to set up rival banks in order to supply the public with the notes they wanted. The public must therefore be induced to accept them willingly if option clause notes are to circulate. At first sight, one might suppose that the public would always prefer notes that were convertible on demand to ones whose convertibility was restricted, but on closer inspection there are several reasons why they might prefer notes with the option clause:

(1) The noteholders would be compensated if a bank suspended convertibility, and this would help maintain the demand for them — and hence their general acceptability — during the suspension period. On the other hand, when a bank that issues fully convertible notes is forced to suspend, it would be in legal default of its obligations, the noteholders might receive no compensation for the inconvenience, and consequently there may be some doubt about the value and general acceptability of the notes.
(2) The presence of option clauses would reassure risk-averse noteholders that they would lose little or nothing if they failed to be first in line in a note run, and this would relieve them of much of the pressure to participate in one.
(3) As explained in the previous paragraph, suspensions are less likely to occur when banks have the benefit of option clauses because speculators would be less willing to take a bear position as the prospective suspension approaches.

These considerations suggest that option-clause notes benefit note holders because suspensions are less likely and they are less costly when they do occur. (For further discussions of these issues, see Chappell and Dowd 1988 and Dowd 1988d.)[11] It is therefore reasonable to suppose that the public might accept them.

This completes our discussion of how banks under *laisser-faire* conditions are able to protect themselves from runs. We have suggested that a *laisser-faire* banking system is not inherently prone to bank runs and can handle them even if they do occur. This suggests that the instability we observe historically is due to outside (i.e. state) intervention. The principal forms of intervention have been: restrictions on the note issue, restrictions on the role of banks as financial intermediaries, compulsory membership of note and deposit insurance schemes, the use of the monetary system to raise revenue, and the operation of a lender of last resort. We shall now consider each of these in turn.

Restrictions on the Note Issue

We have seen that if deposit runs occur, and banks are free to do so, they can deal with them simply by printing extra notes to satisfy the increased demand for currency. The banks would readily do that in order to make capital gains from the temporarily low price of bills, and they would sell the bills and retire the notes as the crisis subsided. *Restrictions on the note issue are potentially destabilising because they interfere with this mechanism by which the free market would automatically correct a deposit run.*

There are a number of ways in which the note issue has traditionally been restricted. One way is to give a single bank a monopoly; this is destabilising in several respects. To begin with, it creates the need for a lender of last resort, and this is potentially destabilising because it replaces the quasi-automatic free market ajustment mechanism with an alternative which is much less reliable. When a deposit run occurs under a monopoly note regime only the monopoly bank can create additional notes to satisfy the demand. Normally, however, the monopoly-central bank will be trying to keep control over the supply of notes and bank reserves (i.e. 'base money'), or else it will be trying to maintain the exchange rate, and an appropriate response will usually require it to make a conscious decision to depart from its normal policy and create the additional base money needed to satisfy the higher demand for it. Whether it wants to be or not, the monopoly bank is responsible for the solvency of the banking system because only it can create the additional notes which may be needed in a crisis. It must therefore develop a set of rules to carry out this responsibility. In short, the *monopoly bank of issue is forced into the role of lender of last resort precisely because it has a monopoly*. The operation of a lender of last resort function can destabilise the banking system in various ways, but we shall defer our discussion of them till later in the chapter. Suffice it at this point simply to note that its potential to destabilise the banking system arises because no lender of last resort policy can match the quasi-automatic response of the free market.

The granting of a note monopoly also destabilises the note issue in that it removes an automatic check on over-issue — the note-clearing system — that would have arisen spontaneously had the note issue been unrestricted. We shall discuss this in more detail in the section on over-issue, but the main point is that when a competitive bank of issue over-expands its notes, it will face reserve losses at the regular clearing sessions between the banks, and these losses will force it to correct its policy. A monopoly note issuer faces no clearing process and so an over-issue of notes takes longer to correct, and can do more damage in the meantime.

State intervention in the note issue has seldom stopped at restricting the note issue to a monopoly. The monopoly itself has often had its note issue restricted, and this can limit its ability to respond appropriately to a sudden increase in the demand for notes. One such restriction is the requirement that banks redeem their notes on demand. As discussed earlier, this is potentially destabilising because it deprives banks of the protection of option clauses and thereby leaves them vulnerable to note runs. The public's knowledge of that in turn makes runs more likely.

Another example of destabilising restrictions on a monopoly note issue is provided by the 1844 Bank Charter Act in the UK. This Act gave the Bank of England an effective monopoly of the note issue, but it also divided the Bank into an Issue Department (responsible for the note issue) and a Banking Department (responsible for the rest of the Bank's business), and these two departments were to be entirely separate from each other. The principal purpose of these measures was to prevent the Bank over-issuing notes (and thereby, among other things, preventing note runs). The effect was to leave the Bank wide open to deposit runs since the Banking Department had no access to additional notes (or specie, for that matter) if it were faced with a run on its deposits. This created the absurd possibility that the Bank of England might default on its obligations to redeem its liabilities despite the fact that the vaults of the Issue Department were full of gold. Three times subsequently — 1847, 1857 and 1866 — the Bank was faced with such runs and was only saved from failure when the Government intervened to allow the Bank to issue additional unauthorised notes.

A final example is from the USA. After the Civil War the note issue was effectively cartelised under the National Banking System and banks of issue were subject to various limits on their note issues. Deposit runs were very frequent but the banks' ability to deal with them was limited. These runs usually led to suspensions. Over time, however, the banks gradually evolved other means of dealing with these runs — in particular, the issue of clearing house loan certificates. At first these would be used only to settle clearing house balances — which released the reserves which would have been used in the clearing system — and as such they were legal. In the end, however, they were being issued to the general public for use as hand-to-hand currency, and this was widely acknowledged to be illegal. Ironically, however, the issuers were never prosecuted because everyone recognised their usefulness.

We have discussed how each of these restrictions exposes agents — usually holders of bank liabilities — to dangers that could have been avoided had the banks been allowed to take appropriate measures to deal with them. Precisely because of that, each of these restrictions increases the likelihood of the relevant mishap occurring. In each case the public would be more likely to demand redemption because they would have reason to doubt that the banking system could withstand the strain. Individuals would reason that if a crisis occurred, only the quickest would be able to redeem their notes or deposits, and they would be tempted to run as soon as they were sufficiently worried that other people might run first. This creates the possibility of 'self-fulfilling' bank runs — situations where (rational) people run on banks simply because they think that other people will. Thus restrictions on the note issue not only make bank runs more damaging when they do occur, but also make them more likely to occur as well.

Restrictions on Banks' Activities

Banks also sometimes face restrictions on their activities which weaken them in various ways and thereby expose them to a greater risk of failure. This seems to be a particular problem in the USA. One instance of this is the system of interstate and intrastate banking laws which, for the most part, restricts banks to operate within the state or county in which they are chartered.[12] This limits the scope for banks to reap the economies-of-scale benefits of a branch-banking system. Perhaps the most important of these benefits is the ability to diversify risks to reduce the chances of failure, but they also include the benefits of operating an *interbranch* reserve market. The principal advantages of an interbranch market are that the lender does not need to worry about the soundness of the borrower, and that it enables reserves to be held at lower cost. The ability of the interbank market to function as a substitute for branch banking requires, however, that interbank interest rates be allowed to equilibrate the supply of reserves and the demand for them. Unfortunately, for most of the period since the 1930s, the payment of interest on interbank deposits has been prohibited, and this 'crippled' the interbank system (O'Driscoll 1988, p. 174). The interbank market began to recover only with the development of the fed funds market and the recent relaxation of interest rate controls. A final effect of branching restrictions is that they: 'prevent an optimal deployment of equity capital in a banking system. Because individual bank exposures in a small bank often are geographically concentrated and relatively large when compared to its total assets, the small bank needs a higher equity capital ratio to protect itself . . .' (Ely 1988, p. 50).[13]

The ability of the branch-banking system to diversify risks and exploit economies of scale is well illustrated by the comparative experience of the USA and Canada during the 1930s. The Canadian banks' greater freedom had led to a stable branch-banking system with a few prominent nationwide banks, and Canada experienced no bank failures at all during the thirties. The US banking system, on the other hand, consisted of a multitude of small *unit banks* whose merger was restricted by laws against branch banking, and literally thousands of them failed. Ely (1988, p. 55) also points out that the Canadian banks were able to maintain branches 'smaller in terms of deposits and population per branch' than their US counterparts.

Another instance of the way in which restrictions on banks' activities can weaken them is provided by the American Glass–Steagall Act.[14] This separates commercial and investment banking by prohibiting deposit-taking institutions from trading in investment securities (equity and commercial paper). This has led to the growth of a dual banking system in the USA with *commercial banks*, which issue deposits but cannot deal in investments, and *investment banks*, which may deal in investments but may not issue deposits. Ironically, it was introduced in the belief that the combining of investment and commercial banking activities had contributed in a major way to the banking collapse of the early 1930s, but it actually increases the risk of bank failure by restricting banks' ability to diversify their portfolios.[15]

State-Sponsored Liability Insurance Schemes

A common response of states to the problems of banking instability that they themselves cause is to force banks to enter into state-sponsored liability insurance schemes. Proponents argue that holders of bank liabilities would be less likely to run on banks if they were insured against loss in the event of failure, and conclude that this would make the banking system more stable. This type of reasoning is superficially plausible but it is based on the questionable premise that runs are a cause of instability rather than a symptom of it. The essential problem with these schemes is that, though they may protect banks against runs in the shorter run, they have the side effect of encouraging policies more likely to produce failure, and so they tend to promote longer-run instability.

These schemes typically have several other weaknesses. The first is that they make no attempt to discriminate between different classes of liability or institution. Institutions that take more risks pay the same premiums as those that pursue safer policies. At the margin, a bank gets free insurance for any extra risks it takes — a clear inducement to take them. The more it takes, the more likely it is to fail so the system has the perverse effect of encouraging more failures. With deposit insurance, the pressure to take risks is intensified because those banks that take more risks have higher expected returns and can therefore offer higher interest rates to attract depositors. The latter have little incentive to monitor banks by withdrawing their deposits since they are already insured against loss. A natural check against excessive risk-taking — the threat of a bank run — is thus substantially eliminated. An aggressive bank can usually count on keeping its depositors simply by offering them a higher return in the knowledge that the public will show little concern about the risks it takes. These higher deposit rates will also put pressure on more cautious banks to raise their deposit rates in order to keep their depositors. As a result, they may feel obliged to cover their higher costs by taking more risks than they would otherwise have chosen to take. The failure to discriminate therefore encourages the banking system as a whole to take more risks, and this makes bank failures more likely.[16]

The second weakness of these schemes is that they are usually actuarially unsound. This implies that the insurance corporations must eventually go bankrupt themselves or be bailed out by the government. Either way there is an eventual crisis. If the insurance scheme does go bankrupt, some of the banks will suddenly find themselves deprived of a pillar on which they had come to rely — protection against bank runs — and they may not have sufficient time to rearrange their portfolios to reduce their exposure. The public would be understandably nervous, and a major bank run is then a very real possibility. Alternatively, the government could intervene to try to discourage a run by announcing some interim support package and assume the debts of the insurance corporation as well. In North America the liabilities of the main deposit insurance corporations are back-stopped by the federal governments, so the taxpayer has effectively assumed the burden already. The costs of this appear to be very substantial indeed. Some indication of these costs can be gleaned from the fact that, as of 31 December, 1983, after allowing for unrealised mortgage losses, the net worth of mutual savings banks and S&Ls alone in the United States was minus $96 billions (Kane 1985, Tables 4.5 and 4.6). Not all of this negative net worth represents a federal liability, of course, but since then these liabilities have mounted very considerably. A recent article in the *Miami Herald* (23 September 1988) gave an estimate of federal liabilities of $100 billion. To these losses must also be added the losses from the FDIC. To make matters worse, excessive secrecy and dubious bail-out operations mean that their liabilities are growing at an alarming rate — a situation described by one Congressman as a 'Constitutional Cataclysm' (*Miami Herald* 23 September 1988) of uncontrolled spending. Even if the US government can stop its losses escalating much further, the longer-term problem still remains of how to dismantle the incentives to excessive risk-taking without provoking a run on the more exposed banks in the process.[17]

A couple of examples will illustrate these points. In 1829 the safety fund system was set up in New York State. This scheme obliged banks to co-insure each other's note liabilities, but there was no regard for the riskiness of different banks' portfolios or the solvency of the safety fund system as a whole. The system was effectively bankrupted after the first wave of bank failures hit it in 1840–3, though the New York legislature managed to delay the formal collapse by coercing the other banks to prop the system up for a while. (For more on this episode, see King 1983.) More recently, insurance schemes were established in the USA and Canada (in 1934 and 1967, respectively) to insure deposit holders against bank failures, but once again, neither sought to make insurance premiums, or the system as a whole, actuarially sound. The bank failures of the early to mid 1980s made both effectively insolvent, but neither was legally bankrupt because the Governments of both countries were responsible for keeping them in operation. Besides the cost they had assumed, both governments still have the problem of dismantling the incentives to take excessive risks.[18]

The Use of the Banking System to Raise Revenue

Another cause of instability has been the state's use of the banking system as a source of revenue. History provides many examples of this. A notable example occurred in Britain in the the period 1793–7. At the time William Pitt's government desperately needed funds with which to finance the war against France, so it pressed the Bank of England repeatedly for loans. These seriously depleted its reserves, and rumours of French invasion in 1797 caused a run the Bank had not the resources to withstand. The Government then had to step in to save the Bank from failure by relieving it of its legal obligation to redeem its notes. Something similar happened in the USA at the start of the Civil War. In order to finance its expenditures the federal government issued large amounts of treasury notes which it obliged the banks to redeem in specie. The pressure of this and forced loans to the government proved too much for the banks' reserves, and the banks had to be allowed to suspend convertibility within a year. In both these cases, the governments' demand for revenue had destroyed the convertibility guarantee that protected the value of the currency. Governments have also tended to weaken banks by undermining their capital bases. This happened in some states in the USA during the so-called 'free banking' era before the Civil War: the free banks were obliged to back their note issues with certain eligible assets — generally state bonds — and this requirement exposed them to capital losses if the prices of these bonds fell. Some in fact fell very severely, and these losses appear to have contributed in a very large way to the 'free bank' failures. We shall return to each of these episodes again in Chapter 5.

The Lender of Last Resort

Finally, there is the question of the *lender of last resort* (LOLR). It has long been part of the folklore of the subject that without an LOLR it would be a case of 'every man for himself' in a panic with everyone trying to increase his liquidity at the expense of everyone else. The effort would be self-defeating and the banking system might easily collapse as a result. The solution, supposedly, is to have a centralised reserve — an LOLR — to be used in such emergencies. I suggested earlier that this argument is theoretically incorrect because a *laisser-faire* banking system has features that can handle bank runs more or less automatically: there is no question of everyone hoarding liquidity and letting the banking system dry up. We have also seen that the 'necessity' for the LOLR arises in the first place only because the monopolisation of the note issue suppresses the automatic stabilising mechanisms of the free market. Remove restrictions on banks and the problem does not even arise. One could also maintain that the argument for an LOLR is inconsistent with the historical evidence. The experience of relatively free banking — in Scotland, Canada, Sweden and, to some extent, the USA in its free banking period — appears to lend no support to the claim that systems without a state-sponsored LOLR are more prone to crises in which it is a case of 'devil take the hindmost', and liquidity dries up.[19] On the contrary, that experience strongly suggests that the banking system is quite capable of protecting its liquidity provided it is left free to evolve the means to do so.

We have given reasons to believe that an LOLR (which is state-sponsored) is quite unnecessary and that the *problem* to which the LOLR is a *solution* is best handled by relaxing restrictions against note issue.[20] This is an attractive solution because it leaves the problem to be solved by the market and imposes on no one in particular the responsibility to solve it. If we retain the note monopoly, however, then we are forced to develop an LOLR policy and deal with some of the problems this raises. The standard recommendation is given in Bagehot's advice to the Bank of England in 1873. As he put it:

> Theory suggests, and experience proves, that in a panic the holders of the ultimate Bank reserve . . . should lend to all that bring good securities quickly, freely, and readily. By that policy they allay a panic; by every other policy they intensify it . . . The end is to stay the panic . . . And for this purpose there are two rules: First. That these loans should only be made at a very high rate of interest . . . Secondly. That at this rate these advances should be made on all good banking securities, and as largely as the public ask for them . . . The only safe plan for the Bank is the brave plan, to lend in a panic on every kind of current security...

He then noted rather ominously: 'This policy may not save the Bank' but added by way of a sort of recommendation 'but if not, nothing will save it.'[21] Bagehot's view[22] — and this has now become standard central banking doctrine — was therefore that the holder of the 'ultimate reserve' (that is, the monopoly note issuer) should lend freely on all good security at a penal rate of interest, and he advocated this policy, not because it would always manage to allay a panic but because he thought it gave the best chance in the circumstances of surviving it.

However, there is another side to Bagehot's analysis of the LOLR problem. He also recommended that the Bank augment its reserves in 'normal' times to be able to withstand reserve drains during panics, but he gave relatively little specific advice on how it should do that. The Bank was to hold 'adequate' reserves, but it was not particularly clear what an 'adequate' level of reserves was, or how the Bank was to be encouraged to hold it. The problem is that there is no market on which the 'insurance' provided by the Bank is traded, and this means that there is no mechanism to ensure that the potential benefits of this insurance are properly appropriated. The presumption must therefore be that many of them are not. In principle, this means that reserves could be over-provided as well as under-provided, but there are several reasons to believe that the latter outcome is more likely.

We must bear in mind, for instance, that the Bank bears the full costs of holding reserves (i.e. in the form of foregone lending opportunities), but many of the benefits (for example, in the form of increased security) flow to others. If the Bank looks only at its own private interest and equates its marginal costs and benefits, then it will hold less than the socially optimal level of reserves. In effect, the protection afforded by the reserves has the *appearance* of an underprovided public good[23]. Perhaps public opinion or the threat of legislative intervention might encourage the Bank to increase its reserve holdings — though the history of the Bank of England in the 19th century does not necessarily bear that out — but until the effects of these factors can be established there must still be a presumption that reserves are too low. In addition, the Bank could also cut down its reserves in the almost certain knowledge that if it were faced with an imminent banking collapse the government might be forced to intervene to suspend convertibility or declare a banking holiday. The Bank also has the option of 'bribing' the government to bail it out in a crisis (e.g. in return for cheap loans, for instance) and it might be cheaper for it to 'buy' implicit insurance from the state in this way than it would be to hold explicit reserves which bear no interest.

In effect, the government and the bank can form a cartel at the public's expense and use the state's bailout powers to generate 'extra profits' (rents) that they can share out between them. For both these reasons, then, the LOLR could probably be expected to over-economise on the reserves it holds, and thereby leave the banking system under-protected against a crisis.

But there is another problem with Bagehot's rules which is perhaps even more important. The problem is that they conflict and there is no reliable way to resolve the conflict. As Rockoff (1986, pp. 160–1) says in a penetrating essay:

> The main problem . . . is this. There are really two Bagehots, even though we remember only one. There is, of course, the Bagehot who tells us to 'lend freely at high rates' in a panic, but there is also the Bagehot who tells us to 'protect the reserve' when the market is merely apprehensive. Both speak authoritatively, but to whom should we listen? It is here that Bagehot fails us, for nowhere does he supply an explicit guide for recognizing the state of the market that calls for one policy rather than the other. [The source of the problem is that:] . . . Bagehot's schema makes everthing depend on the Bank's 'psychoanalysis' of the market. If the Bank mistakes apprehension for real panic and lends freely, then the reserve will fall and the level of apprehension will rise. On the other hand, if the Bank mistakes panic for mere apprehension, the Bank will starve the market of funds and the panic will intensify. (p. 163)

Unfortunately, there are no set rules to tell the Bank when it is dealing with a 'panic' and when it is dealing with mere 'apprehension'. This is the fundamental weakness of the Bagehot rules. Everything hinges on the Bank using its judgement properly, but there is little to guide it and an ever-present danger that a misjudgement could provoke a major crisis. The banking system can only avoid the kind of crisis it is meant to prevent if the management of the LOLR has an unending run of good fortune. The real last resort is therefore a lot of very good luck.

This instability is aggravated even further by the banking system's likely response to the LOLR. As we mentioned earlier, the very existence of an LOLR involves an implicit — or, to be more precise, non-market — system of bank insurance, and this leaves considerable scope for moral hazard problems to arise. Banks might be tempted to take more risks because they might reasonably expect the LOLR to bail them out. They would appreciate that the LOLR would be reluctant to allow a bank failure — especially a big one — for a number of reasons. It would, for instance, be concerned about the possibility of the failure undermining confidence in the banking system and starting a bank run. It would also be acutely aware that public criticism of controversial decisions could lead to political intervention in its affairs which it would prefer to avoid. These worries about contagion and public criticism would encourage the LOLR to avoid difficult decisions, and it is almost always more difficult to refuse assistance and allow an institution to fail than to arrange a temporary rescue package and hope the problem goes away. Furthermore, a crisis will usually erupt quite suddenly and the LOLR will find itself forced to make a decision with very imperfect information on which to base it. This might also encourage the bank to err on the side of caution and put off a failure in any particular instance. These reasons would all encourage the banks to have a reasonable expectation of a bale-out if they got into difficulties, and this would be a strong inducement to take greater risks.[24]

The monetary authorities tend to respond to this moral hazard problem by trying to control banks' risk-taking activities. The result is a growth of regulation to define the limits of 'safe and sound banking' and to make sure the banks stay within them. The monopoly bank is then gradually transformed into a central bank with extensive regulatory powers. This growth of control seems to accompany all LOLR systems. In some countries — such as the UK and Canada — a considerable part of it tends to be informal and take the form of 'gentlemen's understandings' between the LOLR-central bank and the big banks. Much control is then exercised through the medium of what is curiously called 'moral suasion'. These arrangements are also backed up by an extensive explicit regulatory system, and no doubt much of the force of moral suasion comes from the knowledge that the Governor's requests can be backed up by further measures to which the offenders can be compelled to submit. In the USA, on the other hand, the smaller size of most banks makes the informal approach less feasible so there is a greater emphasis on explicit regulation backed up by legislation.

We have already discussed some of the effects of bank regulations. In their favour, it can be said that they might and probably would prevent some instances of excessive risk-taking; but against them, it must be said that they restrict banks' portfolio diversification and impose various other compliance costs on banks which can make them more liable to fail. One must also bear in mind that it is very difficult in practice for a regulator to distinguish an excessive risk from an acceptable one. The risk a bank takes with a project depends not just on the project itself, but also on the rest of the bank's balance sheet. To monitor risk properly, therefore, requires that the regulators monitor all bank activities, and evaluate clearly how each project affects each different bank. This is a massive undertaking, and it is not clear how the regulators could get the information to do it properly, or why they would have the incentive. In practice, regulation boils down to the application of more or less arbitrary rules of thumb. In any case, as markets get more sophisticated, banks can increasingly evade regulations by 'off-balance sheet' operations over which the regulators seem to have little control.

Markets appear to be finding loopholes in regulations at a much faster rate than the regulators can patch them up. At best, regulation is therefore a very imperfect and counterproductive way to handle the incentives to take excessive risks, which the existence of the LOLR creates. The only effective way to stop banks taking excessive risks is to eliminate the incentives for them to do so. That means eliminating the LOLR, and that in turn means eliminating the note monopoly which creates the need for the LOLR in the first place.

2.5 Over-Issue in Central and Free Banking Systems

We turn now to discuss the over-issue of notes. This has been a contentious issue since the early 19th century, with free bankers and central bankers each claiming that the system advocated by the other would weaken the discipline against the over-issue of notes. At the centre of the controversy is the free bankers' claim that the note-clearing system under free banking would provide an effective check against over-issue. Their basic argument is as follows.

Suppose that we start from an initial multi-bank equilibrium[25] and a particular free bank expands its note issue. It does this by expanding its lending, and placing additional notes in the hands of its new loan customers. Suppose, also, that it does nothing to raise its reserve holdings and that other banks continue to act as before. An individual with the additional notes can either redeem them, deposit them at another bank, or keep them as balances to spend. If he adopts the first course of action, the bank faces a direct loss of reserves. If he adopts the second, the bank with whom he makes the deposit will present the notes for redemption at the next meeting of the clearing house, and the issuing bank will face a reserve loss then. Adopting the third course simply means that the person from whom he buys will have the same set of decisions to make. If the bank is small, relative to the market, then most of the people who get the notes would have accounts at other banks, and most of the notes would be deposited elsewhere and returned to the issuer via clearing. The bulk of the reserve loss would therefore come through the clearing system, and the frequent clearings would imply that it would not take long for this loss to make itself felt. This would force the issuing bank to cut back its note issue to maintain its solvency. As Sir Henry Parnell put it in the 1820s: 'It is this continual demand . . . by the banks on one another, that gives the principal of convertibility full effect, and no such thing as an excess of paper . . . can take place for want of a sufficiently early and active demand for gold.'[26]

The proponents of central banking have sometimes claimed that the clearing house restraint on over-issue was an illusion. Perhaps the most famous example of this was the argument of Longfield (1840) which Smith (1936) summarised as follows:

> If one bank increases its issues by a given proportion, its business will increase in the same proportion, and therefore the larger amount of loan repayments it will have falling due in any week will give it the

same number of claims on rival banks as they have on it, so that no differences arise in the clearings and no claims on reserves. (p. 158)

From this he concluded that a bank which failed to expand would increasingly lose business to a competitor that did, and it would be forced to expand in self defence. An expanding bank could therefore drag others along with it. This is a weak argument because it presupposes that *lending more* is sufficient to increase the bank's note circulation.[27] This is not the case. The bank could certainly lend more, but if the public is not willing to hold the extra notes they will come back for redemption. As we have already seen, the bank can only increase its circulation if it increases the demand to hold its notes. Another weakness of this argument, as Smith pointed out, was that it ignored the strain on the expanding bank's reserves between its initial expansion and the repayment of its loans. A bank could only expand if it could withstand the interim loss of reserves.

To this Charles Goodhart (1985) responded that: 'neither Smith, nor apparently earlier economists, had considered the possibility of more thrusting banks seeking to prevent the clearing house losses that would result from rapid expansion *by making their liabilities relatively more attractive*' (my italic, p. 43). He then concluded that the 'market discipline imposed by a well-functioning clearing house . . . was not capable of preventing banking cycles and financial crises' (p. 9).

It seems to me that Goodhart's point about more aggressive banks making their liabilities more attractive might be correct, but it misses the main point. Let us suppose, for the sake of argument, that a bank expands its note issue and makes them more attractive at the same time. (How it would do that is problematical, however, because there are difficulties involved with paying interest on notes which we discuss below in the last appendix to Chapter 4.) It then invests the proceeds in additional loans. Let us also assume that the notes are sufficiently more attractive that demand for them increases to match supply, so the bank manages to avoid reserve losses. Making its notes more attractive will presumably raise its marginal costs. If we assume that the bank takes on marginally less attractive loans as it expands then its marginal revenue will fall.[28] If we assume that the bank was initially in a profit-maximising position then the combination of increased marginal cost and decreased marginal revenue will decrease its profits. *The fact that the bank could conceivably expand and remain liquid is beside the point; the bank would not choose to do so because it would reduce its profits.* The weakness underlying the clearing-house-discipline-is-illusory argument is therefore that it ignores the bank's own private interest.[29]

There is a related argument that also needs to be considered. This is the argument that competition among banks of issue is likely to make the note issue less stable. This is an old theme in the free banking controversies. A modern proponent of this view is Goodhart (1985). He cites approvingly the argument that: 'competitive pressures would drive the banks to seek to maintain and expand market share during normal [i.e. non-crisis] periods. Moreover, during such periods of normal business the more conservative banks would lose market share . . . [and] there was no guarantee that the more conservative banks could recover during panics and bad times the market share lost in good times (p. 59).' This process of bank expansion would therefore lead to a reduction in banks' reserve ratios, and at some point the banks would want to pull in their horns and protect themselves. This would then produce a crisis that would not have occurred but for the competition among the banks.

It seems to me that Goodhart's argument here is open to objections which are similar to those levelled at his argument against the discipline of the clearing system. It is one thing to suggest — validly, in my opinion — that a free banking system might experience cycles, but it is quite another to demonstrate that it would experience more pronounced cycles than an alternative central banking system. For the latter, he needs to focus on the difference in industrial structure and show precisely what enables the central banking system to dampen down the cycles that the free banking system would experience. Furthermore, he needs to show not only that a central banking system *might* be able to dampen down those oscillations, but also that we could reasonably *expect* it to as well. In my opinion he fails to do this. The argument that competition *per se* would create banking instability therefore remains unproven.[30]

We now turn to the free bankers' argument that central

banking is the less stable system. This is best illustrated by supposing that a monopoly bank of issue over-expands its notes. If its notes are convertible it will face reserve losses from noteholders demanding redemption, but not from clearing losses. (Since there is only one bank of issue, there is no note-clearing system.) Yet, as we saw earlier, a competitive bank that over-issued notes was likely to be checked sooner by the clearing system than by direct redemption alone. The difference between competitive and monopolised note issue is that this second, more effective discipline is lacking under central banking.[31] The situation with a monopoly bank of issue is comparable to what would happen under free banking if all the banks could form a cartel and expand their note issues together to prevent a note-clearing mechanism coming into play to discipline them. Eventually, of course, the pressure of direct redemption would suffice to stop them, but the process of checking the over-issue would obviously take longer.

With a monopoly bank there will therefore be a greater, and more persistent, over-issue before demands for redemption bring it into line. This, in turn, seems to imply that the over-issue will be that much more disruptive, and that interest rates, prices, and output will move further out of line before being checked by the bank's measures to counter its loss of reserves. This seems to be consistent with the historical experience of (relatively) free banking as compared with central banking. Countries that had relatively free banking systems — Scotland, Canada, Sweden and, to some extent, the USA before the Civil War — apparently experienced no major problems of over-issue, but a country like England, which had a heavily restricted note issue, experienced a series of monetary crises during the same period that destroyed a large number of English banks, and almost, on occasion, the Bank of England itself. These crises were associated with large fluctuations in interest rates, prices and the balance of trade in gold bullion — all symptoms of disturbances caused by over-expansions of notes.

We have so far assumed that the monopoly bank issues convertible notes. However, there is nothing to force a monopoly bank to make its notes convertible — by definition, the competitive pressures that force free banks to make their notes convertible are absent. Once people become used to using its notes, a monopoly bank can simply abandon convertibility and issue whatever notes it pleases. In practice, all that was ever required was a co-operative government willing to relieve it of the burden of redemption. As a matter of fact, no major central bank has issued even a nominally convertible currency since the collapse of the Bretton Woods system in the early 1970s, and even before then the discipline imposed by the exchange rate regime was weakened by periodic exchange rate changes caused by a general reluctance to sacrifice domestic policy goals to maintain the exchange rate. When notes are inconvertible there is nothing to stop over-issue: however many notes are issued, they can never be returned for redemption because they are not redeemable against anything else. Even the relatively weak restraints against over-issue that exist when the monopoly bank redeems its currency are totally absent, and we are all familiar with the consequences. Irving Fisher was all too right when he said that irredeemable paper money has usually proved a curse to the country employing it.[32]

Notes

1. Quoted from Hayek (1976b, p. 79).
2. In addition, there is no reason why private intermediaries could not arise to fill the information gap. Banks might employ outside monitors — 'auditors' — who could issue credible reports to the public. To be believed, these monitors would have to be independent, with reputations to defend. They might also accept extended liability for their reports to strengthen their credibility. Experience would presumably indicate the appropriate frequency of auditing, the circumstances in which *ad hoc* audits were called for, the information the auditors should look for, and so on. If there was a shock which affected a bank's value then the auditor could be called on to issue a report. If he considered the bank insolvent he would have to say so, and the bank's creditors could run on it. If he gave it a clean bill of health the public would be reassured and there would be no need for a run. Either way the problem of the information asymmetry would be solved and the appropriate outcome achieved. The problem of the public running on sound banks would then no longer arise.

   One might also note that government agencies do not have the same incentive to monitor efficiently (see, for example, Kane 1985, pp. 149–53 and Benston *et al.* 1986, pp. 205, 215, 253–4). Indeed, they have all too often been known to collude in 'cosmetic' accounting exercises that are intended to *mis*inform other agents about the state of banks' balance sheets. A recent example is the FSLIC's innovative accounting, designed to avoid the consequences of a straightforward admission of the scale of its losses. FSLIC officials refused to give congressional committees details of recent bale-out operations. These were said to be so shrouded in secrecy, according to the House Banking Committee chairman, that 'the intelligence committees should take lessons'.

3. Even if one accepts the information-carrying role of the note market, an additional problem with Gorton's analysis is that the gradual superseding of notes by deposits is simply not sufficient to eliminate that role — however relatively unimportant notes may become, their prices would still convey information about the banks' capital values. To eliminate that information would seem to require the *total* replacement of notes by deposits, and this did not happen.

4. In his book he ascribes the comparative success of the Scottish and Canadian banking systems in part to: (i) their branch-banking, and (ii) their 'oligopolistic' structure, which *might* have reduced destabilising competitive pressures (p. 62). These explanations do not appear to be particularly convincing, at least to me. It seems to me that point (i) tends to ignore the argument that branch banking was a direct consequence of (relatively) free banking, and certainly not an alternative to it, while point (ii) is valid only if we suppose that competitive pressures are destabilising, and we discuss that argument in the text. In any case, the evidence seems to suggest that the 'oligopolistic' Scottish free banking system was in fact highly competitive (as Goodhart himself readily acknowledges, loc. cit.). He also ascribes the success of the Scottish and Canadian systems to their ability to withdraw funds in a crisis from London and New York. We discuss this argument in the appendix to Chapter 5 when we review the recent controversy over Scottish free banking.

5. I cannot therefore agree with Goodhart (1985, p. 9) when he says that the case for free banking 'collapses' because 'it depends on the existence of perfect, costless information, or at least on the availability of much greater information than is actually available.' In fact, one cannot easily explain the existence and role of financial intermediaries unless one explicitly acknowledges the role of information problems (see, for example, Fama 1985 and Chant 1987).

6. In fact, it is far from clear just what bank contagion really is, or how it differs from the contagion faced by other kinds of firms. As Benston *et al.* (1986, p. 78 n. 2) say:

Contagious insolvencies are not unique to banking. Whenever a seller cannot meet customer demand for a good because of an actual or perceived shortage, and the customers cannot readily obtain the good in other shops, there is likely to be a run on the remaining shops. Any stock will quickly disappear until replenished . . .

This suggests that contagion is more likely to occur when supply is restricted, and this perhaps explains why we only seem to observe major contagion problems in the presence of attempts to regulate the market (e.g. when banks' activities are restricted, or when price controls are imposed that are expected to lead to shortages).

7. One might also note that Schwartz (1988, pp. 591-2) examines two centuries of US and UK monetary history, and nearly a century of the monetary histories of a dozen other countries, and finds that it is relatively rare for runs to be contagious and lead to widespread panics.

8. For an alternative analysis of deposit runs, see Selgin (1988a, b).

9. It is interesting to ask why such a run might occur in the first place. While one would expect continuous shifts between notes and deposits, a 'random' shift sufficient to cause a deposit run is rather implausible. I would suggest that a deposit run might arise if the public had doubts about the soundness of deposit banks, but these doubts did not extend to the note-issuing banks, or if the public were concerned that notes might become difficult to obtain (although there would be no reason for such concern under free banking). Note also that I have not ignored the possibility that the public might want to redeem notes as well as deposits: one could think of that as a combination of a note run and a deposit run.

10. There is little gain in insight from assuming that the banks issue option clause notes with different features. In any case, one might expect that 'competition' among them would lead them to converge on similar option clauses.

11. For more on option clauses, see Cowen and Kroszner (1988b) and Schuler (1985, 1988a).

12. Branching restrictions have been a persistent theme in US monetary history. In the early days of the Republic, banks were generally permitted to operate only in the state or even county where they were chartered. Restrictions on bank branching were reaffirmed by the legislation establishing the National Banking System in the early 1860s, by the McFadden Act of 1927, and by the Banking Act of 1933. Savings and Loan Associations were subject to similar restrictions (see, for example, Barth and Regalia 1988). It is only in the 1980s that restrictions on branching have started to be relaxed significantly.

13. To some extent, banks can also get round branching restrictions by creating umbrella holding companies, but this can create additional

problems of its own (see, for example, Benston *et al.* 1986, Chapter 6).

14. Strictly speaking, the term 'Glass–Steagall Act' refers to the legislation of 1932 that governed the collateral for Federal Reserve note issues. The term is, however, usually used to refer to the provisions of the 1933 Banking Act that separated commercial and investment banking. These provisions were strengthened by the Bank Holding Company Act of 1956, and reaffirmed again by the amendment to that Act in 1970.

15. In addition, banks are often subjected to minimum reserve ratios, capital adequacy requirements, quantitative credit ceilings, and so on. We discuss capital adequacy in note 4 to the appendix on deposit insurance.

16. Note, however, that adequate failure resolution policies — policies to close down insolvent institutions — can to some extent be seen as a substitute for risk-related deposit insurance premiums. As Kaufman (1987, p. 26) writes:

> federal deposit insurance is not really insurance but a guaranty. Thus, to the extent that insurance premiums are required and intended to be actuarially fair to cover the insurance agencies' expected losses, they need to be scaled to the difficulty of monitoring the activities of the bank and public policy with respect to the timing of closure rather than to the riskiness of the particular activities of the bank. (p. 26)

For more on the failure resolution issue, see also Benston *et al.* (1986), Litan (1988) and note 17, below.

17. An additional problem with the US and Canadian deposit-insurance systems is inadequate failure resolution procedures. This is a problem because the managements of insolvent institutions have little to lose and much to gain from taking wild risks before the insurance agency moves in to close them down. The cost of these gambles is borne by the insurers, and appears to be quite substantial (Kaufman 1987, pp. 22–3). Part of the reason for this is that the institutions that charter banks do not bear the costs of delayed closings. Indeed, if they view bank failures as a blot on their record, they may have an incentive to delay closings as long as possible (see, for example, Kaufman 1987, p. 26). Kane (1985, p. 19) also suggests that the resolution problem may be exacerbated by the regulatory authorities' attempt to stem excessive risk-taking by imposing 'escalating administrative penalties' on suspect institutions, but, he adds:

> The rub in this approach is that the mix of political and economic incentives that governs the behavior of government bureaucrats greatly lengthens the inevitable lag of examiner recognition

behind the true importance of emerging forms of yet-to-be-regulated risk. . . If their agency's economic viability were not backstopped by other federal resources, deposit insurers would have to take cognizance much sooner of emerging risks.

18. Some excellent discussions of these episodes are given in Kane (1985) and Kaufman (1987) for the USA, and the Canadian Senate Report (1985) for Canada. See also Dowd (1988c).
19. We shall discuss the Scottish and US experiences in more detail in Chapter 5.
20. This is not to deny that private institutions will sometimes provide 'lender of last resort functions' on their own. The Royal Bank and the Bank of Scotland provided such support to other Scottish banks during the Ayr Bank episode, for instance (see White 1984b, p. 32), while the clearinghouse associations provided similar support to US banks during the repeated crises of the National Banking System period (see Cannon 1901, Timberlake 1984 and Kaufman 1987, p. 16). One might also add that a private LOLR probably has more incentive to support the banking system than a government-sponsored one which, in the final resort, can expect the government to bail it out. A perceptive analysis of the problems of a monopoly bank LOLR is given in Selgin (1988a, pp. 626–32).
21. Quoted in Fetter 1965, p. 274.
22. In *Lombard Street* (1873) Bagehot favoured free banking in principle, but believed it would be useless advocating it because no-one would take it seriously. He therefore set himself the task of making the existing system work as well as it could. While Bagehot's later free banking sympathies are well known, most writers seem unaware that the earlier Bagehot rejected it quite emphatically. In his first published essay (1848, p. 48), he acknowledged the 'great wisdom' of the currency monopoly as an 'exception to the principles of Free Trade'. See also his approving comments on the 1844 Act on p. 186. If supporters of free banking wish to claim Bagehot as one of their own, they should at least acknowlege his earlier objections to it.
23. Bank protection satisfies neither 'non-rivalness' nor 'non-excludability' conditions (p. 85). It only *appears* to be a public good because there is no market on which it is traded.
24. It is true that Bagehot tried to guard against the LOLR being dragged into bale-outs by recommending that last resort loans be made at a penal rate of interest on good security — the idea being that sound banks would be willing to comply and unsound banks would be unable to — but central banks in practice have frequently failed to insist on these conditions. Perhaps they felt that forcing the insolvent banks into liquidation would give the impression that their policies had failed, and leave them open to the criticism that 'problem banks' should have been sorted out long before that point.

25. The assumption that we start from a competitive equilibrium is important to the argument that follows. There is no insight to be obtained in starting from a position of general disequilibrium, but a possible objection is that there might be a natural monopoly. I doubt there would be, but defer that question to Chapter 4.

26. Quoted in Smith (1936, p. 63).

27. I should like to thank Larry White for pointing this problem out to me.

28. The assumptions that marginal cost rises and marginal revenue falls are not crucial *per se*. What is important here is that the bank is already maximising profits, so, unless external factors altered any change in policy would not increase its profits, and would probably reduce them instead.

29. Another problem with this argument is that if it is correct, it proves too much. It is sufficiently general that it applies to deposits as well as notes, but it then contradicts the textbook analysis that over-issues by deposit banks are disciplined by the cheque-clearing system.

30. Underlying Goodhart's argument here seems to be the claim that bank reputation is a public good (see, for example, pp. 24–5): 'good' banks have the incentive to distance themselves from 'bad' ones, and can do so in many ways (as discussed in appendix 1 to this chapter). Bank reputation does not really satisfy the non-excludability condition for a public good.

31. Goodhart disputes the claim that a central bank prevents a (note-) clearing system arising and points out to me in a letter that central banks were sometimes established, in part, to develop a clearing system (e.g. Reichsbank). I would certainly accept that, but the real issue is what prevented a clearing system arising in the first place, because we would have expected one to have arisen under free competition. One suspects the answer is government-imposed regulation.

32. See Chapter 3, note 2.

Appendices to Chapter 2

Appendix 1: The Theory of Deposit Insurance

This appendix re-examines the Diamond–Dybvig (DD) (1983)[1] analysis of deposit insurance and the conclusions about the feasibility and desirability of state deposit insurance usually drawn from it. This paper is an important one which has come to provide the standard justification for state-sponsored deposit insurance. I shall suggest that there are generally other means of protecting deposit holders against capital losses than deposit insurance, but that deposit insurance may still have a complementary role to play. If there is to be deposit insurance, however, private insurance is probably superior to a government scheme.

The Diamond–Dybvig Model[2]

The DD model has three periods ($T = 0$, 1, 2) and a production technology that yields 1 unit of output for each unit deposited in period 0 and withdrawn in period 1, and $R > 1$ units of output for each period 0 deposit withdrawn in period 2. This captures the idea that early withdrawals interrupt the production process, and depositors have to decide in period 1 whether they wish to withdraw in that period or the next one. All consumers are identical in period 0, but are revealed to be of one of two types in period 1. Type-1 agents derive utility only from period 1 consumption, and type-2 agents derive utility only from period 2 consumption. All agents can privately store consumption goods at no cost, and no storage is publicly observed.

Type-1 consumers will therefore withdraw their deposits and consume them in period 1; type-2 consumers will consume in period 2 any deposits they withdraw in that period and anything they might carry over from the previous period. If agents' types are publicly observable in period 1, DD show that it is possible to design an optimal insurance contract for period 0 that enables agents to insure against the 'unlucky' event of turning out to be a type-1 consumer. They show that agents will buy this contract because it improves on the autarky outcome, whereby each agent avoids trade with any others. They also show that this contract satisfies the 'self-selection' constraint that no agent has an incentive to misrepresent his type.

The problem is to implement this contract when agents' types are not publicly observable. DD suggest that agents might be able to implement the optimal contract by establishing a bank which would take in deposits and invest them in the production process, but promise depositors a reasonable return if they withdraw their deposits in period 1. They therefore suppose that banks offer a demand deposit contract that promises to pay $r > 1$ for each deposit withdrawn in period 1, provided that the bank still has assets to liquidate. The bank is assumed to serve demands for withdrawals sequentially, in random order, until it runs out of assets. Provided it has assets left, they are liquidated in period 2 and divided pro rata among remaining deposit holders. It is important to stress that the bank is a mutual fund in which there is no distinction between depositors and shareholders, and we shall return to this later.

DD find that the demand deposit contract can support the optimal insurance contract as a Nash equilibrium, but unfortunately the equilibrium is not unique, and there exists an alternative bank run equilibrium in which all the bank's assets are liquidated in period 1. This equilibrium occurs when type-2 depositors panic and withdraw their deposits because they anticipate that the bank will run out of assets. It is a worse outcome for both types of agent than the initial autarky equilibrium because certain returns of 1 and R for each type are replaced by uncertain returns for both of mean unity. As DD explain, 'Bank runs ruin the risk-sharing between agents and take a toll on the efficiency of production because all production is interrupted at $T=1$ when it is optimal for some to continue until $T=2'$ (p. 409). DD then suggest that a state deposit guarantee could eliminate the incentive to take part in a run. We can think of this guarantee as a system of deposit insurance.

Investor Capital as an Alternative to Deposit Insurance

We shall now outline an alternative way in which depositors could be protected against runs. Suppose that we introduce another agent — an investor — who derives utility from second-period consumption and is endowed with K units of capital. He has the option of establishing a bank which would invest his capital and the deposits the bank takes in the production process. Let us also suppose that if he does so he would agree to pay depositors the optimal consumption bundles that our previous mutual fund bank would have agreed to pay them. Depositors would therefore be no worse off than if they were to establish a mutual-fund bank of their own along DD lines. We can therefore suppose that they would deposit their capital in the new bank. The investor will then go ahead and set up his bank, provided that he is not too risk-averse and provided that the probability of a typical depositor turning out to be a type-1 agent is not too high.[3]

In the DD model, the possibility of bank runs arises because depositors would be aware that if a sufficient number of them withdrew their deposits, then those who failed to withdraw would suffer capital losses. The prospect of these losses arises in turn because the bank has insufficient capital to redeem all its deposits in the first period at the rate of r per deposit. If the bank had sufficient capital to do this, on the other hand, then the public would have no need to fear capital losses and no reason to participate in bank runs. For this to happen the bank's capital would have to suffice to cover its liabilities in the 'worst case scenario' when everyone withdraws their deposits in period 1. If this condition holds, no type-2 depositor would have any reason to withdraw in period 1. The self-selection constraint would therefore be satisfied and there would be no bank runs. Runs arose in the Diamond–Dybvig model precisely because the zero value of K meant that this condition could not hold.

Private Guarantees for Depositors

We have seen, therefore, that the introduction of investors who are willing to pledge their capital can eliminate the problem of bank runs without any apparent need for state intervention to guarantee the liabilities of the banking system. For this to happen, private agents need to have sufficient capital to pledge, an adequate inducement to pledge it and an appropriate means of pledging it. We also require a legal system that enforces any contracts which private agents make among themselves.

There are a number of ways in which private investors might pledge their capital. One is simply to invest and maintain an adequate 'cushion' of equity capital in the bank. Creditors of the bank could then observe the bank's capital–assets ratio and they would have little reason to run if this was high enough.[4] Before the days of deposit insurance it appears that bank creditors did look at factors like these in judging banks' safety. As Kaufman (1987, pp. 15–16) reports, there is:

> evidence that depositors and noteholders in the United States cared about the financial conditions of their banks and carefully scrutinized bank balance sheets. Arthur Rolnick and his colleagues at the Federal Reserve Bank of Minneapolis have shown that this clearly happened before the Civil War. Thomas Huertas and his colleagues at Citicorp have demonstrated the importance of bank capital to depositors by noting that Citibank in its earlier days prospered in periods of general financial distress by maintaining higher than average capital ratios and providing depositors with a relatively safe haven. Lastly, an analysis of balance sheets suggests that banks took, at least, less interest rate risk before the establishment of the FDIC.

Banks might also maintain an adequate capital cushion by issuing subordinated debt that would be automatically converted into equity when a bank's net worth fell to a level that threatened depositors' confidence. As Litan (1988, p. 302) notes, this:

> could provide for an automatic recapitalization of the bank in the event the bank 'failed' (that is, in the event its equity capital were exhausted). In effect, mandatory convertible subordinated debt would provide a parachute that would ensure a soft landing for the payments system . . . The covenants on the debt that trigger the mandatory conversion into equity would be the ripcord.[5]

In addition to this, private depositors might want to reassure depositors by assuming liability for the bank beyond the extent of their equity investments. In the USA, for instance, it was customary until the 1930s for bank shareholders to be 'doubly liable' for their investments,[6] and there is some evidence that this extended liability did reassure bank creditors (see, for example, Benston *et al.* 1986, p. 61, Kaufman 1987, pp. 13–14). It would have done so by increasing shareholders' incentive to monitor managements and decreasing their willingness to go along with shoot-for-the-moon strategies once banks' net worth became negative (see, Benston *et al.* (1986, pp. 242–3)).[7]

State or Private Deposit Insurance?

We have suggested that there are other ways in which banks could reassure their creditors besides deposit insurance, but this does not rule out a possible complementary role for deposit insurance as well. If there is to be deposit insurance, however, we need to investigate whether it should be provided by the state or the private sector. DD support a state system on the grounds that 'the government may have a natural advantage in providing deposit insurance' because private companies that have no power to tax would have to 'hold reserves to make their promise credible' (p. 416).[8] This is a questionable argument. As our previous discussion indicated, it is a question of pledging property in a credible manner rather than holding reserves, and in principle any form of marketable property would do. In any case, the argument that private individuals hold insufficient reserves seems to undermine *all* schemes for deposit insurance, and not just private ones. In the final analysis, it is the private sector on which the government relies to obtain resources as it needs them. The government would therefore cover all its deposit insurance liabilities from taxation, but this presupposes that private agents have the resources that the state can tax. But if private agents have the reserves to meet the government's deposit-insurance liabilities, they would presumably have sufficient reserves to meet their own deposit-insurance liabilities,[9] and there is no obvious reason why they could not provide deposit-insurance themselves. In any case, it is not so much a question of holding reserves but of bonding property that one owns, and the private sector does this already with many other forms of insurance. Lloyds, for example, does a reasonable job of insuring much of the world without any government guarantee behind it. When we also bear in mind that we are not even sure that we want deposit insurance in the first place, and that it has an extremely dubious historical track record anyway, then the argument for state deposit insurance seems to dissolve entirely.[10]

Notes

1. For other analyses of the theory of deposit insurance, see Kareken and Wallace (1978), O'Driscoll (1988) and Garrison, Short and O'Driscoll (1988).
2. For more details on the theory and proofs, see the DD paper.
3. For more on this, see Dowd (1988a).
4. An interesting question is whether free banks would tend to maintain the socially optimal level of capital. One argument that is sometimes made is that they would maintain capital–assets ratios that were too low. This lies behind some of the fears that banks are 'prone to fail' without government support. We have discussed that kind of argument in the main text. However, one occasionally meets with the opposite argument that free banks would hold *too much* capital, and that this 'social waste' could be eliminated by some kind of government scheme. Historical instances of high capital ratios are sometimes held to lend support to this. To give but one example, it was not uncommon for Australian banks to hold capital ratios of 20–30 per cent in the last century. (I should like to thank Mervyn Lewis for this example.) This line of reasoning seems rather implausible to me. The bank bears a very clear cost when it keeps capital in reserve — the profitable lending opportunities it forgoes — and it is far from clear why banks would tend to underrate those costs or overrate the benefits of holding capital reserves. Nor can we simply assume that the government can come in as a *deus ex machina* and somehow provide security for the banks at less cost. And if banks have sometimes maintained high capital ratios, they presumably did so for good reason, and we cannot say that they held excess reserves unless we know what the optimal reserves holdings actually were. See also our discussion of externality arguments in Chapter 4.
5. For more on the possible advantages of subordinated debt convenants, see Benston *et al.* (1986, pp. 192–5).
6. Double liability for the shareholders of national banks and some

state banks was repealed in 1933 for new shares and in 1937 for old shares (Benston *et al.* 1986, p. 78, n. 1). 'Double liability' persisted for remaining shareholders into the 1950s (Woodward (1988, p. 689)).

7. The potential usefulness of extended liability is argued by Benston *et al.* (1986, pp. 61, 242–3), while Woodward (1988, p. 689) argues that it would be a 'bad idea' because of the difficulties of 'chasing' the shareholders of failed banks. It seems to me that it might be useful, but it is surely up to the free market to find out; what we want is a legal system that allowed banks with different forms of shareholder liability to compete freely against each other. I fail to see why the liability structure that shareholders adopt needs to be imposed on them.

8. They acknowledge that this would not *prevent* private companies from offering deposit insurance, and suggest that 'the deposit guarantee could be made by a private organization with some authority to tax or create money to pay deposit insurance claims, although we would usually think of such an organization as being a branch of government' (p. 413). They therefore conclude that there might be 'a small competitive fringe of commercially insured deposits, limited by the amount of private collateral' (p. 413).

9. One must also bear in mind that a state-run deposit insurance corporation would be likely to accumulate a larger liability than a private one. As we discussed elsewhere, it could be expected to adopt inferior failure resolution policies, encourage 'cosmetic' accounting, and so on. State bureaucrats have less incentive to look after taxpayers' funds than private managers do to look after their shareholders'.

10. An interesting question is why instances of private deposit insurance seem to be historically so rare. The answer, I would suggest, is that alternative means of protecting banks and depositors are more cost-effective, perhaps because of the scale of the moral hazard problems that deposit insurance creates. From time to time state governments in the USA have encouraged the establishment of deposit insurance systems in their jurisdictions, but by and large these cannot be regarded as 'private' deposit insurance systems. For more on these experiences, see Kane (1985, pp. 4–5) and Benston *et al.* (1986, pp. 78–9, 190–2, 247–8).

Appendix 2:
Free Banking and the 'Real-Bills' Doctrine

This appendix examines the relationship of free banking to the real-bills doctrine. This is an important issue because the real-bills doctrine is a dangerous error, and advocates of free banking have sometimes been accused of supporting it. We shall see that there is no necessary connection between the two, and some supporters of free banking have advocated the real-bills doctrine while others have rejected it. The touchstone is their position on convertibility: the real-bills doctrine is fundamentally incompatible with a commitment to convertibility, and therefore the real-bills charge cannot be levelled at those free bankers — or anyone else — who consistently support convertibility.

To start with, we must outline what we understand by the 'real-bills doctrine'. This term has been used to apply to a body of related doctrines, but the essence of it has been aptly summarised by White (1984b, p. 120):

> banks may properly create any quantity of bank notes and deposits so long as they create them only in purchases of the real bills offered to them. Real bills were commercial IOUs, issued by a second firm in payment for material inputs received from a first firm higher in the structure of production, to be paid off with the proceeds of sales to a third firm lower in the structure.[1]

Its attraction lay in the supposedly elastic supply of notes and deposits it would generate: 'The intuitive appeal behind the doctrine was that in a system operating on real-bills principles the supply of bank money would supposedly expand in step with real output and the demand for bank money'. (White, loc. cit.)

This doctrine is unequivocally false. As stated here, it involves a number of serious problems:

(1) It fails to recognise that the consequence of linking the quantity of bank money to another nominal quantity — like the quantity of bills offered for discount — is an indeterminate price level. This is so because the quantity of bills offered for discount itself depends in part on the quantity of money and the general price level. In short, it fails to recognise that there is nothing to 'tie down' the three nominal magnitudes — the supply of bank money, the supply of bills offered for discount, and the price level.

(2) It fails to recognise that the quantity of bills offered for discount depends on the discount rate charged by banks.

(3) It fails to recognise that a rule governing the *way* in which bank liabilities are introduced into the system does not provide a check on the *amount* of bank liabilities that the banks can keep in circulation.

(4) It fails to provide banks with an operational decision rule since banks, in practice, cannot distinguish 'real' bills from 'fictitious' ones.

The origins of the real-bills doctrine are to be found in the theories of John Law in the early part of the eighteenth century,[2] and it played perhaps the central role in the bullionist controversy in Britain in the first decade of the nineteenth century. It was adopted enthusiastically by some of the Directors of the Bank of England who used it to claim that, regardless of whether the currency was convertible or not, the Bank could not over-issue notes provided it only discounted real bills. Its fallacy was spelt out by Thornton (1802) and by the Bullion Committee of 1810. They appreciated that it provided no limit to the note issue, and recommended instead that the Bank of England limit its note issues by making them convertible. They also perceived quite clearly that the failure of the real-bills rule to provide an effective limit to the note supply opened the way to inflation. This analysis was widely accepted, and the real bills doctrine was rightly discredited as a recipe for potential disaster.

To understand how free banking relates to the real-bills doctrine, let us first recall how free banks would operate. As we discussed in the previous chapter, these banks would issue convertible notes, and the extent of their note issues would be limited by the demand to hold them. A persistent issue of notes beyond the demand for them would then be impossible because the excess notes would flow back to them — the 'law of reflux'. The fact that the note issue is demand determined in turn implies that there is no scope for any other rule — like a real-bills policy — to govern the note issue. A bank can follow a real bills policy or maintain convertibility, but it cannot do both. The real-bills issue therefore arises only if the commitment to convertibility is abandoned, and since competitive forces would force free banks to maintain convertibility, it should not arise at all under genuinely free banking.

A problem is that not all those who considered themselves

free bankers were unequivocal supporters of convertibility, or thought that competitive pressures would force the banks to redeem their issues. Rothbard (1988, pp. 233–41) appears to be quite right when he mentions that some of the most prominent 19th century free bankers supported various versions of the real-bills doctrine and either opposed the gold standard outright or, at best, were lukewarm and ambiguous in their support of it.[3] There is no denying that free banking, in that form, is unsound, and the opponents of the real-bills doctrine were right to criticise it. However, adherence to the real-bills doctrine was by no means a monopoly of the inflationist wing of free bankers. It was shared also by some members of the banking school, as well as by some of the earlier anti-bullionists, and these were certainly no free bankers. There therefore seems to be no connection between support for free banking and support for the real-bills doctrine. One finds writers who supported one or the other, or both, or neither. These real-bills advocates were opposed by members of each of the currency, banking and free banking schools whose commitment to convertibility was irreproachable.[4] Whoever else supported free banking, one must never forget that there is a 'hard money' wing to the free banking school that is every bit as committed to convertibility and every bit as opposed to the real-bills fallacy as any supporter of the currency school.

One suspects that much of the confusion on these issues can be related to the failure of some members of the banking and free banking schools to clarify the precise nature of the 'laws of reflux' on which they were relying to establish the limits to the note issue. Not all of them appreciated that it depended crucially on convertibility, and some of them were outright real-bills advocates, who believed that convertibility was not only useless, but positively harmful. The confusion was probably added to by talk — some of it quite correct — of the desirability of the note issue responding to the 'needs of trade', a position that resembled the real-bills doctrine, but is not the same as it.[5] It was all too easy to confuse sound versions of the law of reflux and the needs-of-trade doctrine with the unsound real-bills doctrine. The members of the currency school were right to insist upon the paramount importance of convertibility, and right to suspect that some of those opposed to the theory were ambiguous in their support for it. One can therefore understand why they were inclined to suspect their opponents of being closet inflationists, and to dismiss as unsound any doctrine that even resembled the real-bills fallacy. We must also bear in mind that most of the histories of those controversies were written by currency school supporters. We should be wary of historical accounts of these controversies that treat the errors of the currency school as if they were Gospel truth.

Notes

1. It is unfortunate that Sargent and Wallace (1982, p. 1212) define the 'real bills prescription' as 'unfettered private intermediation or central bank operations designed to produce the effects of such intermediation'. This effectively identifies the real-bills doctrine with free banking. This is most unfortunate because the association of the two discredits free banking and allows for a spurious rehabilitation of the real-bills fallacy. One might note, however, that Sargent and Wallace's *analysis* shows that free banking is Pareto-optimal while restrictions on the money supply are not.
2. Adam Smith is often wrongly identified as the author of the real-bills fallacy. While he was not always fully consistent, Smith was a strong supporter of convertibility who appreciated the importance of the law of reflux in limiting over-issue in a convertible system (see, for example, the *Wealth of Nations*, 1776, p. 265). He clearly understood banks could not operate a real-bills policy in practice because they could not distinguish 'real' bills from 'fictitious' ones (pp. 277–8). He went on to criticise the true author of the real-bills doctrine, John Law, for imagining that the problems he sought to cure could be solved simply by creating more money (pp. 282–3). Unfortunately, Smith did his own cause no good with his notorious real-bills passage (p. 269) where he talks of a bank discounting a 'real bill of exchange drawn by a real creditor upon a real debtor'. I would suggest, however, that if one reads this passage in context it becomes (reasonably) clear that the policy rule he is recommending banks to follow is to protect their reserves, not to try to tell which bills are real and which are not, and then discount only the former.
3. For more on these writers, see Chapter 5, note 6.
4. Thomas Tooke among the members of the banking school was a consistent supporter of convertibility (see Laidler 1975). Sir Henry Parnell and Robert Mushet among the free bankers were hard money men who supported convertibility (see Rothbard 1988, p. 237).

5. At one extreme, this needs-of-trade doctrine can simply mean an elastic note or deposit issue, and this is sound enough in principle. (In the system we outline, for instance, the supply of notes and deposits would be perfectly elastic.) Sound versions of the doctrine therefore exist, but one must also bear in mind that at the other extreme it can be difficult to disentangle from the real-bills doctrine. One must therefore be clear which version of the doctrine one is dealing with.

3

The Problem of Monetary Policy

Quis custodiet ipsos custodes? *Somewhere power must remain. But is it to be a Government Department, an independent National Bank guided by a directorship of merchants, a Nationalised Central Bank inspired by the Treasury, a quasi-public Corporation guided by Mr Keynes?* Who *is to take the final responsibility? How is such a body to deal with a constitutional opposition, certain to arise, represented by City Editors, Friendly but Critical Economists, Unfriendly but Critical Business Men? These are the kinds of questions which must be faced . . .*

(Sir Theodore Gregory 1926)[1]

Irredeemable paper money has almost invariably proved a curse to the country employing it.

(Irving Fisher 1920)[2]

3.1 Introduction

Once a monopoly bank of issue has been established there arises the problem of what it should do — the *monetary policy problem*. We have already discussed one aspect of this problem in the previous chapter — the problem of lender of last resort policy. This chapter deals with the macroeconomic and fiscal aspects of monetary policy. We begin by explaining what the monetary policy problem actually is and how it differs from the policy problems faced by banks under a regime of *laisser faire*. While a competitive bank would simply maximise its profits, it is not immediately obvious what a monopoly bank should do, or within which institutional framework it should operate. But whatever that framework might be, it rests on the suppression of competition, and the resulting outcome is likely to be inefficient. We then investigate how monetary policy affects private agents and outline some of the problems it causes. This prepares the ground for our discussion of monetary reform in the last chapter. We then turn to the fiscal uses of monetary policy and examine whether the inflation tax should be used to raise revenue for the state.

3.2 The Problem Defined

Every economic agent needs to follow rules which tell him what to do in any given situation. He does not have to be able to articulate the rules he follows, and he may not even be consciously aware of them (like many social conventions) but the essential point is that he follows rules regardless of whether he is fully aware of them or not. This applies to banks as well as to anyone else. Banks must adopt rules to govern the assets they buy, the liabilities they issue, the interest rates they charge and pay, and so on. Both competitive and monopoly banks of issue thus face the problem of choosing appropriate rules or policies. They differ, however, in that:

- The freedom of manoeuvre of a competitive bank is heavily constrained by the competition of rivals. The freedom of manoeuvre of a monopoly bank is not, and this gives it — or whoever controls it — the problem of choosing from among a wider variety of alternatives.
- The competitive bank is likely to get more feedback on its policies than a monopoly bank to enable it to correct mistakes (for example, a competitive bank gets feedback from the note clearing system which a monopoly bank lacks, it observes that its market share changes, and so on). On the other hand, a monopoly bank lacks this kind of feedback, and whatever feedback it gets is also likely to

operate with long and variable lags which complicate its task of disentangling the 'signals' from the 'noise'.

- Any mistakes the monopoly bank makes could be more serious for other parties because of the bank's unique position. The bank will have to adopt an LOLR policy, for example, and if the currency is inconvertible then the bank will have ultimate control over the price level, and mistakes in either capacity could be very serious indeed.

- Most important of all, perhaps, a competitive bank has a clear objective — to maximise its profits — but it is not immediately obvious what the objectives of a monopoly bank should be. If it is not to maximise profits, then someone has to decide what else it should do and someone (else?) has to decide who that should be. These are the virtually intractable questions that arise and need to be answered once competition is suppressed and a monopoly bank established.

These questions are what distinguishes the monetary policy problem from the policy problems of individual banks of issue. In effect, they are what the monetary policy problem is all about.

3.3 Monetary Policy and Welfare

Before we get into any detailed discussion of particular monetary policies we should pause and bear in mind that the issue of monetary policy only arises in the first place because free competition has already been suppressed. We would normally presume that the prohibition of competition leads to a suboptimal outcome unless we have specific reason to believe the contrary.[3] If we adopt the Pareto criterion, for instance, then an optimal outcome is one in which it is impossible to make some people better off without making others worse off, and an outcome will only be Pareto-optimal if all mutually beneficial trades have been entered into. This suggests that a competitive outcome is Pareto-optimal. It also suggests that a currency monopoly will not deliver a Pareto-optimal outcome because of the mutually beneficial trades it suppresses, and these conclusions seem to be supported by the analysis of Sargent and Wallace (1982, p. 1212).[4] This alone makes it very difficult to give a convincing intellectual defence for the monopoly in base money: it is extremely difficult to defend a rule or an institution that delivers a particular outcome when a superior outcome is also attainable — one has to explain why one does not go for the superior outcome instead. In addition to this, the work of Dean Taylor (1982a, b) strongly suggests that central banks can be viewed as inefficient, loss-making nationalised industries[5] whose attempts to manipulate exchange rates have given money away to speculators in the private sector who were smart enough to bet against them.

The monetary policy problem is therefore an exercise in second-best optimisation in which one seeks to find the best policy among the remaining possibilities to which one has chosen to restrict oneself. It is then natural to ask what this second-best monetary policy looks like and how it compares with the monetary policies which central banks tend to adopt. In order to address these issues we need first to investigate how monetary policy affects agents.

3.4 How Monetary Policy Affects Private Agents

We start by investigating how monetary policy affects a typical individual. Such an individual will maximise his expected welfare or profits subject to the constraints he faces, and subject to the expectations he forms of variables that affect him but which he does not observe. Monetary policy affects him principally by altering these expectations. There are two ways in which it does this and we shall examine each in turn.

The Effects on Relative Price Perceptions

First, monetary policy can affect an individual's perceptions of relative prices. The basic mechanism by which it does this is explained most easily using Lucas' (1972) 'island story'. The idea is to view household-workers as living on an island where they specialise in the production of one good. They trade this good in a centralised market and import a wide variety of other goods. The household-firm observes the price of its own good but not the prices of other goods. It therefore has to form an expectation of the general price index to guide its production and sale decisions. Since the household-firm is rational it will form the best possible expectation (a 'rational expectation') given the information it has. This consists of its knowledge of past prices and its observation of the current price of its own product. It will produce more when it thinks the relative price of its own output is high; less when it thinks it is low. Monetary policy can affect agents by influencing their perceptions of these relative prices. For instance, an unanticipated increase in the money supply will cause an unexpectedly high demand for goods and lead agents to over-estimate the relative prices of the goods they sell and increase their output. Unanticipated rises in money supply thus tend to increase output and unanticipated falls tend to decrease it. Anticipated rises (or falls) in the money supply tend to have no effect, on the other hand, because agents would continue to perceive relative prices correctly. The basic message that comes from this story is therefore that monetary policy affects agents by 'fooling' them into misperceiving relative prices.

The fact that an agent would have done something else had he been better informed indicates that he considers that alternative to be preferable. If we accept that he is the best judge of his own welfare then the conclusion must be that the monetary policy made him worse off. Note that this is so regardless of whether the misperception increases output or reduces it. The essential point is that it fooled him into doing something he would not otherwise have chosen to do.

This suggests that activist monetary policies which influence people's behaviour probably only make them worse off,[6] and what we need, therefore, is a monetary policy that makes prices as predictable as possible. This implies that the central bank should adhere to some fixed rule which the public could use to predict its actions with the maximum possible accuracy. There are two types of rules the bank could follow:[7]

(1) *Monetary growth rules*
In this instance the monopoly bank chooses a particular

definition of the money supply and commits itself to keep the growth of that target aggregate within certain limits. In principle[8] such a rule might make the target money supply reasonably predictable, but it is *prices* rather than the money supply that the public want to predict. To achieve a monetary target would probably require that the central bank be able to predict the demand for money, and this requires not only that there be a stable demand-for-money function, but that the demand for money be predictable *ex ante* as well. Recent regulatory and technological changes appear to make this a very stringent condition. These changes also make it very difficult even to come up with an operationally useful definition of money any more. And even if these problems could be overcome, we cannot simply invert a demand for money equation to predict prices or inflation.[9]

In addition, we cannot simply adopt a monetary target and assume that the behavioural relationships on which it depends will continue to hold — the Lucas critique of econometric policy evaluation (1976) indicates that behavioural rules estimated for one policy regime may be of limited or no use in predicting behaviour under another. One might therefore expect a money demand equation to shift once the corresponding aggregate is adopted as a target. These problems clearly make monetary targetting an extremely difficult task indeed.

Another problem with a commitment to a monetary target is that it can seriously hinder the monopoly bank's role as lender of last resort. This problem is most acute when the target monetary aggregate is the monetary base. (Such a target has been proposed, for example, by Friedman (1984) and Selgin (1985).) A monetary base target is incompatible with the central bank's LOLR role because the former ties down the monetary base but the latter requires it to be flexible. A fully credible monetary base target would therefore require that the bank explicitly abandon its LOLR function, but this would leave the banking system with little defence against a liquidity crisis. The 'need' for the LOLR would remain for as long as the restrictions on note supply continued in place. The problem is less acute when the target aggregate is broader because it would be possible in principle to increase the base without necessarily compromising the target, but that would be difficult to do in practice because of the need to predict other agents' actions with the required degree of accuracy. There would still be considerable tension between the LOLR role and the monetary target.[10]

(2) Price stabilisation rules:
An alternative is for the bank to stabilise a particular price. This could be the price of a particular good (like gold or a foreign currency) or the price of a bundle of goods (like Hall's (1981a) ANCAP bundle). The bank may peg the price by maintaining convertibility (as under the gold standard) or else it may adopt some kind of feedback rule to increase base money when the target price is too low and decrease it when it is too high. There are a number of technical issues involved which have been extensively discussed in the literature (Hayek 1943, Friedman 1951, Hall 1983), but in this context it suffices merely to note that price stabilisation rules exist which avoid both the drawbacks of monetary growth rules — they make prices more predictable and they avoid the conflict with the LOLR role of the monopoly bank. This suggests that the right kind of price stabilisation rule is better than any monetary target.

There is one final point to consider while discussing monetary policy and relative price predictability. The Lucas–Sargent–Wallace story yields the recommendation that monetary policy should make prices as predictable as possible, but it says nothing that would enable one to prefer one particular inflation rate to another. If one takes that story literally, then one inflation rate is as good as any other, provided that it is as predictable. However, there are other considerations which the island story leaves out that would lead us to prefer one particular inflation rate — a zero rate — to any other. Prices in most markets do not change continuously, but at discrete intervals, and the process of changing prices is costly: notices need to be changed, customers informed, forms changed, coin and note-taking machines altered, and so on. These costs are obviously minimised when inflation is zero. There are also accounting costs — the costs of reckoning and keeping track of prices and keeping books in order — and these are also minimised when prices are stable. In any case, it is not clear that one can talk realistically of different rates of inflation and assume that relative prices remain unaltered. A number of writers have suggested that relative price dispersion might rise with the inflation rate (see Graham 1930) and the issue still appears to be unsettled (see Hercowitz 1981). These considerations lead us to the conclusion that we should seek a monetary regime that delivers stable prices rather than merely predictable ones.

The Time Consistency Issue

We now turn to another way in which monetary policy impinges on private agents. Monetary policy can also affect them if they doubt what the monetary authority says and if these doubts lead them to change their plans to protect themselves against the possibility that it might do something different from what it said it would do. This basic problem of time-inconsistent policy has long been understood in other economic contexts. In the case of capital taxation, for instance, a government might want the freedom to impose capital levies, but at the same time it would not want to discourage private investment. It might, therefore, promise not to impose future levies to encourage people to accumulate capital, but if the promise was not credible the public would lower their investment anyway to reduce their exposure to a possible future levy. A sub-optimal outcome would then arise because the government could not credibly promise to refrain from imposing a future levy. Kydland and Prescott (1977) explain the problem as follows:

> Even if there is an agreed-upon, fixed social objective function and policymakers know the timing and magnitude of the effects of their actions, discretionary policy, namely, the selection of that policy which is best, given the current situation and a correct evaluation of the end-of-period position, does not result in the social objective function being maximised. (p. 619)

The reason for this is that while it may be optimal to make a promise, it may not be optimal to honour it later once people have acted on it:

> The reason that such policies are suboptimal is not due to myopia.

The . . . entire future is taken into consideration. Rather, the suboptimality arises because there is no mechanism to induce *future* policymakers to take into consideration the effect of their policy, via the expectations mechanism, upon *current* decisions of agents. (p. 627)

Barro and Gordon (1983a) have shown that one feature of this sub-optimal outcome is an excessive and variable inflation rate. The socially optimal rate of inflation is likely to be zero, as we discussed earlier, but a central bank operating with an inconvertible currency is almost certain to engineer a higher rate than that, and possibly a much higher one. To see why, let us suppose that we start from a position where people expect zero inflation. In that case the costs of inflating to the central bank are likely to be very low while the benefits — like reducing unemployment from 'surprise' inflation or raising revenue — could be quite substantial. It would therefore have an incentive to inflate. Knowing this, the public would not rationally expect zero inflation. Instead, they would expect the inflation rate that the central bank has an incentive to produce — the rate that equalised the marginal costs and benefits of inflation to it. This rate would be greater than zero and vary with changes in the factors that determine its marginal costs and benefits. Barro and Gordon plausibly suggest that factors which might influence these costs and benefits and cause higher inflation include a recession, a rise in the natural rate of unemployment, greater government spending, and an increase in the outstanding stock of nominally denominated state debt.

This analysis carries a clear implication for reform: a superior outcome can be achieved if a means is established to enable the central bank to commit itself. The rule would need to be imposed from outside: the only alternative — that the central bank's concern for its reputation might suffice instead — is discussed in another paper by Barro and Gordon (1983b) and rejected. They suppose that the bank benefits from having a reputation for honesty, and instances of 'misbehaviour' impair that reputation, but they find that having a reputation to defend only reduces the monopoly bank's 'misbehaviour' and does not eliminate it entirely. The bank will still break a promise if the incentive to do so is big enough.

It is therefore necessary to impose an outside rule on the bank to compel it to honour its promises, but it is not clear how such a rule could be credibly established. It is not enough for the state simply to pass a law ordering the bank to fulfill its commitments. To be fully effective, the public would have to believe that the law was more than just a trick that the government might later revoke when it suited it. The public would recognise that the monopoly bank would have an incentive to pay politicians later to free them of their constraints (such as passing a law to suspend convertibility), so they would only fully believe the law if they were confident that the chances of such deals were sufficiently remote. And since they could not trust the politicians to refuse such offers, the politicians would probably have to be deprived of the ability to make such deals and renege on commitments. In other words, the public would have to be convinced that the law was sufficiently entrenched to withstand a future coalition of politicians and bank officials who might seek to undermine or remove it. The law prohibiting such deals would somehow have to be 'cast in stone', and it may well need to have the status of a constitutional amendment. This raises a number of issues to which we shall return in the last chapter. Suffice it, for the moment, to note that we have at least indicated the importance of pre-commitment and the problem of protecting commitments against future attempts to undermine them.

3.5 Are There Macroeconomic 'Externalities'?

Our discussion so far indicates that we want a monetary framework in which commitments can be credible and prices are likely to be stable. There is, however, a long tradition that maintains that monetary policy can, and should, do more than that. According to this, we want an activist monetary policy to counter the (alleged) failures to which the free market is prone. It claims, in effect, that monetary policy can generate external benefits that the free market does not appropriate, and that these benefits are sufficiently high to be worth the costs they involve (like the costs of 'fooling' people or regulating them). Monetary policy is said to be able to create two kinds of macroeconomic externality:

The first externality is to reduce unemployment (or, more or less equivalently, to increase output). The problem with this argument is that monetary policy is not an appropriate instrument to reduce unemployment, even if one accepts the Keynesian diagnosis of unemployment itself. As we saw earlier, the Lucas–Sargent–Wallace story indicates that monetary policy can only reduce unemployment if it delivers a positive money shock, and if the public is rational there is no systematic way in which it can do this. On average, monetary shocks are as likely to be negative ones, which increase unemployment, as positive ones which reduce it. We should not, therefore, expect monetary policy to reduce average unemployment. If one wishes to reduce unemployment one has to resort to other measures instead to improve the general functioning of the economy. Possible structural reforms that would help to do this include reforms of the tax-benefit system to improve incentive structure and eliminate poverty traps, the deregulation of labour and housing markets, and the abolition of the legal privileges of trade unions. Whatever one might do to reduce unemployment, though, the important point is not to try using monetary policy to do it.

The second possible externality is to improve macroeconomic stability. This is another common argument but it is open to both logical and historical objections:

(1) The logical argument is that it lacks theoretical plausibility. The Lucas–Sargent–Wallace story suggests that monetary policy works (influences agents' behaviour) by creating 'noise' that distorts agents' perceptions of relative prices. This must be presumed to be destabilising because there is no plausible way in which the government can stabilise the economy by creating noise to offset shocks arising in the private sector.[11] The time-inconsistency literature also suggests that if it has any effect, monetary policy will be destabilising. As Kydland and Prescott put it, 'stabilization efforts (might) have the perverse effect of contributing to economic instability' (Kydland and Prescott 1977, p. 620)

because there is no guarantee that the 'repeated game' between the central bank and the private sector is stable, and if it is not, there could be severe fluctuations as they thrash about reacting to each other.

(2) The historical evidence also suggests that monetary policy is a major cause of macroeconomic instability rather than a cure for it.[12] Friedman's assessment of the US evidence up to 1960 seems also to apply to later US experience and the experiences of other countries:

> Every [major economic fluctuation] has been accompanied by a significant monetary disturbance. There has been no significant monetary disturbance not accompanied by a severe economic fluctuation. The monetary disturbances have had a largely independent origin in enough cases to establish a strong presumption that they are contributory causes rather than simply incidental effects of the economic fluctuations; that, while influences ran both ways, there was nothing in the nature of the economic fluctuation that made the monetary disturbances inevitable ... Finally, almost all the monetary disturbances have arisen either from inadequacies of governmental monetary policies or from controversy about them. Governmental intervention in monetary matters, far from providing the stable monetary framework for a free market that is its ultimate justification, has proved a potent source of instability. (pp. 22–3)

It seems to me that this undermines the externality argument and, with it, any plausible defence of activist monetary policies. Our previous conclusions therefore appear to remain valid: what we need is a monetary framework that makes commitments credible and prices stable, and which avoids creating additional instability of its own. As Friedman continued:

> the central problem is not to construct a highly sensitive instrument that can continuously offset instability introduced by other factors, but rather to prevent monetary arrangements from themselves becoming a major source of instability. What we need is not a skilled monetary driver of the economic vehicle continuously turning the steering wheel to adjust to the unexpected irregularities of the route, but some means of keeping the monetary passenger who is in the back seat as ballast from occasionally leaning over and giving the steering wheel a jerk that threatens to send the car off the road. (loc. cit.)

3.6 Monetary Policy as a Means of Taxation

State-controlled monopoly banks of issue can use monetary policy to raise revenue by increasing the supply of high-powered money (currency and deposits at the central bank). This raises revenue in three ways: (i) through the additional high-powered money itself, (ii) through 'fiscal drag', that is, where the extra money causes inflation and people get pushed into higher tax brackets because of a progressive tax system, and (iii) where the inflation it causes reduces the real value of outstanding government debt issued at interest rates that did not make adequate allowance for the lowered value of money. Friedman and Schwartz (1986, p. 56) estimate that the revenue to be obtained through the first category is likely to be quite small — they give a figure of about 0.7 per cent of national income as an upper limit. The revenues to be obtained from the second category depend on how well-indexed the tax system is, but Friedman and Schwartz believe the revenue to be gained from the third is 'extremely important' and they note as an indication that: 'At the end of World War II, the funded (US) federal debt amounted to 6% more than a year's national income. By 1967 it was down to about 32% of national income despite repeated 'deficits' in the official federal budget. Since then it has risen as deficits have continued and increased, but even so only to about 36% currently' (p. 57).

The (ab)use of the monetary system to raise revenue for the government is probably the most recurrent theme in the history of state intervention into the monetary system. 'A Government can live for a long time . . . by printing paper money. . . . The method is condemned, but its efficacy, up to a point, must be admitted. A Government can live by this means when it can live by no other. It is the form of taxation which the public find hardest to evade and even the weakest government can enforce, when it can enforce nothing else' (Keynes 1923, p. 41). Printing money is therefore an easy way to raise revenue, and an especially attractive one when alternative sources of revenue are hard to find. It is also a highly dangerous expedient that has frequently led to disaster. Inflation disrupts the process of economic co-ordination by injecting noise into price signals that are normally reliable guides for agents to follow. When it is unexpected it also produces arbitrary redistributions from those with assets to those with liabilities denominated in nominal terms. This is damaging enough, but the real danger is that once a government has resorted to the inflation tax it might become dependent on it and be forced to inflate at an accelerating rate.[13] Once the government gets trapped on this treadmill the almost inevitable result is a monetary collapse. As Keynes put it when discussing the German hyperinflation of the early 1920s:

> Reliance on inflationary taxation, whilst extremely productive to the exchequer in its earliest stages . . . gradually broke down the mark as a serviceable unit of account, one of the effects of which was to render unproductive the greater part of the rest of the revenue-collecting machinery — most taxes being necessarily assessed at some interval of time before they are collected. The failure of the rest of the revenue rendered the Treasury more and more dependent on inflation, until finally the use of legal-tender money had been so far abandoned by the public that even the inflationary tax ceased to be productive and the Government was threatened by literal bankruptcy. (1923, p. 61)

This process can destroy the very basis of society. To quote Keynes once again:

> Lenin is said to have declared that the best way to destroy the Capitalist System was to debauch the currency. By a continuing process of inflation, Governments can confiscate, secretly and unobserved, an important part of the wealth of their citizens . . . As the inflation proceeds and the real value of the currency fluctuates wildly from month to month, all permanent relations between debtors and creditors, which form the ultimate foundation of capitalism, become so utterly disordered as to be almost meaningless; and the process of wealth-getting degenerates into a gamble and a lottery.
> Lenin was certainly right. *There is no subtler, no surer means of overturning the existing basis of Society than to debauch the currency. The process engages all the hidden forces of economic law on the side of destruction, and does it in a manner which not one man in a million is able to diagnose.* (1919, pp. 77–8; my italic)

These views are echoed by the late Graham Hutton[14]. As he wrote, all too prophetically, in 1960:

> The working-out of inflations in history caused big social changes

and injustices, from which . . . little real economic progress . . . came. In some cases, especially that of Rome, the entire social fabric and civilization came down in ruins. . . . But in most cases of uninterrupted, progressive and rapid inflation — from ancient Rome[15] to modern Germany — the causes were appreciated, the inflation became policy, and the government utilized it for purposes of politics, ie, power. The ends of such policy-inflations were socially cataclysmic (p. 160).

[He added:] Planned, progressive inflation as a policy ends in unplanned, unvailed, but inescapable — and above all, unforeseen, disaster. That is the lesson of all inflations in history (p. 161).

Despite these considerations against the inflation tax there is an argument in its favour which deserves very serious consideration. According to this, an inflation tax may sometimes be justified in a world where the government has to finance itself by distorting taxes. (This argument has been made by Phelps (1973) and others. Obviously, if the state can subsist on non-distorting taxes then efficiency considerations indicate that only those taxes should be levied, but the point at issue is what the government should do when this option is not available.) Given that the alternative is to levy a tax that has distorting side-effects, it is *conceivable* that the inflation tax may be worthwhile because the costs it involves *may* be less than those implied by the next-best tax. This is an intellectually respectable argument which demands a response.

One response is that the disruption caused by inflation is so high and the dangers associated with it so great that there should never be any resort to it — at least outside of emergencies like a major war, and possibly not even then. This argument can be buttressed up with the evidence provided by many historical experiences of inflation to provide a persuasive case, but not — unfortunately — an airtight one. While the anecdotal and historical evidence is certainly impressive, the fact remains that the effects of inflation are not well-understood and there is still some room for dispute about how serious they might be. One still has the problem of *proving* to a sceptic that the inflation tax is not worthwhile.

The solution appears to have been provided by Kimbrough (1986) and Faig (1988).[16] They show that the argument for the inflation tax in a world with distorting taxation is not valid (under reasonable conditions, at least) because it fails to take account of the fact that money is an 'intermediate good' which yields utility only indirectly. Their point is basically an application of a well-known theorem in public finance that states that it is inefficient to tax intermediate goods. Applied to inflationary finance, the argument is that money is used to reduce transaction costs, and inflation raises these costs while the use of other taxes does not. The resort to inflation is therefore never optimal because it effectively throws away the resources consumed by the higher transactions costs it causes. This appears to answer the argument that inflationary finance might be theoretically worthwhile even when the alternative is to levy distorting taxes.

Notes

1. Quoted from Gregory (1926, p. 44).
2. Quoted from Fisher (1920, p. 131).
3. It seems reasonable to maintain that there is a prima-facie case for the superiority of the competitive outcome provided there are no plausible grounds for externalities that cannot be appropriated by the free market, and whose existence might invalidate such a claim. Possible externalities are discussed at various points in the book: last chapter dealt with externalities connected with the instability of the banking system, this chapter deals later with Keynesian-style macroeconomic externalities, and the next deals with externalities relating to the medium of exchange. None of these arguments seems to be particularly convincing, at least to me.
4. Sargent and Wallace (1982) compare 'unfettered private intermediation' (p. 1212) with 'the sort of restrictions suggested by the quantity theorists' (p. 1214). Their results about the inferiority of restrictions appear to hold for any restrictions on the currency supply.
5. Taylor evaluates the central banks' performance using Friedman's profit criterion and finds that their losses in the 1970s ran into billions of dollars. These losses arose because they tried to resist exchange rate movements, and their efforts tended to destabilise foreign exchange markets. His work also suggests that speculation against the central banks both reduced the destabilising effect of their intervention and decreased the welfare loss associated with that intervention.

6. A possible objection is that monetary policy might still be worthwhile if it appropriates beneficial externalities that the market does not. See note 3.

7. A third sort of rule that is sometimes suggested is that the bank should attempt to stabilise interest rates. The problem with this is that if the target interest rate is inappropriately chosen the price level would become extremely volatile, and the correct interest rate — the natural rate — is likely to vary and be almost impossible to identify in practice. I have therefore ignored interest stabilisation rules.

8. In practice, this raises serious problems. Only the monetary base can be directly controlled by the central bank. If the target aggregate is broader than the monetary base then the bank has to manipulate the base (or interest rates) to meet its targets. This is far from easy as it would have to be able to predict the behaviour of the rest of the banking system and the general public. On the other hand, as we explain in the next paragraph, the adoption of a monetary base target undermines its LOLR role.

9. As Hendry (1985, p. 80) says:

   A standard blunder with [standard money demand] equations . . . is to 'invert' them to 'determine' one of the price level or nominal income or interest rates etc. . . . The equation is predicated on the assumption that agents could obtain the M1 balances they desired and is a *contingent* behavioural rule *given interest rates, inflation and incomes*. Then agents choose to hold on average the amounts of M1 predicted by the equation. . . . *Such equations cannot be inverted and still remain constant.*

10. As we discussed in the previous chapter, there is also the non-trivial problem of ensuring that the LOLR has the right incentive structure to carry out its LOLR function in the most desirable way.

11. It is sometimes said that the government can do this if it has an informational advantage over the private sector (see Fischer 1977). However, as Barro (1977a) points out, the obvious first-best solution is for the government simply to give the information away. In any case, it is not clear why the government should have an information advantage in the first place. If it arises because the government has monopolised the collection of information then that monopoly should presumably be abolished. If the information is valuable, private agents would have an incentive to collect it for themselves, and competition would presumably ensure that it was collected in the fastest and most efficient way.

12. I am not suggesting that monetary factors are the *only* cause of economic fluctuations. There is a long literature on the non-monetary causes of business cycles (see the summary in Haberler 1941), and more recently there has been considerable interest in 'real business cycles'. I am suggesting only that monetary factors are a major source of *avoidable* instability.

13. Capie (1986, p. 156) notes that all major inflations have been

associated with social unrest leading to deficit spending and thence to rapid inflation. He also notes that a:

> striking feature common to all the episodes [of very rapid inflation] is that of an unbacked paper currency. . . . Without a paper currency, the technology available would not allow a sufficient expansion of the money supply or a rise in velocity sufficient to produce the rapid rise in prices. All experiences with unbacked paper money resulted in inflation, though they did not always degenerate into very rapid inflation. . . . But vast increases in unbacked paper characterize all very rapid inflations. (pp. 140–1)

14. It is unfortunate that most economists have ignored Hutton's book *Inflation and Society* (1960). It is one of the best pieces ever written on the subject.
15. Roman inflation during the third century — its worst period — averaged about 3–4 per cent per annum (Capie 1986, p. 117). It is most disturbing to note that this would be considered reasonably low by modern standards.
16. Faig (1988) explores further the conditions under which the inflation tax is dominated by a linear commodity tax. He implies (p. 146) that they probably hold, at least in the industrialised countries.

4

An 'Ideal' Monetary System

How to discover a banking system which will not be the cause of catastrophic disturbances, which is least likely itself to introduce oscillations and most likely to make the correct adjustments to counteract changes from the side of the public, is the most acute unsettled economic problem of our day.

(Vera Smith 1936)[1]

4.1 Introduction

It is sometimes claimed that state intervention into the monetary system can be justified because the use of money generates external benefits that cannot be appropriated by the free market, or that the production of money is a natural monopoly, or that state intervention is required to provide a 'unit of account' in which prices can be expressed. This chapter begins by examining these claims. In doing this, it is convenient to drop the ambiguous term 'money' and instead distinguish between the *medium of exchange* (MOE), the *medium of account* (MOA) and the *unit of account* (UA). The MOE refers to the debt instruments which are transferred in the exchange process, the MOA refers to the commodities in terms of units of which prices are quoted, and the UA refers to those units. It is important to make these distinctions because very different considerations apply to the MOE and the MOA: the use of an MOE normally requires the use of an instrument that cannot be used for some other purpose at the same time, but an MOA is free of this limitation and can be used by any number of people simultaneously. The

MOA is in the nature of a social convention, and the economies it brings are economies of standardisation[2] rather than of production. It follows from this that arguments about production externalities or natural monopoly are not strictly applicable to the MOA, though they can apply to the MOE; because of such considerations we must treat the MOE and the MOA separately.

Our objective is to develop an idea of the roles of the MOE and the MOA in an 'ideal' monetary system. We begin by taking the MOA as given, and examine whether externality and natural monopoly considerations apply to the MOE. We shall see that there are no plausible arguments for these would justify state intervention into the provision of the MOE. We then discuss the role of the MOA, how the MOA and the MOE relate to each other, and how state intervention has replaced a commodity-MOA with an inconvertible paper one. We should then be able to set out our ideal monetary system and outline how it could be established. Its characteristic features are unrestricted competition, a convertible currency, and a commodity-definition of the MOA.

4.2 Externalities

The first argument we wish to consider is that state intervention in the production of the MOE is justified because the MOE has 'public good' characteristics which would lead to a sub-optimal output under *laisser faire*. A public good is a good with one or both of the following characteristics:

- Its consumption by one individual does not reduce the consumption available to another ('non-rivalness').
- Once it is produced, the producer cannot restrict its consumption ('non-excludability').

Public goods are sometimes claimed to provide a justification for state intervention because they can lead to externalities which are not appropriated by private agents in a free market. According to the standard Pigovian analysis, these agents only look at their own private (marginal) costs and benefits, and a sub-optimal outcome results because these differ significantly from the corresponding social costs and benefits. Some form of intervention is then supposedly required to bring these private costs and benefits into line with the social ones.[3]

Three types of externalities are usually put forward: externalities arising from the exchange process (transactions externalities); confidence externalities; and information externalities. We shall now consider each one of these in turn.

Transactions Externalities

These arise from the use of a medium of exchange. The usual argument is that externalities arise from the liquidity services of money, but the problem here is that the liquidity services of money tend to accrue to the owner rather than to anyone else. However:

> It might nonetheless be argued that an individual's use of a *common* medium of exchange confers non-appropriable external benefits to others who can now trade with him more cheaply, and that therefore a free market monetary system will underproduce the quality characteristic of commonness or general acceptability in exchange media. (White 1986b, p. 12)

Having set out the argument, White then proceeds to demolish it:

> If we assume that some fraction of the transactions cost savings accomplished through use of a common money are enjoyed by the marginal money user, the remainder being enjoyed by those with whom he transacts, then there is no divergence between what is privately optimal and what is 'socially optimal' in the choice among exchange media. [In any case, he adds:] This argument runs up against the historical fact that the market did *not* fail to produce commonly accepted media of exchange prior to government involvement in money. Gold and silver emerged as near-universal monies because of strong *private* incentives for individuals to use as exchange media the commodities that other traders most readily accept. (p. 12)[4]

Confidence Externalities

The confidence externalities argument takes two basic forms: (i) that government intervention is necessary to increase the insufficient level of confidence that would be provided under the free market; and (ii) that private provision of confidence involves a 'social waste' that could be eliminated by the state.

The first argument can mean *either* that an individual bank has insufficient incentive to promote confidence, *or* that the banking system, as a whole, will not promote sufficient confidence. The first interpretation runs up against the fact that banks have very strong incentives to promote public confidence — each bank will appreciate that if it loses confidence it will face a run which, at best, will force it to borrow liquidity at short notice and, at worst, will drive it out of business. Given this, there is no a priori reason to believe that a bank will take insufficient measures to promote public confidence. In any case, like similar arguments, if this one is correct it proves too much: if it justifies the suppression of competitive banks of issue, then it justifies the suppression of competition among banks of deposit as well. Indeed, in addition, it may justify suppressing competition in any other industry that also depends on public confidence (such as insurance or medicine), and one wonders whether many of its advocates would be willing to take their logic that far. The second intepretation implies that there is some systemic failure which prevents the system as a whole from producing sufficient confidence, and this seems to imply that there is a 'contagion mechanism' which spreads lack of confidence in one bank to others. The reader will recall, however, that we discussed this issue in Chapter 2 and found that no plausible case could be made for such a mechanism when markets exist to price bank-specific risk.

We turn now to the argument that the private provision of confidence is wasteful. This usually takes the form that private issuers of money — media of exchange in this context — would need to keep reserves of specie to promote confidence, and these reserves are a social waste that could be eliminated if the state abolished the convertibility requirement. There are several problems with this line of reasoning:

(1) It ignores the fact that the commitment to convertibility, and the reserves needed to support it, serve a very useful purpose — they offer a guarantee of the real value of the currency, and this plays a major role in helping to promote confidence in it. Proponents of fiat money ignore the main issue when they assume that the state can intervene by suppressing convertibility and maintain confidence at little or no cost. Confidence is not something that can be created by state fiat. As Klein (1978, p. 75) puts it: 'Consumer confidence . . . is not a free good that can be created by mere assertion'. If the state destroys the guarantees that promote confidence, then it inevitably undermines that confidence itself. Any reserves the banks keep to maintain convertibility are therefore far from wasted.

(2) If it is correct that convertible currencies involve a social waste, then one might expect that inconvertible currencies would drive out convertible ones through a process of free competition. There is no evidence to support that — indeed, there does not appear to be a single historical instance of fiat money supplanting convertible currency through competition rather than state coercion.[5] The evidence all points the other way, in fact, and there are plenty of examples of the public giving up inconvertible currencies and adopting convertible or commodity currencies instead during rapid inflations.

(3) An inconvertible currency involves considerable resource costs of its own. As Friedman (1986, p. 642) puts it, the argument that an irredeemable paper currency involves 'negligible real resource costs . . . is clearly false as a result of the decline in long-term price predictability'. The costs of this price unpredictability include the costs of the disruption caused by inflation as well as the costs of taking precautions against future price instability (like the resources used up in markets which exist to provide people with assets to protect themselves against inflation).

(4) In any case, competitive banks have an incentive to economise on their reserves because they represent forgone lending opportunities. A good example of this is provided

by the Scottish free banks which were able to operate successfully on very low reserve ratios. Checkland (1975, p. 237) reports that the average ratio of specie to total liabilities for the Scottish banks in March 1772 was 6 per cent, while Cameron (1967, p. 87) gives figures for the free banking period as a whole of 1–5 per cent. These figures indicate that the potential gain from eliminating reserves would be quite low anyway, and it is quite possible that more sophisticated short-term reserve markets would lead modern free banks to operate on even lower reserve ratios.[6] Indeed, it is quite possible that reserve costs could be substantially *eliminated* if the banks substitute contracts for future deliveries for (spot) commodities. As Barro (1979, pp. 30–1) points out, 'The use of futures not only eliminates significant storage costs, but also removes the entire resource cost (except for transactions costs in futures markets) from this part of the monetary base. . . . It is, in fact, imaginable to have a commodity reserve that is based entirely on futures'.

Information Externalities

It is sometimes argued that a competitive banking system would impose large information requirements on private agents (Laidler 1986, p. 311). This argument states that the uniformity of money is a public good which reduces the information burden on transactors, and the conclusion usually drawn is that the best way to provide the good is for the government to suppress the variety of monies that would arise under free competition. However, as White (1983) points out:

> The argument proves too much . . . It holds equally against proliferation of a variety of products or brands in any industry. It amounts to arguing that too much choice makes life difficult for consumers and ought to be suppressed by government choosing for them. This sort of intervention in fact eliminates the only process available — market competition — for discovering which products and how many brands best serve consumer preferences. Even if the market process will eventually converge on a single type of money . . . the time spent converging is not a wasteful aspect of competition that may efficiently be supplanted by government

edict. Government would not be in a position to know what the market process would have selected as most suitable. If the market will instead support a number of brands, as under competitive conditions it has in the production of coins and inside money, entry barriers serve no welfare-enhancing purpose. (pp. 292–3)

4.3 The Natural Monopoly Argument

These considerations indicate that externality arguments for state intervention in the monetary system are not particularly plausible. This leaves the argument that state intervention can be justified because the business of issuing money is a natural monopoly. A natural monopoly arises when marginal costs decrease as output rises. Declining marginal costs lead to a single producer because, at some point, one producer would take advantage of his falling costs and expand his output to try to drive his competitors out of the market. Other firms might expand in retaliation, but the resultant fall in prices would make production unprofitable for everyone, and by some point all but one firm will have decided to cut its losses and pull out of the market. The result would be a market with a single producer — a 'natural monopolist'. There are two versions of the natural monopoly argument that have sometimes been made regarding the issue of notes.

The first argument is that issuing notes is a natural monopoly because the marginal cost of issuing a note is simply the cost of printing it (or less, if one thinks of it as the cost of adding a zero to a dollar bill). But this only applies to a fiat money issuer, and we have already seen that under competitive conditions a fiat money issuer would eventually be driven out of business. A fiat note issuer is thus a *real* monopolist — one whose business is protected by legal restrictions against competitors — and not a natural one, as such: remove legal privileges and the monopoly will disappear.

It becomes readily apparent that the marginal cost of a note is much more than the cost of the pen and ink needed to print it, when one appreciates that freely competitive banks would issue convertible notes. Granted this, the relevant marginal cost is not the cost of printing an additional bill and putting it into circulation, but the cost of keeping it there, as we discussed in Chapter 1. This marginal cost includes the cost of increasing the demand for the bank's notes as well as the cost of simply putting additional notes into circulation. Unlike the costs of printing another note, there is no particular reason to suppose that these marginal costs are decreasing.

The second version of the natural monopoly argument is based on the economies of scale of reserve holdings. (One sometimes finds this argument in implicit form, but I am not aware of it being spelt out in detail anywhere.) Assuming that banks would issue convertible notes, the argument would be that there are economies of scale in reserve holdings because of the well-known theorem that optimal reserve holdings rise with the square root of the scale of transactions. This implies that larger banks would have a competitive advantage over smaller ones, and one could argue that the note-issuing business is a natural monopoly because there is no apparent limit to these economies. While the argument for *economies of scale* in note-issuing seems both theoretically plausible and historically well-attested, it is premature to jump from that to the conclusion that the industry is a *natural monopoly*. The size of the potential economies is likely to be quite small, in my opinion, because banks would tend to operate on quite low reserve ratios anyway, and it is plausible to suppose that other factors (like organisational diseconomies) might produce decreasing returns to scale beyond some point.[7] This would put a stop to the growth of firms and the emergence of a natural monopolist. In any case, it seems to me that the logical implication of the economies of scale argument is the centralisation of reserves (e.g. in a clearing house association) rather than the emergence of a natural monopolist, as such.

Be that as it may, if the note-issuing business was a natural monopoly, we would expect to see a single producer emerge under conditions of free competition, and there is no evidence of such a tendency from the historical experience of relatively free banking in Scotland, Canada, Sweden or New York State during the free banking period (see White 1984b, Schuler 1985, Jonung 1985 and King 1983, respectively). The market structure that did emerge was a stable one with a few relatively large note-issuing banks, but there was no tendency for any one bank to drive the others out.[8]

In any case, it would still not be optimal to prevent entry to the note-issuing business — even if it were a natural monopoly. The *threat* of entry is still required to encourage the natural monopolist to operate efficiently. Restrictions on entry therefore need to be abolished to make this threat effective. As Vaubel (1984) puts it:

> the optimum does not require restrictions on entry, or other forms of legal currency discrimination, not even with respect to the currency unit. Since we do not know the characteristics of an optimal money . . . there is a case against restrictions on entry. Since, finally, we cannot even be sure that money or the currency unit is a natural monopoly, the case against restrictions on entry is overwhelming. Only if a governmental producer of money can prevail in conditions of free entry and without discriminatory subsidies is he an efficient natural monopolist.[9] (pp. 46–7)

4.4 The Medium of Account (MOA)

This completes our discussion of MOE arguments and we turn now to those relating to the MOA. By definition, all prices take the form of bilateral exchange rates: 'so many units of good x for one unit of good y'. This can become cumbersome when there is a large number of goods, so it is helpful to select one good and express prices in terms of one unit of it (in other words, select a medium of account (MOA) — the terminology is Niehans' (1978).) This has the advantage that it reduces the number of bilateral exchange rates — i.e. prices — that an agent needs to consider. It is often said that the choice of MOA is a matter of definition, analogous to the definition of units of temperature or length, and it is sometimes inferred from this that the choice of MOA is an arbitrary matter devoid of any economic significance. This, however, ignores the costs of the time or resources used up in the process of comparing exchange ratios. These accounting costs are important in understanding why a particular MOA is chosen in preference to others (see Niehans 1978, Chapter 7).

Once a good is chosen as an MOA then the prices of other goods will alter as the relative price of the MOA-good changes. If we wish to minimise this kind of price volatility — as we presumably would — then we would want to choose as an MOA a good whose relative price was reasonably stable. The choice of MOA has real economic significance because some MOAs imply more stable prices than others. The correct analogue to the choice of units of length is therefore the choice of units in which to measure the MOA — i.e. the UA — and not the MOA itself.

Our first task is to sort out the relationship to each other of the MOA and the MOE. They are often the same commodity, but they do not have to be. (To give a trivial example, the MOA traditionally used in auctions in England is the guinea, but the MOE is an instrument of exchange denominated in pounds sterling.) This may seem an obscure issue, but we need to sort it out in order to understand the forces at work in a monetary system, and thence to form a clear idea of the 'ideal' monetary system which we seek. To clear up this issue we need go back to the origins of the monetary system and consider how it evolved.

4.5 The Early Evolution of the Monetary System

A useful place to start is with White's (1984a) 'conjectural history' of the evolution of the monetary system. He begins with a primitive barter economy driven by private interest. Individual traders seek to avoid double-coincidence-of-wants problems by resorting to indirect exchange in which they exchange their own goods for an easily disposable (saleable) intermediary good and then seek someone who has the goods they want and who is willing to take the intermediary good. The most saleable good would normally be preferred, and its use as an intermediary good would make it even more saleable. In the end, one good is likely to become dominant as an intermediary, and this good could be regarded as a medium of exchange. In the course of this process, a medium of account would emerge as a means of economising on accounting costs. White's argument is that traders would naturally post prices in terms of the good they were willing to accept in exchange. This is so because:

> Posting prices in terms of a numeraire commodity not routinely accepted in payment [i.e. using an MOA that was not the MOE — K.D.] . . . would force buyer and seller to know and agree upon the numeraire price of the payment media due. This numeraire price of the payment medium would naturally be subject to fluctuation, so that updated information would be necessary. A non-exchange-medium numeraire commodity would furthermore be subject to greater bid–ask spreads in barter against other commodities, as by hypothesis it is less saleable, than the medium of exchange. It would therefore serve less well as a tool of economic calculation. (p. 704)

White's conclusion is that: *'a unit of account emerges together with and wedded to a medium of exchange'* (p. 704, my italics). He also stresses that the 'process is self-reinforcing: a buyer or seller who communicated bid or ask offers in nonstandard units would impose calculation costs on potential trading partners' (p. 711), so that other people have an incentive to adopt the MOA that is already being used. This being so, the market would converge on an MOA without any need for state intervention to sponsor one.

4.6 The Development of the Banking System

The next stage[10] in the process is the development of inside money — bank notes and deposits — based on convertibility into the outside money (gold). At first there are only a few metalsmiths who keep gold safe and issue depositors with receipts in return for a fee. The practice spreads, however, and as it does, people begin to exchange the receipts instead of redeeming their gold and then redepositing it every time they want to trade. The receipts become banknotes and the goldsmiths become bankers. In the meantime the goldsmith–bankers realise that they could make a profit by lending out the gold deposited with them. They therefore start competing for gold by offering the public interest-bearing deposit accounts. In order to make them more attractive, they will allow the public to use these deposits as exchange media by writing cheques on them. Banknotes and deposits thus evolve as alternative MOE to gold, but they are valued in terms of gold, and they may continue, for a while, to be redeemable in gold.

It is important to stress that gold continues to be the sole medium of account, principally because it is not worthwhile for an individual to change the MOA he uses. An agent who introduces a new MOA imposes additional accounting costs on those with whom he trades and, unless there are sufficient gains to compensate for these costs, the agent will have to operate on wider bid–ask spreads to get people to trade with him, but if he does that he will be out-competed by rivals who stick to the old MOA. This perhaps explains why the public appears to be so reluctant to adopt new MOAs, except in circumstances where the old one was faring extremely badly (e.g. under hyper-inflations).

Notes and deposits have the advantage of being cheaper to store and transfer than coins, and deposits have the additional advantage of bearing interest. As the public gets used to banks, and trusts them more, it increasingly prefers to use inside money as MOEs instead of gold. The public preference for inside money is borne out by its readiness to hold the money wherever it is allowed to. Indeed, in some cases, notes have sold at a considerable premium: for instance, W. Graham (1886, pp. 131–2) reports that in the town of Wick in western Scotland, in 1825, the fishermen would sell barrels of herrings at a price which was 1s. to 5s. cheaper if they were paid in local notes — which they knew and trusted — rather than coins, which were less familiar to them. Ultimately, it is possible to envisage a fully-banked economy in which gold is entirely replaced as an MOE by notes and deposits. Gold would continue to be the medium into which notes and deposits were denominated, but it would fall into disuse as an MOE.[11,12]

Another feature of this *laisser-faire* banking system to be noted is that at no point does the system ever abandon convertibility. Convertibility satisfies a need (to guarantee the value of a bank's liability) and that need continues to exist for as long as the bank does. As discussed in Chapter 1, a bank that abandoned convertibility would be out-competed by rivals, and the banks would be unable to keep out competitors if they abandoned convertibility in concert. Writers like Meulen (1934, pp. 239–41) and McCallum (1985, p. 29) appear to be mistaken when they rather casually suggest that the banks might eventually just give it up.[13] As an aside, it is possible that banks might change the medium of redemption (MOR) if an alternative seemed to be superior (for example, they might start to redeem in platinum rather than gold), but the principle of convertibility would still remain intact.[14]

In reality, of course, the banking system never got to the point we described because the state intervened to alter its development. This intervention took place in two steps. In the first, the state intervened to establish a bank with a monopoly of the note supply, but the notes of the monopoly bank continued to be convertible into gold. Over time, however, the bank's notes replaced gold in everyday exchange and in most agents' reserves, and most gold disappeared abroad or into the vaults of the bank of issue. Once this process had been substantially completed, the state then intervened to suppress the convertibility of the monopoly bank's notes into gold. The MOA had changed from being a particular commodity to become an inconvertible paper liability issued by a particular bank. It bears stressing that *nowhere* did convertibility disappear as part of a spontaneous market process: in *every case* it disappeared because the state suppressed it.

4.7 An 'Ideal' Monetary System

We are now ready to outline our ideal monetary system and how it could be established. On the basis of our earlier discussions I suggest that it be based on the principles of unrestricted competition, a convertible currency, and a commodity-definition of the MOA:[15]

- Competition is desirable on the same grounds that competition in any other commodity is (usually) desirable: it is the most effective way to provide the public with the monetary services they want. There appear to be no plausible grounds for externalities or natural monopolies in the provision of MOEs that might have justified state intervention to prevent competition. Agents would also be entirely free to use whichever MOAs or MORs they wished.

- Convertibility is required to give legally-binding guarantees of value to the holders of bank liabilities. As we saw earlier, however, there is no need for convertibility to be imposed because competition among banks would lead them to adopt it anyway, and there is no need for the state to restrict the choice of convertibility contracts which banks might offer their customers.

- A commodity-definition of the MOA is needed in order to provide a stable anchor for prices,[16] because the alternative of a fiat MOA creates a considerable amount of unnecessary price instability.

We shall now outline how such a monetary system could be established.

Redefining the MOA

Since we start with an intrinsically worthless MOA, the first reform would be to (re)define the MOA in terms of an intrinsically valuable commodity-bundle. It is very important that the existing MOA — the dollar, or pound, or whatever — be redefined rather than a new one introduced, because introducing a new MOA would impose substantial costs on the public. The adoption of a new MOA would mean that prices would have to be re-posted, forms and records changed, people would have to make an effort to get used to it, and so on. Switching over to a new MOA could also be very disruptive. Since the old MOA is inconvertible, its value depends on its supply and demand, and the fall in demand for it would produce a major inflation unless appropriate measures were taken to contract its supply in line with the fall in demand. If this is not done, the inflation might soon accelerate out of control, with inflation reducing the demand for the MOA and the reduced demand pushing inflation up further. In any case, there is no guarantee that the public would actually switch over to a new MOA — what incentive would they have to adopt it? — and if they did not, we would be left more or less where we started, with the disadvantages of a paper MOA whose longer-term value was very uncertain. In short, the introduction of an alternative MOA would cause a number of potentially serious problems which could all be avoided if the existing MOA was simply redefined instead. There would be no adjustment costs and the public would continue to use the MOA it was used to.[17]

Then there is the question of what the commodity bundle should be. Perhaps the best criterion that could be used to select an appropriate commodity bundle is that it be expected to deliver a reasonably stable general price level. The choice is basically between a bundle of commodities which is large enough for changes in the prices of individual goods to cancel out and produce a reasonably stable average price, and a single commodity (or perhaps a small group of commodities) whose price(s) could be expected to remain stable because supply is highly elastic. The exact choice of the commodity bundle is obviously a matter of some judgment, of course. If we wanted a large commodity bundle we might go for the goods and services whose prices make up the consumer or producer price indices, for instance. We could also go for something like the ANCAP commodity bundle suggested by Hall (1981a). This is made up of a particular combination of ammonium nitrate, copper, aluminium and plywood, and Hall shows that the price of the ANCAP bundle moved very closely with the cost of living in the USA in the postwar era. Whether it would continue to do so is another matter, of course, but the ANCAP and others like it clearly deserve to be considered. Alternatively, if we wanted to go for a single good we might go for a commodity like bricks, as suggested by Buchanan (1962).

It must be stressed that the *sole* purpose of the redefined MOA would be to function as a (stable) value-measurer. It would *not* be to provide either an MOE or a *medium of redemption* (MOR). The choice of both of these would be left entirely to the free market. The MOA, the MOE and the MOR each perform fundamentally different functions, and it would be fortuitous if one good (or group of goods) turned out to be efficient at more than one of these functions. There is no reason to expect the most efficient MOA to be the same as the most efficient MOE(s) or the most efficient MOR(s), and there is certainly no reason to impose more than one function on any one good. In the present context, this means that in choosing the MOA, there is no reason to restrict the choice to meet requirements that MOEs or MORs would have to satisfy (like whether or not people would be willing to accept it in payment, or whether it could be 'warehoused' or transferred easily). To repeat, therefore, the *only* requirement the MOA would have to satisfy is that it be a stable measurer of values.[18]

A related issued is whether the commodity definition of the MOA should be revised periodically. I would suggest that periodic revisions are desirable because the commodities chosen and the weights attached to them would otherwise be frozen to reflect the prices and patterns of demand at the particular point in time when the MOA was established, and as time passes the value of the MOA might diverge from (other?) general price indices. Future patterns of demand can never be predicted with much precision, and a commodity index that seemed ideal *ex ante* might turn out to be less satisfactory than it was anticipated to be. Furthermore, there is always the possibility that certain goods might cease to exist at all. If this happened then the good in question would obviously cease to have a price, and so the price of the commodity bundle of which it was a part could not be determined. Since we could never be sure that each of the goods in the bundle would continue to exist, this factor alone requires that there be some procedure to revise the MOA.

The next matters to be decided are who would select the commodity definition of the MOA and how the revisions should be made. I recommend the establishment of an expert commission to decide on the initial definition of the MOA, and to meet periodically to make any revisions. The objective of the committee would be to come up with a commodity definition of the existing MOA that could be expected to keep prices stable, but it would have to select a commodity bundle of the same value as the pre-existing MOA at the time of the changeover. This would prevent any disruption caused by sudden jumps in the value of the MOA — and hence in prices generally — as the changeover to a commodity definition of the MOA is made. The machinery setting up the committee would also need to have safeguards to prevent groups with vested interests from 'capturing' it and using it to manipulate the price level. Among these groups with an interest in manipulating the price level is the state itself, which is the biggest debtor of all. A major safeguard would be to stipulate that any revised MOA should have the same market value as the old one,[19] which would prevent sudden jumps in the price level as the revised definition takes effect. This, in turn, would reduce, but not entirely eliminate, the scope for interested groups to use the committee to influence the price level, and we would still have to guard against revisions being adopted that were expected to cause major price movements in the medium or long term. To address these problems we might give the commission quasi-judicial status to protect itself from the executive and legislative branches of the government, and we might diffuse the power to appoint members in some way. It might also help to give the committee an inbuilt conservative bias by specifying voting rules that would require substantial majorities for any changes to the definition of the MOA to be carried through. This would make it more difficult for interest groups to 'capture' the committee and control its decisions.

The Provision of Media of Exchange

We now leave aside the MOA and turn to consider the banks. As mentioned earlier, there would be no restrictions at all on the liabilities the banks could issue, or on the MORs into which they could be redeemed. The sole requirement that they — or anyone else — would have to satisfy is that they honour any commitments they freely enter into. The role of the state would be simply to provide the judicial machinery to allow such commitments to be enforced. The contracts which banks make with their liability-holders would have the following features:

- They would specify the conditions under which the liability could be redeemed. The liabilities might be redeemable on demand, for instance, or they might give the bank the right to demand prior notice under certain conditions.
- They would specify the commodity bundle — the medium of redemption (MOR) — into which bank liabilities could be redeemed. As we discussed already, the MOR might be the

same as the MOA, but there is no particular reason why it should be.[20] The choice of MOR is best left to the free market as there is no way to tell what the most appropriate MOR might be, or whether it has changed over time. In this respect, as in so many others, the market is the only available discovery mechanism for finding out what the most appropriate MOR might be, and the best way to ensure that we get it. The MOA would probably be an instrument or commodity (bundle) that is standardised and valuable, relative to storage costs, and financial instruments — like equities and claims to physical commodities — come readily to mind, as well as precious metals like gold and platinum.

- These contracts would also specify the value of the MOR into which a given liability could be converted, as measured in terms of units of an agreed MOA. The law would not force the bank and its customers to use a particular MOA but, as we suggested already, if the MOA in general use is reasonably stable they would almost certainly choose to use it.

Having established an MOA and suggested that banks should be free to do as they wish, we then have to explain how prices are determined and what forces exist to return them to their equilibrium levels if they are 'shocked' away from them.[21] To do this, let us first assume that a particular bank issues a note worth one unit of the MOA (which we shall call a dollar). Let us also suppose, for the sake of argument, that the MOA is a commodity bundle that is traded in a particular market.[22] The bank stands ready to buy and sell its notes for a price of $1, so the equilibrium price of the MOA is clearly unity. Given this, we can think of all other nominal prices as being pegged down by the exchange rates of the goods in question to the MOA. This explains how prices are determined.

Now, suppose that the price of the MOA, in terms of the banknote, is shocked above unity. Let us suppose, for instance, that the price of the MOA rises to $1.2 in bank notes: this would make the MOA overpriced, compared to the banknote. In that case an arbitrageur would sell a unit of the MOA on the MOA-market for $1.2 in notes; he or she would then go to the bank and exchange his/her notes for 1.2 units of the MOA. (Recall that the bank would buy its notes at face value.) In this way, the arbitrageur would have converted one unit of the MOA into 1.2 units. He or she might then sell the 1.2 units for $1.44, and so on. In the process, the bank would lose reserves and its notes would be retired. Market operators would continue to make capital gains in the same way until the banknote price of the MOA was restored to par. Conversely, if the price of the MOA fell below unity, market operators would make profits by selling it to the bank, since the bank would be willing to buy it for a higher price (i.e. unity) than the market. They would do this for as long as the price remained below unity, and thereby return it to par. This establishes that a mechanism exists to return prices to their equilibrium levels.

We turn now to the issue of legal tender (the issue of what constitutes the legal payment of a debt). The general rule to be adopted is that the law would consider as payment of a debt whatever the two parties to the contract agreed should constitute payment, but no-one would have the right to force someone else to accept a particular MOE or to insist on being paid in that MOE unless the contract covered it. (This is necessary to protect creditors from being forced to accept dubious credit instruments like bad cheques, and to protect debtors from creditors who unreasonably refuse to accept the MOEs they are offered in payment.) A slight problem is that it is often costly to make contracts fully exlicit, so it would be better if these costs could be avoided by incorporating 'default clauses' in the relevant law of contract which would specify a certain class of instruments that would be considered as constituting legal payment unless a contract explicitly specified that payment was to be made in some other medium. Exactly what instruments this law should include needs more careful thought, but one possibility is that it should simply define the default instruments as 'all commonly accepted media of exchange' and leave it to an evolving body of case-law to give judgments on what that does and does not include.

Such a default clause would not only reduce the costs of writing contracts, but it would also solve several other problems that have sometimes arisen in discussions of prospective monetary reforms. One of these is what MOEs the state should be willing to accept in payment of taxes. The answer, presumably, is that the state would accept the MOEs covered in the default clause, as currently interpreted by the courts. A second issue is whether agents might find themselves forced to accept payment in terms of a bundle of physical commodities. This is a frequent concern for monetary systems with MOAs defined in terms of commodity-bundles; for example, in discussing Hall's ANCAP scheme, White (1984a, p. 702) says that if the commodity bundle is legal tender:

> Any sufficiently wide divergence between the market price of the standard commodity bundle and one dollar will trigger demands by creditors to receive commodities rather than paper dollars (or deliveries by debtors of commodities in place of paper dollars). Transactors choosing to contract in ANCAP dollars would be exposing themselves to the risk of being forced to deliver, or to accept delivery of, physical bundles of the standard commodities.

This problem is easily avoided by excluding the MOA from the list of instruments covered by the default clause. Payment in physical commodities could then only be insisted upon if it was explicitly specified in the contract. Thus the problem discussed by White no longer arises.[23]

Notes

1. Quoted from Smith (1936, p. 171).
2. I am grateful to White for suggesting the term 'economies of standardisation' to me.
3. One might also mention in this context that the Coase theorem (1960) suggests that externalities tend to disappear when property rights are appropriately defined. This implies that the presence of externalities requires the redefinition of property rights, rather than intervention, to equalise marginal private and social costs or benefits. In a sense, most of the following arguments can be interpreted as different ways of working through this insight.
4. White also mentions another transactions cost argument and proceeds to dismiss it:

> The most that could be argued on transaction–cost–externality grounds is that market convergence on a common money may

occur too slowly because of limited information about the exchange media accepted by one's potential trading partners. If this argument went through, it might be used to make a utilitarian case for collective subsidy of convergence-speeding information additional to the information that would be privately produced. It could not be used to justify government imposition of a monetary standard by edict, however, because an unbiased market process is necessary in order to discover what type of money traders will find most suitable. In order to enhance 'social utility', of course, government would have to know (magically?) what information was in fact socially valued more than its cost of production even in the absence of any revealed willingness to pay for it, and would have to spend less (angelically?) on its production than the information was worth. But even if that were possible, government's limited publicity role would disappear entirely once the economy had fully converged on a common money. (1986b, p. 13)

5. Steve Russell of the University of Georgia maintains that such an instance may well have occurred during a ten-year period in the 1820s and 1830s in North Carolina. He develops this theme in his forthcoming PhD dissertation (University of Minnesota, 1989). I am not convinced that this is a genuine counter-example, but I haven't yet seen his work.

6. Also, it is quite possible that banks would hold other assets as MORs, whose holding costs were lower, thereby lowering reserve costs even further. The Scottish free banks apparently did this (see note 14 below.)

7. An excellent survey by Lewis and Davis (1987, pp. 202–10) of recent empirical work on economies to scale in (principally deposit) banking indicates that there are substantial, but not unlimited, economies to scale. This suggests that we would expect large firms but not a natural monopoly.

8. The historical evidence of relatively free banking shows some tendency towards 'pyramiding' (i.e. some banks acting as bankers to others), and some writers read such evidence as indicating a natural monopoly (e.g., Laidler 1987, p. 17). Bank pyramiding and natural monopoly are quite separate issues, however, and they must be clearly distinguished. In any case, there always tends to be more than one bank at the head of the pyramid (that is, there is pyramiding but no natural monopoly).

9. Fischer (1986, p. 435) challenges this sort of argument by suggesting that it does not apply when there are substantial fixed costs of entry. That response seems to miss the point. Even if there are substantial entry barriers, the threat of intervention limits the extent to which a natural monopolist can exploit the market or allow itself to operate inefficiently. In any case, the presence of

entry barriers in the free market does not constitute an argument for adding legislative barriers as well.

10. For the sake of brevity I have omitted to discuss how competitive mints would arise to convert the lumps of precious metal into coins. For more on that, see White (1984a) and Dowd (1988b). To avoid unnecessary complications I have also assumed that all coins are gold.

11. This conclusion — that the MOA and the MOE would separate — runs counter to the majority view (e.g. Barro 1985, p. 50, McCallum 1985, p. 17; and White 1984a, pp. 699, 712). McCallum concludes that the same commodity would serve as both MOA and MOE because he seems to restrict himself to a commodity-MOE. On the basis of that restriction, his conclusion is correct but it does not apply to a more sophisticated banking economy. White, however, insists that his conclusion does apply to a sophisticated economy, but in my opinion he fails to appreciate the crucial role played by the potential dominance of inside money as an MOE over physical commodities.

12. An interesting issue is what would have happened to the relative price of gold, and hence the price level, had the process of replacing gold as an MOE been allowed to run its course without state intervention. The gradual supplanting of gold as an MOE would have reduced its demand directly, as the demand for gold as an MOE declined, and indirectly, as this reduced demands on the banking system for redemption and enabled banks to reduce their reserve ratios. Other things remaining equal, the fall in demand for gold would reduce its relative price, and hence raise the price level. As this happened, the price level would also become relatively more dependent on those factors that determine the 'non-monetary' demand for gold — like fashions in jewellery or technology in dentistry. How serious a problem this might have become, or how the banking system would have responded to it, are fascinating questions which demand further exploration.

13. Incidentally, McCallum's suggestion — that the Bank of England's suspension of convertibility during the period 1797 to 1821 is a possible example of this — is very misleading. In fact, the Bank was forced to suspend principally because of the scale of government demands upon it, not because convertibility became obsolete.

14. It is interesting to note in this context that the Scottish free banks found it worthwhile to adopt new MORs, though they apparently did not abandon specie entirely as MORs: Checkland (1975, pp. 186) points out that the notes of the public banks were used by the other banks as redemption media, while the public banks themselves often used drafts on London to redeem their liabilities (Fetter 1965, p. 122). The newer MORs were presumably adopted because they were cheaper to hold than specie.

15. An option to be avoided at all costs is to maintain the inconvertible

note issue while allowing everyone to issue identical notes. This would effectively be the same as giving away the central bank's note-issuing plates to anyone who cared to use them, and the result would be the hyper-inflationary nightmare mentioned by Friedman (1960), in which people keep printing additional dollars until the marginal revenue from doing so — their purchasing power — is driven down to the marginal cost (virtually nothing) of printing them. This disaster would arise because everyone would effectively be liable for everyone else's notes and so there would be no private incentive to restrict their issue. As our discussion of a *laisser-faire* system indicates, this outcome can be avoided simply by allowing people to issue notes for which they alone are liable.

16. This fills an important gap that some other schemes for free banking have left open. For example, Selgin (1985) proposes to establish free banking but leaves the MOA issue in an unsatisfactory state by advocating the freezing of the monetary base. As mentioned in the text, that effectively leaves prices at the mercy of the very uncertain future demand for the MOA.

17. The redefinition of the existing MOA we propose also avoids a major difficulty that arises with the alternative monetary systems of Fama (1980) and Hall (1981b). Both papers discuss model economies in which a major role for the state is to determine the MOA, but neither of them explains why the private sector would adopt the state-sponsored MOA as an MOA. The 'spaceship tax' discussed by Fama would create a demand for the government's fiat MOA, but would not in itself make the private sector use it *as an MOA*, while Hall seems to imply — in my opinion very unreasonably — that the mere definition of an MOA by the state would suffice to make the public use it.

18. This highlights another advantage of our monetary system: the value of the MOA commodity bundle is not affected by its adoption as MOA. When the MOA is tied to the MOE or MOR — as it is, for instance, under our current monetary regimes — then changes in policy with respect to the MOE or MOR affect demand for the MOA, and that can lead to changes in its relative value, and hence in prices generally. To give an example, the adoption of a gold standard in which gold was used as either an MOE or MOR would increase the demand for gold and raise its relative price, possibly quite significantly. This change in relative price would be very difficult to predict and, consequently, so would the price level generated by this kind of gold standard. This is another example of the Lucas critique of econometric policy evaluation (1976).

19. In suggesting that the MOA be revised in a way that keeps its value constant, my scheme avoids a major drawback that affects schemes for 'constant dollars' whose value would be altered from time to time to keep their purchasing power constant. (These have been proposed, for example, by Fisher (1920) and Hall (1981a).) The problem is that the revisions would be predictable, and this would

cause considerable disruption to interest rates as the revisions approached: as a revision came up, speculators could anticipate increasingly large capital gains, and short-term interest rates would have to rise to very high levels to keep pace with them. My proposal would avoid this problem because it would avoid any jumps in the price level as the revisions take effect.

20. A convertible system in which the MOR and the MOA differ might be called *'indirectly convertible'* (see Yeager 1985, p. 106). Note that in such a system the MOA-price of the MOR will generally fluctuate — the MOE will be convertible into the MOR as valued in terms of the MOA. For the record, the system proposed here borrows much from the system Yeager proposes in that paper, but it differs from him in dispensing entirely with the notion of a monetary authority.

21. This meets a criticism that McCallum (1985, p. 28) has levelled at Hall (1981a). Hall maintains that the state would define an MOA but would do nothing itself to maintain its exchange value. He insists that arbitrage opportunities would do this, but does not explain how they arise; he implies that they would arise (somehow?) from the legal tender definition of the dollar, but leaves it at that. In my system the exchange value of the currency is maintained by the banking system's offering convertible liabilities whose nominal value is tied to the exchange rate of a commodity-MOA.

22. This assumption is made only to illustrate the mechanism at work in the simplest possible way. A similar but more involved logic still applies, even if the MOA is traded in a set of markets rather than just one: the key arbitrage opportunities on which the basic mechanism depends would still remain. Another simplifying assumption is that the bank redeems the notes immediately on request (that is, it does not invoke any option clause, if it has one). Again, this does not affect the basic mechanism at work.

23. Even this precaution might not be necessary under my system. The problem could only arise if all the commodities in the MOA were warehousable and transferable; if even one were not — and many commodities are not (like labour services) — then it would be physically impossible to make payment in terms of the MOA, and the problem could never arise.

Appendices to Chapter 4

Appendix 1: Counterfeiting

It is sometimes claimed that the multiplicity of bank notes under free banking would make counterfeiting more of a problem because the public would find it more difficult to recognise forgeries. However, this argument seems to be based on a misconception: counterfeiting becomes more of a problem not so much when there are more note issuers, but when the average circulation period of a note is longer. The longer this period is, the more counterfeit notes that can be put into circulation without detection. As White (1984b, p. 40) indicates, Scottish bank notes during the free banking period circulated for a very short period of time before being returned via the clearing system, and instances of counterfeiting were relatively few as a result. (Counterfeiting did not appear to be a major problem with free banking in New York state either, see King 1983, p. 155.) The harm done by counterfeits to the public was reduced even further because the banks tended to adopt a policy of honouring counterfeit notes if they were tendered in good faith. Apparently, this was an act of self-interest: they realised that the cost of honouring counterfeits would be quite low and that the policy would encourage people to accept their notes and thus increase the demand for them. By contrast, Bank of England notes of the same period tended to have relatively long circulation periods, and the counterfeiting of Bank of England notes was a very serious problem, especially during the Restriction period (see Fetter 1965, pp. 71–3).

Appendix 2: The 'Separation' of the MOA and the MOE

In a recent paper Greenfield and Yeager (1983) have argued that *laisser faire* would permit a 'separation' of the MOA and the MOE that would allow macroeconomic stabilising mechanisms to arise that are suppressed when the prices of the MOA and MOE are tied together. (They actually use the term 'unit of account' in this context but for reasons explained earlier it is more accurate to use the term 'medium of account' instead.) Their argument is as follows:

> Our existing monetary system is subject not only to inflation but also to stagflation, deflation, and depression because the unit of account and the medium of exchange are tied together and because the actual quantity of money can fail to correspond to the total of money holdings desired at the existing price level . . . Market-clearing forces do not work very well to maintain or restore equilibrium between money's supply and demand because money does not have a single price of its own that can adjust on a market of its own. Instead, the medium of exchange has a fixed price in the unit of account (each dollar on the money market has a price of exactly $1). With no specific price and market to impinge upon, imbalance between money's supply and demand must operate on the dollar's purchasing power, that is, on the whole general price level. This process requires adjustments on the markets and in the prices of millions of individual goods and services . . . failure to keep the quantity of money correctly and steadily managed can have momentous consequences. (Greenfield and Yeager 1983, p. 309)

If correct, this would suggest another reason for the superiority of *laisser-faire* banking in correcting macroeconomic disturbances. This analysis is not entirely convincing, however. To begin with, we should note that the Greenfield–Yeager arguments do not apply to MOEs in general, but only to non-interest-bearing ones (or, strictly speaking, to MOEs whose interest rate is not allowed to adjust to equilibrate the market). When an MOE bears interest (like a demand deposit), and the interest rate is allowed to adjust freely, then it can be used to equilibrate the market without imposing unnecessary and costly price adjustments in other markets. The 'spillover effects' which Greenfield and Yeager talk about would therefore seem to apply only to the currency whose rate of return is not allowed to adjust sufficiently. The question then is whether the market for this currency can adjust to shocks without imposing these spillover effects on other markets. Greenfield and Yeager suggest that this can be done by varying the MOA-value of the MOE, but we have already seen in our discussion of note runs that a *laisser-faire* banking system could do this easily and automatically by increasing or decreasing the note supply to satisfy any demand at the same price. (The supply of notes is perfectly elastic, in other words.) The fact that the MOA and the MOE are tied together (i.e. have a fixed exchange rate) does not force prices elsewhere to adjust, provided that banks are free to adjust the note supply. Greenfield and Yeager have highlighted an important problem — that the note market might not be able to equilibrate without imposing costly price adjustments in other markets — but the cause of it is restrictions on the note supply rather than the tying together of the prices of the MOA and the MOE.

Appendix 3: Legal Tender

In the text we proposed that legal tender (what would constitute the legal payment of a debt) should be whatever the parties to the contract agreed it should be, and in the event of this being unspecified there should be a default list of possible instruments which would be considered as legal tender. This approach to legal tender would dispense with legal-tender laws, as they are conventionally understood. Such laws tend to restrict agents' freedom to enter into mutually beneficial contracts and they are sometimes used to redefine currency units in ways that award arbitrary gains to some groups and inflict arbitrary losses on others. They therefore violate the state's presumed duty to protect the security of contracts. In the former case, this duty is violated because certain classes of contracts are denied the protection of legal enforcement. In the latter case, the state becomes an accomplice to the violation of a contract that two agents had freely entered into. According to this view, there is no need for legal-tender laws anyway because legal tender is already covered by existing laws of contract:

> The ordinary law of fraud does all that is necessary without any law giving special function to particular forms of currency . . . If I promised to pay 100 sovereigns, it needs no special currency law of legal tender to say that I am bound to pay 100 sovereigns, and that, if required to pay the 100 sovereigns, I cannot discharge the obligation by anything else. (Lord Farrer 1895, quoted in Hayek 1976b, p. 32)

It follows that to the extent that legal tender laws force people to accept what they had already agreed to accept, then they needlessly duplicate existing laws of contract, and to the extent that they force a creditor to accept or a debtor to pay what he had not agreed to accept or to pay, then the original contract is violated and there is an arbitrary redistribution from one to the other.

The view of legal tender which I have articulated might be described as a libertarian, *laisser-faire* approach. There are, however, several alternative schools of thought we should consider. The first is a kind of metaphysical approach which would not deserve serious consideration but for the fact that elements of it still appear to be widely accepted. According to this view, legal-tender laws are necessary to make money acceptable. As Hayek (1976b, pp. 30–1) puts it, this view of legal tender: 'is surrounded by a penumbra of vague ideas about the supposed necessity of the state to provide money. This is a survival of the medieval idea that it is the state which somehow confers value on money that it otherwise would not possess.' This view of legal tender was revived by Knapp (1905), and made fashionable in the English-speaking world by the sympathetic attitude Keynes took towards it (see the *Treatise on Money* (1930), volume 1, pp. 3–6). It is closely related to the chartalist view that 'money is the creature of the state', in the sense that it is the state that gives money value. This view of legal tender is decisively refuted by both historical evidence and a priori reasoning. As Menger (1892) demonstrated, money arose quite spontaneously so there is no logical necessity for the state to create it. As for the need to compel people to accept money, reason tells us — and history abundantly confirms — that people do not need to be compelled to accept a 'good' money that they trust. This suggests that we ought to provide them with a framework that would produce a money they trusted instead of trying to force a currency on them they did not want.

The second alternative view is that legal tender laws should be employed to encourage people to use a particular money because of externalities. (This appears to be implicit in Hall (1981a), for example.) The argument is that legal tender enables the economy to benefit from the use of a common money, or that it would make the market converge faster on a particular money. We have already seen, however, that the uniformity argument is dubious because the benefits of using a common money are privately appropriable, and this implies that a uniform money would be adopted anyway, even without the assistance of legal tender. And, as the White quote in note 4 clearly suggests, the speed-of-convergence argument at best implies that there should be a subsidy to provide more information to encourage faster convergence — and even that is debatable — but it provides no basis for continuing intervention once the convergence has been completed.

Appendix 4: The Future of the Monetary System

A major concern of much recent literature (e.g. Fama 1980, Greenfield–Yeager 1983, White 1984a) is with the prospective future evolution of the payments system and, in particular, with the replacement of cash by other financial instruments. It seems to me that this has been a major issue because people are concerned that the declining currency/deposit and (bank) reserve ratios that would accompany such changes would imply a rising price level in an outside money economy, and because at the limit — that is, when these ratios are zero — the price level would become indeterminate.

Two points need to be made here. The first is that the problems of the declining demand for currency pushing up prices and a possibly indeterminate price level do not arise in our system because it is a convertible one. Prices are determined by the relative price of the MOA, not by the supply and demand for currency. Hence the question of whether currency would disappear does not have the same importance in my system that it does in some other monetary systems, although it is obviously not without interest. The second point is that my previous analysis continues to hold pretty much regardless of what new financial instruments arise and whether the ones in current use disappear or not. As mentioned in the second chapter, when we talk of a *note* we really mean any financial instrument that is convertible into some outside redemption medium, and where we talk of a *deposit* we really mean a financial instrument that is convertible into another. Similarly, a *bank* is just an institution that issues these instruments. Whether notes, deposits and banks, as we know them, continue to exist or not does not fundamentally affect how one would analyse the monetary system. (The only difference I can think of is that it may be easier to pay interest on future 'notes' than it is to pay interest on the notes we have today — see Appendix 5 — but whether that counts as a major analytical difference is doubtful.) The reader should therefore not be misled by the talk of 'notes', 'deposits' and so on to think that we are discussing a monetary system that is likely to become obsolete as financial innovation continues. Financial innovation should not affect the way we analyse it in any fundamental way.

Appendix 5: Competition, the Rate of Return and the 'Optimal Quantity of Money'

This appendix deals with some issues that have been raised regarding the manner in which competitive banks compete away the surplus profits from issuing notes, and whether or not the competitive outcome is Pareto-optimal.

In a competitive equilibrium it will be worthwhile for an individual bank of issue to put out its last note, but it will not be worthwhile for it to issue another. This is because an extra note would come back sufficiently quickly not to be worth the expense and effort of putting it into circulation in the first place. If the bank wanted to increase its circulation it would have to increase the demand for its notes by opening more branches, advertising more, making its notes more attractive, and so on. However, one would presume that if the bank were in equilibrium, the number of branches, the amount spent on advertising, and so on, would be optimally chosen, and so the bank would have no incentive to try to expand its note circulation further.

This establishes that the 'excess profits' of note issuing will be 'competed away', but it does not tell us *how* they are competed away. It has been suggested in the literature that banks might do this by paying interest on their notes or by engineering a price deflation so that the real value of a note of fixed nominal value would rise over time. A perceptive analysis of the interest-bearing notes issue is given by White (1986c, pp. 7–9). He argues that they involve a certain amount of inconvenience to the public because of the need to calculate the present value of the note. Given this, there would be some threshold denomination below which it would not be worth an average individual's while to collect the interest accruing on the note. He then proceeds:

> A thumbnail calculation indicates that this threshold value would in practice exceed historically common currency sizes, given historically common interest rates. On a note whose initial value equals two hours' wages, held one week while yielding interest at 5% per annum, accumulated interest would amount to less than 7 seconds' wages. If the noteholder's wage rate indicates the opportunity cost of his time, then he will not find it worthwhile to compute and collect interest if to do so twice (once at the receiving end and once at the spending end) takes seven seconds or more . . . To indicate the same point less generally, a $20 note held one week at 5% interest would yield less than 2 cents. Notes held in cash registers by retailers generally turn over much more rapidly than once a week, of course, so that the threshold denomination may well be extremely high. (pp. 8–9)

This argument strongly suggests that interest-bearing notes will not circulate except perhaps for relatively large denominations, and this appears to be broadly consistent with historical experience.

That leaves the issue of whether banks would pay a return on their notes by engineering a price deflation. It seems to me that they would not. If banks tried to denominate their notes in terms of an asset whose value rose over time, they would have to offer one denominated in a new MOA, unless the MOA currently in use had a value that just happened to be appreciating at the desired rate. Barring this fortuitous circumstance, the notes denominated in the new MOA would impose additional accounting costs on the people who used them. Calculation problems would therefore arise similar to those which arise with interest-bearing notes. There is, however, a vital difference between the two cases. With interest-bearing notes, the noteholder is in principle guaranteed his return, but in the second case he is not. This is because prices do not usually change continuously, but rather at discrete intervals, so the noteholder would only get the benefit of the rising real value of the note if the prices of the goods he wanted to buy fell (relative to the note) over the short period for which he held the note. Even during a rapid inflation, many a noteholder will find that the value of note he holds does not change at all over the particular period for which he holds it. This leads one to suspect that if noteholders are to receive pecuniary returns, then they would probably prefer to receive them in the form of explicit interest payments — that way they can be sure of getting their return. And if it is not worthwhile to pay interest, then it will not be worthwhile to introduce notes denominated in an MOA with a rising real value. We would therefore expect to observe agents using non-interest-bearing notes denominated in the standard medium of account, and that seems to be what we find.

This analysis suggests that it is misleading to talk about competitive banks of issue offering liabilities with a 'competitive real rate of return', at least as far as note liabilities as we know them are concerned. (Here, I refer to 'notes' as we know them, not necessarily to hypothetical future 'notes'.) It also suggests that the 'optimal quantity of money' literature (e.g. Friedman 1969) may be of limited applicability to the problems we have discussed here, the reason being that it presupposes that banks compete along only one dimension — the pecuniary rate of return on notes — and that is the very dimension along which our discussion leads us to believe they will *not* compete.

In the absence of any obvious grounds for externalities, I would suggest that there is a prima-facie case that the individual bank's (and noteholder's) optimum outlined above translates into a Pareto-optimal general equilibrium. Before we can safely draw that conclusion, there is a possible objection to be considered. That concerns Samuelson's so-called 'non-optimality of money holding under *laisser faire*' (1969). The starting point of the argument is that agents under *laisser faire* will choose levels of real money balances that reflect their private opportunity costs of holding money. The argument is then that all agents could benefit if they could be induced to hold more money balances by mistake, and hence it is concluded that *laisser faire* is non-optimal. However, this analysis treats the cost of increasing money balances as trivial, and given the costs of expanding note issues under convertibility, this is even remotely plausible only with an inconvertible currency. For reasons explained earlier, this would imply a restricted note issue, and so Samuelson's conceptual experiment does not really apply to *laisser faire*. In any case, we have already suggested that any outcome with a restricted note issue will not be Pareto-optimal. Therefore, our prima-facie case, that we have a social optimum under (genuine) *laisser faire*, still stands.

5

The Establishment of Central Banking

A central bank is not a natural product of banking development. It is imposed from outside or comes into being as the result of Government favours.

(Vera Smith 1936)[1]

5.1 Introduction

We turn now to the historical experience of state intervention into the monetary system. This chapter deals with the establishment of central banking, while the next deals with its historical record. We shall see how British and American monetary history confirms many of the conclusions we reached earlier about the benefits of *laisser-faire* banking and the potential damage that can be done by state intervention. For accounts of other countries' experience, the following references might prove to be useful: for Canada, see Bordo and Redish (1988), Chisholm (1979, 1983), Schuler (1985, 1988a,b) and Shortt (undated); for China, see Selgin (1987); for France, see Nataf (1987) and E. White (1988); for Sweden, see Jonung (1985) and Sandberg (1978); and for Switzerland, see Weber (1988). The experience of these countries appears to be broadly consistent with the conclusions that we draw from British and American monetary history.

We begin with the establishment of central banking in Britain.

5.2 The Early History of the Bank of England[2]

A recurrent theme in English history is the government's perpetual shortage of money. The monarchs could always levy taxes, of course, but only with their subjects' consent, and they were often forced to make concessions to obtain it. Over time the need for taxes grew, but so did the accumulated concessions and the potential for conflict between sovereign and Parliament. The Tudor monarchs were generally skilful enough to avoid major confrontations with Parliament, but the needs of the state continued to grow, and when the relatively inept Stuarts succeeded to the throne a major confrontation was almost inevitable. It came with the Civil War (1642–50).

The war failed to solve the underlying problem. After the Restoration Charles II soon found himself in financial straits and decided to borrow the money he needed from the London goldsmiths, rather than ask Parliament for it. He could not repay and repudiated the debts in 1672. This action caused much distress and badly damaged the Government's credit for years to come. Some twenty years later William III needed money to wage war against France but was faced with high interest rates reflecting the Government's poor credit. He was therefore very receptive when a Scottish financier, William Paterson, suggested a scheme in which he and a group of other financiers would advance the Government a loan in return for the right to set up a bank to issue loans and print banknotes. The bank was to be known as the Governor and Company of the Bank of England, and it was set up in 1694.

The early history of the Bank can be summarised as a series of purchases of privileges by the Bank from the Government. Originally, the Bank made a loan to the Government of £1,200,000 in return for the right to issue notes to the same amount. These amounts were extended in 1697, when it was also stipulated that the Bank should enjoy a monopoly of chartered banking in England and the privilege of limited liability for its shareholders. These were the beginnings of the Bank's monopoly powers. In 1709 these were extended further when a law was passed to limit competition to companies with less than 6 partners with unlimited liability. The capital of any other bank was therefore limited to what could be provided by up to 6 partners, and in an industry where there were economies of scale this meant that English banks were severely under-capitalised. The effects of this were very detrimental:

> The hunger for credit persisted . . . and reliable aggregations of capital from among more than six moderately wealthy persons were impossible. The consequence was that petty shopkeepers and tradesmen set up everywhere as bankers to supply the demand for credit . . . (But) With every threat of a Stuart rising or a foreign invasion the more timid people rushed to the banks to exchange their notes for gold. Only the wealthy banks could stand such runs, and the petty shopkeeping banks failed on all such occasions in scores, dragging down with them their clients . . . (Meulen 1934, pp 95–6)

It was widely believed at the time that the instability of English banks was due, not to their under-capitalisation, but to their freedom to set their own terms of redemption and issue small notes. This led to demands for legislative action, and Parliament responded by prohibiting option clauses throughout the UK in 1765, by prohibiting notes of less than £1 in England and Wales in 1775, and then by extending this ban to notes of less than £5 in 1777. The suppression of option clauses forced banks to redeem on demand and made them vulnerable to runs on their liquidity, while the suppression of small notes meant that the majority of trades now had to conduct business using the more expensive medium of coins. This ban also hindered the growth of small banks since new banks relied, to a large extent, on the issue of small notes to gain acceptance.

The sale of privileges to the Bank continued throughout the eighteenth century. As Smith (1936, p. 11) put it:

> The result of the accumulation of an array of privileges was to give the Bank of England a position of prestige and influence in the financial world such as to cause small private banks to experience difficulties in continuing to compete in the same line of business, and in London the majority of private note issues had been abandoned by about 1780. A further effect was that the smaller banks began to adopt the practice of keeping balances with the Bank of England, which was thus already beginning to acquire the characteristics of a Central Bank.

The process of the Government raiding the Bank's larder eventually culminated in the suspension of the convertibility of the Bank's notes. When the French revolutionary wars broke out, the Government repeatedly applied to the Bank for more loans. The Bank felt obliged to comply, although it did so under protest, but the strain on its reserves proved too much, and in the end the Government had to authorise the Bank to suspend specie payments. In effect, the Government had first made the Bank insolvent, and then legalised its insolvency.

After the suspension, Bank of England notes went to a discount against gold, and specie disappeared from everyday circulation. To all intents and purposes the Bank's notes were legal tender, although they were not made so officially until 1812. The use of the Bank's notes was encouraged further by the authorisation to issue small notes, which was motivated by a desire to economise on specie. Increasingly, the other banks came to look upon Bank notes as backing for their own issues, and they continued to do so even after convertibility had been restored and Bank of England notes again ceased to be legal tender. The nation's stock of gold was therefore concentrated more and more in the vaults of the Bank of England, and this, together with the Bank's unique note-issuing privileges, meant that the Bank came to be looked upon as the ultimate — and indeed, only — source of help in liquidity panics. This was gradually to force the Bank to accept a role as lender of last resort and custodian of the nation's monetary system.

We now leave England for a while and turn to Scotland.

5.3 The Development of Free Banking in Scotland[3]

The development of banking in Scotland took a very different course from that of banking in England. The first Scottish bank was the Bank of Scotland, which received its charter from the Scottish Parliament in 1695. This charter gave it the rights to limited liability and a monopoly of the note issue in Scotland until 1716. Despite its title, the Bank of Scotland was not a state bank, and its charter prohibited it from lending to the Government. Shortly after its foundation, the Act of Union of

1707 merged the Scottish and English Parliaments, and the new Westminster Parliament was distinctly unsympathetic to the Bank because of its suspected Jacobite leanings. It therefore ignored the Bank's pleas not to charter a rival bank — the Royal Bank of Scotland — in 1727.

Warfare between the banks broke out on the same day the second bank opened. Each side tried to drive the other out of business by collecting its notes and presenting them for summary redemption. It became apparent, however, that though these 'note duels' could inflict considerable damage, neither bank was going to put the other out of business. The banks gradually realised this and a more peaceful note exchange began to develop which eventually led to a formal note-exchange agreement in 1751. The competition continued on other fronts, nonetheless, and it led to some major banking innovations. In 1728 the Royal Bank instituted the cash credit account, a form of overdraft which individuals could use, provided they presented evidence of sound character and two or more co-signatories who accepted liability for the loan. This allowed individuals to borrow money without the need for extensive collateral of their own. Meanwhile, in the same year the Bank of Scotland (the 'Old Bank') began offering interest on its deposits, and the following year it introduced a cash credit account of its own. It followed these innovations, in 1730, with the introduction of the option clause to protect itself from sudden demands for redemption.

The next move in the banks' rivalry was the establishment of the Glasgow Ship Bank in 1749 by the Old Bank, to win business away from the Royal Bank. The latter responded by setting up the Glasgow Arms Bank the next year. The two Glasgow banks then turned against the Edinburgh banks by issuing their own notes, and a new bank war followed. The bank war proved inconclusive, so an attempt was made to set up a cartel and agree on a market share-out. That attempt proved to be unsuccessful, and so the banks settled down to an uneasy coexistence. In the meantime, a new chartered bank came on the scene with the British Linen Company, which obtained its charter in 1746. Originally set up to promote the linen trade, it started banking and eventually dropped the linen trade altogether. New banks continued to enter the field in the late

1750s and early 1760s and they began to offer notes for smaller amounts (less than £1) which helped to alleviate the inconveniences caused by the lack of an adequate coinage. The banks also adopted the Old Bank's practice of inserting option clauses into their bank note contracts to protect their liquidity. Both small notes and option clauses were controversial, though, and they were suppressed by Act of Parliament in 1765[4]. After this, Scottish free banking was never entirely 'free'.

The innovations continued. In 1771 all the major Scottish banks finally agreed to accept each other's notes at par and to exchange them at a regular clearing. This helped to promote the demand for each bank's notes, but it also contributed significantly to the stability of the banking system by providing a rapid and effective check against any bank that over-issued its notes. The 1770s also saw the establishment of the first successful branch banks, and branch banking rapidly spread.

The stability of the Scottish system was demonstrated by the episode of the Ayr bank failure. The management of this bank engaged on a reckless expansion of its loan business and soon found itself in serious difficulties. It managed to remain solvent only by borrowing from bankers in London, but its steadily mounting debts forced it into bankruptcy in 1772 just 3 years after it opened. The public suffered no losses from the failure, and all the creditors were eventually paid off in full. Any inconvenience the public might have suffered was reduced by the policy of the Old Bank and the Royal Bank to accept the notes of the Ayr Bank at par; they did this to attract more deposits and to put more of their own notes into circulation. The collapse of the Ayr Bank inflicted serious losses on the bank's proprietors (who were liable for all its debts) and on some smaller banks that had circulated its bills, but the major banks and the public suffered little or nothing. Such were the effects of the most serious bank collapse during the free banking period.

The Scottish banking system was as able to weather external shocks as internal ones. Two of the most significant were in 1797 and 1825–6. The first was when the Bank of England suspended convertibility — this caused a brief panic in Edinburgh, and the major Scottish banks temporarily suspended as well. The panic subsided, however, and the Scottish banks soon resumed their normal redemption policies and maintained them for the rest of the Restriction period. This indicates, incidentally, how competition forced the banks to maintain convertibility. The second shock was the crisis of 1825–6, 'a panic so tremendous that its results are well remembered after nearly fifty years' as Bagehot (1873, p. 138) later described it. This panic shook the English banking system to its foundations, and virtually every bank in the country had to apply to the Bank of England for assistance. The strength of the Scottish banking system is perhaps illustrated by the fact that not a single Scottish bank felt the need to apply to the Bank of England, despite the close links between the English and Scottish financial systems.

Scottish bank notes were widely accepted, not just in Scotland but in much of northern England as well. The esteem in which Scottish notes were held is well illustrated by a memorial sent by the representatives of the border areas of Northumberland and Westmoreland to Parliament, when it was proposed to prohibit the Scottish £1 note in 1826. The memorial outlined the reasons for the strength of the Scottish banks and continued:

> The natural consequence has been that Scotch notes have formed the greater part of our circulating medium, a circumstance in which we have reason to rejoice, since, in the course of the last 50 years, with the solitary exception of the Falkirk bank, we have never sustained the slightest loss from one acceptance of Scotch paper; while, in the same period, the failures of banks in the north of England have been unfortunately numerous, and have occasioned the most ruinous losses to many who were little able to sustain them.[5]

Another indication of the relative losses suffered by the public in Scotland and England is given by White (1984b, p. 41) who reports an estimate of the losses from all Scottish bank failures, up to 1841, of only £32,000. Against this, losses the previous year in London alone were said to have been twice that amount.

The fifty years or so after the Ayr Bank episode saw the further development and consolidation of the Scottish banking system. The smaller note-issuing banks gradually disappeared, and branch-banking continued to spread. The smaller banks that remained tended to be specialist firms which kept accounts with the larger banks and did not issue notes. This indicated that there were substantial but limited economies of scale in the note-issuing business, and there was certainly no tendency for any one bank of issue to drive the others out. In other words, while there were economies of scale there was no evidence of natural monopoly in the note-issuing business or any other aspect of banking.

The system of free banking in Scotland appears to have promoted the country's economic development in various ways: by making credit available to promote industry and commerce; by encouraging habits of thrift and industry among the population; by encouraging the use of bank liabilities as media of exchange to reduce transactions costs; and by providing the people with a stable monetary system which protected them against disturbances. An indication of how much the banking system might have contributed to Scotland's economic development is given by Cameron (1967, pp. 94–5). He points out that per-capita income in Scotland in 1750 was probably only half that in England, and yet it nearly equalled England's income by 1845. Scotland's much more rapid economic progress over this period was attained despite a number of obvious disadvantages — its greater political instability, inferior infrastructure and greater distance from export markets — and Cameron concludes that the only advantages it could have had, relative to England, would have been its superior educational and banking systems. It therefore seems reasonable to suppose that Scotland's better economic progress was due in some considerable part to its superior banking system.

5.4 British Controversies Over Central Banking[6]

While the roots of the free banking idea can be traced to Adam Smith (1776)[7] and Jeremy Bentham (1788)[8], it was not until the 1820s that it began to acquire anything like a significant following. The immediate antecedents to free banking can be found in the agitation in the early 1820s for the 6-partner rule against joint-stock banking in England to be abolished. This agitation appeared to start with James Mill's *Elements of Political Economy*, in 1821, and a pamphlet by Thomas Joplin in 1822. They argued that the joint-stock organisation was more suited to banking than a partnership, and cited the example of Scotland as evidence. Their claims seemed to be borne out by the disastrous crisis of 1825–6 which shook the English financial system to its foundations:

> The crash of 1825–26 brought down a number of England's most reputable country banks and London banking houses as well as scores of smaller banks. A single month in 1825 saw 73 banks stop payment, only 10 of which eventually resumed business. One member of Parliament took note that 700 or 800 country banks — virtually the entire industry — had asked the Bank of England for assistance during the general panic. The Bank of England itself, in the words of Bagehot 'was within an ace of stopping payment' due to depleted specie reserves. (White 1984b, p. 47)

This crisis led the Prime Minister, Lord Liverpool, to declare:

> The present system is one of the fullest liberty as to what is rotten and bad, but one of the most complete restriction as to all that is good. By it a cobbler or cheesemonger, without any proof of his ability to meet them, may issue his notes, unrestricted by any check whatever; while, on the other hand, more than six persons, however respectable, are not permitted to become partners in a bank with whose notes the whole business of the country might be transacted.[9]

The result was the Act of 1826 which allowed joint-stock banks of issue in England — provided only that they were more than 65 miles from London. Thus the Bank's monopoly position was perhaps weakened in one respect,[10] but confirmed in another.

About the same time, proposals began to be put forward to abolish the Bank of England's privileges altogether and establish free banking in England. One such proposal came from Sir Henry Parnell, who put forward the idea in a meeting of the pro-free-trade Political Economy Club in 1826. He argued that the issue of bank notes should be entirely free, and was severely critical of the 1826 Act which left untouched the greater evil to be remedied in the Bank of England. He was much impressed by the evidence brought by Scottish bankers to the Commons Committee of 1826, and repeatedly stressed the role of the note-clearing system in limiting over-issue among competitive banks. Because of this, he wrote:

> no such thing as an excess of paper or as a depreciation of paper can take place for want of a sufficiently early and active demand for gold.

If in England the power of converting paper into gold has not prevented an excess of paper, because the demand does not occur until long after the excess has taken place, this is to be attributed to the system of English banking.[11]

These claims provoked a number of critical responses, all of which disputed the claim that the clearing system would discipline over-issue. J. R. McCulloch (1831), for example, argued that a bank which expanded its note issues under competitive conditions of issue would be able to force the other banks to expand along with it, but the free bankers were quick to counter that this argument ignored the reserve losses which the expanding bank would face in the course of its expansion. G. W. Norman (1837), however, argued that the clearing system would not work because competition would force the banks to expand together. The premise of Norman's argument is dubious, as we discussed in Chapter 2, but in any case the reserve losses of the system as a whole would still exert the necessary discipline. The most famous argument, however, and one to which the free bankers never gave a clear response, was the argument put forward by the Irish economist Mountiford Longfield about the clearing system not disciplining over-issue because a bank which expanded its loans would also expand the payments it had falling due to it. We discussed this argument in Chapter 2, where we noted its invalidity because it is not sufficient to expand loans in order to increase the note circulation, and because the argument fails to allow for the time lag between the loan expansion and their repayment. We now return to the main storyline.

The calls for free banking from Parnell and others acquired additional force because the Bank's charter was due to expire in 1833. This put the Bank's defenders under considerable pressure, and it was doubtful whether Parliament would allow the Bank's privileges to be extended. As early as 1826 Lord Liverpool and Frederick John Robinson wrote in a letter to the Bank's directors: 'With respect to the extension of the term of their exclusive privileges . . . it is obvious . . . that Parliament will never agree to it. Such privileges are out of fashion, and what expectation can the Bank under present circumstances entertain that theirs will be renewed?'[12]

The threat was sufficiently strong that at least one of the Bank's proprietors in 1832 advised his colleagues to agree to give up the note-issuing monopoly in return for some form of compensation.[13] That same year, the Leader of the Commons, Lord Althorp, moved for an investigation in view of the coming expiry of the Bank's charter. The issue to be determined was the conditions under which individuals should be allowed to issue money. A Secret Committee was set up to deliberate the issue, but the Chancellor made a deal with the Bank to extend the charter and pushed the Committee to a quick decision to recommend renewal. The vast majority of witnesses were London bankers and brokers who recommended the renewal of the charter but were hardly in a position to offend the Bank, while many witnesses who would have opposed renewal were not even called.[14] On the Committee, Parnell alone voted against renewal and afterwards complained that the proceedings were 'ex parte and one-sided'.[15] When the issue came back before the House, Lord Althorp then made his position clear: 'My opinion is, that if you contrive an adequate check upon the conduct of a single bank, it will be more advantageous that such single bank should manage the circulation of the country, than that it should be left to the competition of different and rival establishments.'[16] In the event, a majority of MPs agreed with him, and it was decided to renew the Bank's charter until 1844.

In retrospect, this was probably the best chance the free bankers had to abolish the Bank of England's monopoly. The decision to renew the Bank's charter was greeted with many protests, and proposals for free banking continued to come from various quarters, both inside and outside Parliament, but as time went on the focus of public debate appeared to shift from the issue of whether there should be a central bank to the question of what rules it should follow. It was ironic that this increasing antipathy to free trade in banking came at about the same time as the idea of general free trade was gaining ground:

> There was an increasing feeling that the note issue should be concentrated in a single agency, either the Bank of England or a newly created National Bank . . . Spokesmen for the country banks tried to make the most of the idea that there was a conflict between the principles of free trade and a monopoly of the note issue. They had little success, and at the same time that free trade sentiment was

gaining ground in the field of trade and business there was a growing acceptance of the idea that note issue was not a business activity, but a function of government. The idea was expressed in many ways, and by many people, but the summary statement of Thomas Spring Rice, Chancellor of the Exchequer, in the debate on the Bank of Ireland bill in 1839, gave what appears to have been the preponderance of public opinion: 'I deny the applicability of the general principle of the freedom of trade to the question of making money'. (Fetter 1965, pp. 173–4)[17]

Whether or not this view represented the preponderance of public opinion in 1839, it certainly did later.

In the late 1830s the Bank came under renewed criticism for its alleged responsibility for the monetary disturbances of the period. A defence in 1837 of the Bank by one of its directors, John Horsley Palmer, laid the blame with the country banks' allegedly reckless credit policies. This pamphlet itself provoked a lot of criticism, and in the subsequent controversies three different schools of thought could be discerned: the free bankers argued that the problem could be cured by convertibility and competition, and that no fundamental solution could be found while the monopoly of the Bank remained. As one of their leaders, Samuel Bailey, said in 1837, under a monopoly, 'the necessity will exist of having recourse to arbitrary assumptions and empirical expedients', but under free banking, 'the currency will be capable of adapting itself by those insensible contractions and expansions which no human sagacity can ever effect, to the perpetually varying wants of the community'.[18] The second view blamed the monetary disturbances on the Bank of England and especially on the country banks, and recommended legislation to ensure that the note issue was properly regulated. This position was to crystalise into the currency school.[19] Their position is well summarised in the words of S. J. Loyd, one of their leading proponents: 'With respect to a paper currency . . . *a steady and equable regulation of its amount by fixed law* is the end to be sought'.[20] The third point of view put some of the blame on the Bank, but argued that it should simply hold a larger specie reserve. This point of view was put forward by Thomas Tooke and later evolved into the banking school. The currency and banking schools disagreed over the precise remedy to the problem, but they had a common and deep-rooted hostility to the free bankers, and the free bankers, in turn, were hostile to both schools as defenders of the Bank's privileges.

As the Bank's charter came up for renewal in 1844 the controversy tended to focus on the currency school's recommendations to regulate the Bank of England and the banking school's opposition to them. The currency school had a powerful ally in the Prime Minister, Sir Robert Peel, and in 1844 Peel was able to get their proposals enacted. Under this Act, the Bank of England was to be split into completely separate Issue and Banking Departments, and the former was to maintain a 100 per cent marginal reserve requirement beyond a fixed authorised note issue. All the Bank's other business was to be done by the Banking Department. Entry to the note-issue business was closed, and the note issues of banks in England and Wales were to be frozen. If any bank of issue failed or gave up its right of note issue, the fiduciary issue of the Bank was allowed to rise by two-thirds of the lapsed issue. The ban against banks of issue having offices within 65 miles of London also remained in force. It is significant that the main provisions of the Act were suggested to the Government by the Bank, whose management apparently saw the implementation of the Currency School proposals as a way of safeguarding their monopoly and giving them an 'automatic rule' they could apply which would shield them from public criticism. A second Act the next year froze the authorised note issues of the Scottish banks as well, and obliged them to maintain 100 per cent marginal reserve ratios against further issues. These Acts effectively centralised the note issue throughout the whole of the United Kingdom. Free banking in Scotland had been sacrificed to satisfy Peel's desire to unify the UK monetary system.

The reaction to these Acts from those who had advocated free banking was limited. In large part this was because the Acts bought off many of the interested parties. Much of the agitation for free banking had come from bankers, and the Acts effectively made note issuing a cartel by banning new entrants and freezing market shares. The suppression of competition was thus a windfall gain to existing note issuers, and this went a long way to silencing any other criticisms they might have made of the Act. More spirited reactions came from other quarters. James Wilson, the first editor of *The Economist*, condemned the Acts as entrenching the cause of the evil — the monopoly position of the Bank of England — and complained:

> We have never been able to discover any good ground for the objections which appear to exist in the minds of a large portion of even the most uncompromising free traders, against the application of the same principles to banking, and especially to the issue of notes payable on demand. Nor have we ever been able to elicit any satisfactory reasons for their objections; which the more we have considered the more we are satisfied are based on groundless fears and misapprehensions. (Wilson 1847, p. 281)

Further proposals for free banking continued after the setbacks of 1844 and 1845, but it slowly became apparent that the two Acts were there to stay despite the subsequent monetary crises that seemed to bear out their critics. Fewer people were willing to countenance radical proposals for monetary reform, and such proposals therefore seemed increasingly irrelevant. Writers like Herbert Spencer in the 1850s continued to advocate free banking, and Walter Bagehot in the 1870s accepted it in principle,[21] but regarded himself as too much of a realist to think it had any chance of being adopted, and after their generation no-one of any prominence supported free banking, even in principle. The old controversies about free banking were gradually forgotten, and it came to be accepted, more or less without question, that free banking must be unsound.

This completes our discussion of the establishment of central banking in England. We now turn to the history of banking in the United States.

5.5 The Early History of Banking in the USA[22]

While English banking was dominated from an early stage by the Bank of England, and Scotland enjoyed relatively free banking until Peel abolished it, the United States of America experienced a wide variety of monetary experiments that ranged between more regulated versions of free banking and less complete versions of what can only very roughly be described as 'central banking'. If Scotland enjoyed *freedom*, and the English system was *centralised*, the US system was one of 'decentralisation without freedom' as Smith (1936, p. 36) rather aptly described it, and the USA opted for fully fledged central banking only at the comparatively late date of 1913.

The first major monetary experiment in the USA was the founding of the Bank of North America to help finance the War of Independence. After the war was over, however, there was considerable agitation to abolish the Bank. It was argued that the Confederation Congress had no authority to grant bank charters, and that the authority to do so lay with the states because they had had that authority as colonies before independence, and had not granted it to Congress or relinquished it by joining the federation. The agitation eventually had the desired effect and the Bank's charter was repealed.

It was not long, though, before attempts were made to replace the Bank. The leading inspiration was Alexander Hamilton, who submitted a proposal for a new national bank — the (first) Bank of the United States — in 1790. Hamilton had considerable influence on the American banking system, not only on this occasion but later on as well because much later, legislation was based on his original ideas. The proponents of the Bank argued that a national bank would serve a number of purposes: it would help spread banking, and thereby facilitate the conversion of 'dead' gold and silver into productive capital; it would be able to provide the federal government with funds in an emergency; it would assist the federal government in the collection of taxes; and, by setting up branches, it would help to unify the all-too-fragmentary American banking system. Another argument for chartering the Bank was that the federal government would get a free share in it, worth around $2 million. The Act was passed and the Bank came into operation in 1791. The Bank was to be the depository of all federal balances and had the right to open branches in any state it chose. It proceeded to alienate other banks and was steadfastly opposed by the states' rights lobby. Its opponents were sufficiently strong that when the Bank's charter came up for renewal in 1811 they were able to prevent it and let the charter lapse.

In the meantime, many banks were set up under the separate legal systems of different states. The states' legal frameworks varied considerably, but they typically involved applying for a charter from the local legislature. The charter would give the shareholders some form of limited liability (usually fixed at twice the value of the capital subscribed) and placed restrictions on the ratio of note issues to capital. Banks were frequently obliged to make special loans to the states that chartered them, and these loans often weakened their liquidity and undermined their capital values, and thereby made them more prone to fail. The state charter system also had other adverse consequences. The fact that charters only permitted banks to have offices in the state (and sometimes only the county) where they were chartered prevented a branch-banking system from developing, and this caused two major problems:

- It increased banks' vulnerability by restricting their opportunity to diversify their portfolios;
- It raised the costs of redeeming notes. This hindered the development of an effective note-clearing system and created problems of note depreciation and over-issue. Banks of issue were smaller and more numerous, and their notes often found their way to other counties or states where they sold at discounts reflecting the high costs of redeeming them and the unfamiliarity of the banks that issued them. The high cost of redemption in turn reduced the frequency of redemption and relaxed one of the constraints against over-issue;

Had a branch-banking system been allowed to develop (as it was in Scotland and Canada) the banks would have been less vulnerable because they would have held more diversified portfolios, and they could have exploited economies of scale in the note-issue business in order to reduce the number of different notes, and to reduce the costs and increase the frequency of redemption. This, in turn, would have reduced over-issues and helped to 'equalise the exchanges' between different banknotes. As we shall see, these problems caused by a unitary banking system are a persistent theme in US monetary history.[23]

In 1812 war broke out again with Britain. At first, the US

government tried to cover its revenue needs by issuing loans, but it resorted to the issue of interest-bearing Treasury notes when these measures proved insufficient. A large number of banks bought these and used them to expand their own issues. This expansion of paper led to a shortage of specie, and most banks were forced to suspend convertibility. The result was monetary chaos. Different banks depreciated their currencies to different degrees, and it became impossible to maintain any kind of reliable medium of account. One consequence of this was to throw the government's finances into complete confusion:

> The Treasury . . . received duties in the bank notes of the port at which the goods were entered. Consequently there was a further advantage to import commodities at the port of entry where the currency was most depreciated. Hence Philadelphia and Baltimore enjoyed a period of great apparent prosperity, for, in July, 1815, New York paper was at 14% discount, and Baltimore paper at 16%, compared with Boston paper or silver . . .
> The government suffered the greatest loss and embarrassment from the derangement of the currency. Boston was the money market of the country, and there were heavy disbursements there, which must all be made at specie par; but there was no revenue there, all being obtained further south in depreciated notes. If any one had any payments to make at Boston to the Treasury, he bought notes of the suspended banks to the southward with which to do it. (Sumner 1986, p. 66)

Gresham's Law ensured that specie and the notes of specie-paying banks were effectively replaced by depreciated paper.

The combination of the deranged currency and the government's fiscal needs led to new calls for a national bank. A bill to establish such a bank was passed by Congress, but vetoed by President Madison early in 1815. The pressure for it intensified, however, and an Act the next year provided for the establishment of the Second Bank of the United States. This Bank was very similar to its predecessor: the government took a large (subsidised) stake in its capital; it had a 20-year charter and the monopoly of the government's deposits; and it had the right to set up branches anywhere in the Union it pleased. It was expected to provide a 'uniform currency' — i.e. to equalise the exchange rates of different banknotes across the country — and to act as the government's fiscal agent. To provide a uniform currency, it sought not only to provide a note issue of its own, but also to get other banks to peg their notes to it. In order to persuade them to do this, the Bank promised to provide them with support in the event of an emergency. This was the first time that an American national bank had explicitly accepted the role of lender of last resort.

In 1817 there was a temporary resumption of specie convertibility. It was temporary because the Bank, instead of attempting to reduce the state banks' issues, proceeded to encourage them further using its own notes as a basis. In over-extending itself, the Bank fed a further round of inflation and brought itself to the brink of bankruptcy in 1818. Its only possible response was to curtail its lending, which brought on a financial crisis. This produced widespread bankruptcies and a new suspension of convertibility in 1819.

After this inauspicious start, the Bank was gradually able to recover and its performance improved considerably. Convertibility was restored in 1821, and there were relatively few monetary disturbances throughout the 1820s. The Bank's reputation improved, and it began to look as if it would be accepted as an essential feature of the American monetary system. In the late 1820s, however, the Democrats went on the attack again and accused the Bank of violating its charter and meddling in politics.[24] When Andrew Jackson declared war on the Bank, all the old objections about its constitutionality and states' rights took new life again. The Bank, he declared, was 'unauthorized by the Constitution, subversive of the rights of the states, and dangerous to the liberties of the people'.[25] Jackson's election as President made it clear that the Bank was in serious trouble, and in 1833 he ordered the government's deposits to be removed from it. Not long afterwards he vetoed the bill to renew the Bank's charter, and the charter lapsed in 1836.

After this, the federal government abstained from any major attempts to legislate banking for nearly thirty years and left the field wide open to the states. There followed a fascinating period characterised by a wide variety of monetary experiments. This period is generally known — somewhat inaccurately, as we shall see — as the free banking period. We shall deal with this in the next section.

5.6 The Free Banking Period

The federal withdrawal gave the states free rein to pass whatever banking legislation they wished and a number of states then proceeded to enact free banking laws. The first states were Michigan, in 1837, and New York and Georgia in 1838. Others followed suit afterwards. While they varied from state to state, 'free banking laws' had the following general features:[26]

- Anyone could set up a free bank who could raise the capital to do so, subject to a minimum capital requirement which varied from state to state.
- Free banks had to secure their note issues with deposits of certain specified types of bonds that were to be deposited with the state auditor. The types of bonds eligible varied, but they were usually state and sometimes federal bonds.
- The notes of free banks had to be redeemable on demand, and a bank was to be liquidated and its assets sold off to pay its creditors if it refused to honour a single note. The noteholders usually had first preference on the assets of a liquidated bank.
- The shareholders of free banks were generally allowed some form of limited liability. The usual limit was twice the value of their capital subscription.

The first provision made entry to the banking industry free, subject only to a minimum size restriction, but the second and third provisions were potentially destabilising — the second because it forced the banks to buy state bonds and thereby made them vulnerable to fluctuations in their prices, and the third because it implied a prohibition of option clauses with which banks might have been able to protect their liquidity.

The experiences of different states varied dramatically. The free-banking experiments were successful in New York, Ohio and Louisiana, for example, but in others the result was less satisfactory. According to one modern account, 'Banks of very dubious soundness would be set up in remote and inaccessible places "where only the wildcats throve". Bank notes would then be printed, transported to nearby population centers, and circulated at par. Since the issuing bank was difficult and often dangerous to find, redemption of bank notes was in this manner minimized' (Luckett 1980, p. 23). An alleged instance of this 'wildcat banking' was in Michigan, after its first attempt at free banking. There, the bank commissioners complained that, 'gold and silver flew around the country with the celerity of magic; its sound was heard in the depths of the forest, yet like the wind one knew not whence it came or whither it was going . . .'.[27] Dramatic accounts like these left a strong but misleading impression on popular memories of the free banking period. A more accurate view — and a more valuable one, I would suggest, because it is contemporary — was presented by the state auditor of Indiana in his report of 1856:

> The experiment of free banking in Indiana, disastrous as it has been in some particulars, has demonstrated most conclusively the safety and wisdom of the system. The original bill was crude and imperfect, admitting of such construction as held out to irresponsible men inducement and facilities for embarking largely in the business of banking, without the ability to sustain themselves in a period of revulsion.
> That revulsion came . . . and yet the loss to which the noteholder was necessarily subjected, in many cases did not exceed 5%, and in no case exceeded 20% of the amount in his hands.[28]

Two questions then arise: (i) How successful was free banking generally?, and, (ii) Why were some experiments with free banking apparently more successful than others?

A tentative answer to the first question is suggested by the recent work of Rockoff (1974), Rolnick and Weber (1983, 1984, 1985, 1986) and Economopoulos (1988). This suggests that traditional accounts of the free banking period have tended to over-emphasise wildcatting and exaggerate the losses that noteholders suffered. Rolnick and Weber also find no evidence of contagion effects which would lead a run on one bank to spread to another, and they conclude that the main source of the free bank failures was external shocks. (We shall return to these shocks later.) This suggests a reasonably good general track record.

This leaves the question of why some free banking experiments seemed to be more successful than others. The different outcomes can be explained by several factors. One factor is the differences which existed both in the legal frameworks under which banks operated, and in the standards of law enforcement. For instance, in some cases the state auditor was satisfied if banks had the prescribed assets in the right places when he made his periodic — and predictable — visits, and he seldom made much effort to check that those assets were there the rest of the time. This gave wildcatters the opportunity to render the inspections ineffective by passing the same assets around from one bank to another as the auditor made his round.[29] Another, perhaps more important, difference in the legal framework was that some states intervened to suspend convertibility. This was the case with Michigan's first free banking experiment, for instance. This led to wildcat banking because the suspension of convertibility removed the main check against over-issue, and so a monetary explosion was to be expected. (See also Chapter 4, note 15. It is also worth noting that even after this disaster Michigan tried again at free banking, about 20 years later, and this time the experiment was successful.)

The second reason — and possibly the most important one — for the variance in the success of free banking is to be found in the combination of the bond deposit provision and the state of different states' finances. In their papers, Rolnick and Weber have argued that the main cause of the free bank failures was the capital losses inflicted on them by falls in the values of the bonds in their portfolios. These are the shocks that we referred to earlier. Their reasoning is that when falls in bond prices make a bank's net worth sufficiently negative, then it will choose to fail because, by doing so, it can pass on part of the capital loss to the noteholders. They also present empirical evidence that gives their 'falling asset price' theory a considerable amount of empirical support.[30]

The Rolnick-Weber analysis explains the free bank failures in terms of falling asset prices, but it is an incomplete explanation because it does not explain *why* the failed banks suffered the capital losses they did. I suggest that some indication of the reason for the capital losses can be gleaned from the history of state finances at the time. If one looks at bond prices for the period one cannot help being struck by their very wide discrepancies (see Homer 1963, Martin 1856, or some of the data given by Rolnick and Weber). For example, US and Massachussetts bonds tended to trade at or above par most of the time, and they show relatively little price variability, while Illinois and Indiana bonds traded below par most of the time and showed far greater price variability. In the course of 1842, for example, the prices of both bonds fell by over 70 per cent and even after that the gap between the highest and lowest price in any given year was about 20–30 per cent of the price of the bond. These bonds were obviously very risky and their holders must frequently have suffered large capital losses.

The history of the period strongly suggests that these discrepancies between different state bond prices can be traced to differences in states' public finances. In virtually every case, the large falls in bond prices were associated with speculation — which sometimes proved to be correct — that the states in question were about to default on their debts. Indiana, for example, had defaulted on its debt during 1841 and there were fears that it might do so again. This evidence therefore seems to point to the conclusion that the cause of the falling bond prices that put most of the failed free banks out of business was the instability of some states' finances.[31]

This explanation seems to be confirmed by Rockoff (1974, p. 163) who reports 6 cases of wildcat banking out of 18 cases of free banking, and that 3 of these (Wisconsin, Illinois and New Jersey) 'can be traced to the linking of the supply of currency to the debt of another state', while another (ie, Minnesota) was 'clearly due to efforts by the state to force its bonds to a higher price than they were currently bringing in the market'. The last two were Indiana and Michigan after its first free banking law was passed in 1837, and we have discussed these already.

Free banking spread relatively slowly after the initial spurt of free banking laws, and some states preferred entirely different monetary regimes. Some set up a monopoly bank of issue (such as Ohio in 1845), while others, like Arkansas, preferred to prohibit banking altogether. Their residents then turned to out-of-state notes instead. State authorities tried to discourage this but they could not prevent it. Their attempts raised the costs of redeeming notes and thereby weakened the market forces that would have maintained their value and quality. The result was that these states generally ended up with worse currencies than the free banking states, and their governments had no control of the currency either.[32] The success of free banking encouraged other states to adopt it, and there was a pronounced drift towards it in the 1850s. Illinois,[33] Ohio and Massachussetts[34] adopted free banking in 1851, and Indiana and Wisconsin followed them shortly afterwards, while Michigan adopted free banking (again) in 1857, Iowa and Minnesota in 1858 and Pennsylvania in 1860. By the eve of the Civil War, over half the states in the Union had adopted it.

This period witnessed several other interesting monetary experiments besides the free banking laws. One of these was the spread of the Suffolk system which helped to check over-issue and 'equalise the exchanges' by ensuring a speedy redemption of notes.[35] As we have already seen, a major weakness of the US banking system was that it was highly fragmented and this fragmentation raised redemption costs with the consequences we have already discussed. Some banks tried to exploit the possibilities this raised by placing themselves at a distance from large centres of population and putting out large note circulations which were costly to redeem. City banks found themselves at a relative disadvantage because their notes were easier to redeem and they were often frustrated to find that out-of-town banks were able to secure most of the note issue in the cities, and yet still remain liquid. To counter this, the Boston banks tried a number of methods to collect the notes of out-of-town banks and return them for redemption. The most successful of these was the Suffolk system, named after the Suffolk Bank of Boston which initiated it. The idea behind it was that the banks which joined it would have their notes redeemed at par by the Suffolk and contribute to a fund which would be used to pay the expenses of redeeming all other notes they received (principally out-of-town notes).

The adoption of the system ensured that country banks notes were rapidly redeemed and their note issues curtailed. It also had the effect of equalising the exchanges between different notes, both because the Suffolk promised to accept members' notes at par, and because the rapid note return ensured that note issues did not get far out of line. The strength of the system was that non-members had an incentive to join or else to set up rival systems. This was because their notes would be sent for redemption anyway, and the scheme reduced the costs to each bank of redeeming other banks' notes. As a result, the Suffolk system spread quite rapidly to cover most of New England, and was copied elsewhere. The Suffolk system, like the Scottish note-clearing system, demonstrates that many functions often associated with central banking — like the existence of a centralised note exchange to ensure rapid redemption and to equalise the exchanges — do not require central banks to operate them, and arise spontaneously under competitive conditions.

A less successful experiment of the period was the safety-fund system. This was a system adopted in several states in which banks were made to pay into an insurance fund designed to protect noteholders in the event that a bank went bankrupt. Unlike clearing systems, such as the Suffolk scheme, safety fund schemes did not arise from the free market but were imposed on the banks by legislation. They are interesting to modern economists because they are very similar to contemporary deposit insurance schemes and, indeed, can be regarded as forerunners to them.

The most ambitious safety fund, which was set up in 1829, was in New York.[36] Each year banks paid in their subscriptions and there were no claims at all on the fund for the first few years. The system contained the seeds of its own destruction, however, because it involved an implicit subsidy to take risks and because nothing was done to ensure that the insurance premia were actuarially sound. As a result, the fund was in fact accumulating an actuarial deficit while it still seemed to be in surplus, and all that was required to break the fund was a major crisis. This occurred in the early 1840s, when 11 safety fund banks went bankrupt, and the fund could not meet its liabilities. The fund was effectively bankrupted, and while the remaining banks were made to put more capital into it, it never properly recovered and was wound up some years later. Other safety funds elsewhere met similar fates.

This concludes our discussion of the free banking period. As we have seen, the different monetary experiments of this period produced some significant successes but also some costly failures. It is probably fair to say that the successes were due in large part to the freedom the banks enjoyed to respond to the demands of the market-place. The evidence also appears to be consistent with the view that the failures were due either to inappropriate regulations (as with the free bank failures) or to other misguided interventions (as with the safety funds). In effect, there was a process of competition between the monetary systems of different states, and there was a tendency to abandon experiments which failed, and to copy those that worked (like the Suffolk system and New York-style free banking), and this produced a substantial improvement in the quality of American banking as time went on. But then the Civil War came and the federal government once more started to legislate on banking.

5.7 The National Banking System[37]

The start of the Civil War had an immediate impact on the banking system since the southern banks repudiated their debts to northern banks when they seceded from the Union. The northern banks managed to shoulder the loss, but they soon came under renewed pressure again, this time from the federal government. The Secretary of the Treasury was finding it difficult to raise sufficient money by borrowing from the public, so he drew up a plan to borrow $50 million in specie from the banks. At the same time he started to issue US notes which the banks were obliged to redeem in specie. The resulting pressure on the banks' reserves forced them to suspend convertibility at the end of 1861. After this, there followed three issues of irredeemable legal tender of $150 million each and these produced a substantial inflation.

The federal government then decided to raise more money from the banks by adopting the bond deposit principle at the federal level. This was the origin of the National Banking System which was established by the National Banking Acts of

1863 and 1864.[38] Under the new system, any group of five or more could form a note-issuing bank, provided that their capital was not less than $50,000, and provided that their note issues were secured by deposits of United States bonds.[39] (This raised the demand for US bonds, and therefore increased their price.) The Treasury would have first lien on the assets of a failed bank, and shareholders would be subject to double liability. The Treasury would protect noteholders by redeeming the notes of any failed bank, thus maintaining the free circulation of notes, even after the bank that issued them had gone out of business. The national banks also had to maintain a minimum ratio of 25 per cent between their holdings of legal tender reserves and the sum of their notes and deposits, and these reserves included US Government bonds and 'greenbacks' as well as specie. (This also increased the demand for federal liabilities.) Finally, the national banks had to pay a tax of 1 per cent on their notes, and of 0.5 per cent on their deposits and their capital not invested in US bonds. The Act also made allowance for state banks to enter the scheme and become national banks, but as they did not enter sufficiently quickly, another Act of 1865 put a 10 per cent annual tax on their note issues, and this effectively killed off the state banks of issue.

The National Banking System was neither a fully-fledged central banking system nor free banking, though it had some resemblances to each one. It had a number of serious defects:

(1) It explicitly discouraged a branch-banking system by requiring that a bank could only carry on business at the place named on its certificate of association. The USA thus continued to be saddled with the defects of a unitary banking system.

(2) The restrictions it placed on the note issue seriously stunted the development of the banking system because the US economy was still at a stage where the issue of notes was an important source of profits for a bank, and so restrictions on their issue erected a significant entry barrier (see Sylla 1972). These restrictions would therefore have forced the public to use alternative media of exchange — coin, illegal currencies (see Timberlake 1981) and, in more sophisticated circles, cheques — and it would have deprived them of banks that

would otherwise have been established. This in turn would have hindered the contribution that the banking system could have made to the country's economic development, and as Sylla (1972) pointed out, this would have been particularly important in the more backward areas where banks would have had difficulty even getting started. These problems were compounded even further in the early days of the National Banking System because of an arbitrary limit of $300 million which was placed on the note supply. Notes were to be allocated across regions on the basis of population and economic activity, but in practice the banks of the New England, Middle Atlantic and East North Central regions got very disproportional shares, and the rest of the country had to make do with what was left. The $300 million limit was raised by $54 million in 1870, and then abolished altogether in 1875. Shortly thereafter, however, the price of US bonds rose to well above par and it was seldom worthwhile to issue notes anyway.[40]

(3) The bond deposit provision tied the note supply to price of federal debt. The note supply was then forced to contract as the federal government ran surpluses during the post-bellum years and bought back much of its debt, and in the process raised its price. As Cagan (1963, pp. 22–3) put it, the profitability of note issuing:

> depended crucially on the prices of the US bonds eligible to serve as collateral. When from 1864 to 1880 these bonds sold at or just above par, the issuance of notes returned a handsome profit. I have calculated the rate of return on the capital tied up in issuing the notes . . . to be 31% per year in 1879 and 21% in 1880. Shortly thereafter, however, the Treasury began to run a budget surplus . . . As a result, large premiums appeared, which sharply reduced the profitability of issuing notes. . . . In January, 1882 . . . the return to issuing notes fell to . . . 9% per year. Banks earned almost as much on other assets. In subsequent years the return on notes fell even below the average return on other assets. Consequently, new issues ceased, and many banks retired part of their outstanding notes. The total quantity outstanding declined from around $300 million at the beginning of the 1880s to $126 million at the end of that decade. Their circulation expanded again in the 1890s when the high premiums on US bonds fell sharply.

(4) The restrictions on the note supply often prevented it responding appropriately to changes in the demand for notes. This was the problem of the 'inelasticity' of the note supply which attracted increasing attention as time went on. This problem was particularly acute in the autumn when there was a seasonal rise in the demand for notes, but the banks were able to respond only to the extent that they could continue to satisfy their bond deposit and reserve ratio requirements. This led to very considerable interest rate fluctuations and made the US banking system peculiarly liable to panics:

> A series of acute financial crises occurred in fairly quick succession — 1873, 1884, 1890, 1893, 1907. Crises occurred on most of these occasions in London as well, but they were nothing like as stringent. Money rates in New York rose to fantastic heights as compared with London, and there was one other even more marked dissimilarity. In America there took place in three out of the five cases (1873, 1893 and 1907) widespread suspensions of cash payments, either partial or complete, with currency at a premium over claims on bank accounts. (Smith 1936, p. 133)

It is important to stress that these suspensions occurred not because the banks had no specie — they generally did — but principally because they were not allowed to issue additional notes. In the terminology we introduced in Chapter 3, these were deposit runs rather than note runs.

The problem of liquidity shortages in a crisis gave rise to the institution of clearing houses to deal with it. These originated in an agreement among the New York banks during the 1857 crisis to expand their loans together so that no bank would lose reserves to the others. In later crises, the banks agreed to *clearing-house loan certificates* — interest-bearing notes which the banks used to settle accounts with each other. Apart from ensuring that banks did not lose reserves to each other during a crisis, they also contributed to the system's overall liquidity at a time when liquidity was most needed, and clearing houses had very strong incentives to support their member-banks.[41] As time went on, the institution of clearing houses spread, and other types of certificate were invented. The value of clearing-house loan certificates and similar instruments ran into hundreds of millions, and their usefulness was widely recognised. They were also technically illegal, but the government wisely decided not to prosecute their issuers. A contemporary writer summarised the situation in the following way:

> Most of this currency was illegal, but no one thought of prosecuting or interfering with its issuers . . . In plain language, it was an inconvertible paper money issued without the sanction of law, . . . yet necessitated by conditions for which our banking laws did not provide . . . when banks were being run upon and legal money had disappeared in hoards, in default of any legal means of relief, it worked effectively and doubtless prevented multitudes of bankruptcies which otherwise would have occurred. (Andrew 1908, pp. 515–6)

It is an unfortunate state of affairs when the government feels it cannot implement the law because of the damage it would cause.[42]

These repeated crises gave rise to much controversy and numerous plans for reform. A growing school of thought maintained that the solution to the problems of the US monetary system was to establish a central bank on the European model, and the controversy over whether the USA should establish a central bank intensified after the crisis of 1907. Congress responded to that crisis by passing the Aldrich–Vreeland Act to authorise the issue of 'emergency currency' as a stopgap measure, and to establish a National Monetary Commission to report on banking reform. The Commission was particularly impressed by the way in which European central banks were able to handle liquidity crises by centralising reserves and acting as lenders of last resort. It tended to assume that the greater stability of the European financial systems was due to their having central banks, rather than to other defects of the American banking system, and it did not take arguments for free banking particularly seriously. The Commission therefore recommended the establishment of an American central bank — a Federal Reserve System of 12 regional Federal Reserve Banks which would be owned by banks which were members of the System.[43] The Federal Reserve System would be run by a

Federal Reserve Board and would be responsible for issuing notes, keeping the reserves of member-banks and setting interest rate policy. Congress accepted these recommendations and the Federal Reserve Act was passed in 1913. The Federal Reserve started operations the next year.

5.8 Some Conclusions

This completes our account of the establishment of central banking in Britain and the USA. As we have seen, the monetary experiences of these two countries are very different, but they both show similar basic themes:

- Central banking did not arise 'spontaneously' as a result of market failures, but as a consequence of specific state interventions and the problems those interventions created.
- State intervention was generally motivated by the desire to raise revenue or to correct for problems caused by earlier intervention. It was not motivated by market failures *per se*.
- The effect of intervention was to destabilise the banking system and occasionally to debase the value of the currency.
- Free banking (or something close to it) was tried successfully in both nations and suppressed for fundamentally political reasons.

We shall now proceed to the next chapter and consider the historical record of central banking.

Notes

1. Quoted from Smith (1936, p. 148).
2. This section draws heavily on White (1984b), Meulen (1934) and Smith (1936), and to a lesser extent on MacLeod (1896), Andréades (1909) and Clapham (1945).
3. This section and the next are distilled from Cameron (1967), Checkland (1975), Kerr (1918), Meulen (1934), Munn (1981), Smith (1936) and White (1984b). The Scottish free banking experience has

provoked a great deal of recent controversy. To avoid too long a digression on this controversy in the main text, we defer our discussion to an appendix of this chapter.

4. Option clauses have received a bad press since the controversy of the 1760s. I have argued in Chapter 2 and elsewhere (Dowd 1988d and Chappell and Dowd 1988) that this judgment might be premature and that option clauses are potentially very useful.

5. Quoted in Meulen (1934, p. 139).

6. The standard references to the UK monetary debates are Smith (1936), Viner (1937), Mints (1945), Fetter (1965) and, more recently, White (1984b). The reader should also refer to Rothbard's review (1988) of White. According to Rothbard, White 'conflates two very distinct schools of free bankers: (1) those who wanted free banking in order to promote monetary inflation and cheap credit, and (2) those who, on the contrary, wanted free banking in order to arrive at hard, near-100% specie money' (p. 234). He argues that only two of White's heroes, Robert Mushet and Sir Henry Parnell, were clearly hard-money men, and he presents evidence to suggest that a number of the remainder — Sir John Sinclair, Poullett Scrope, James Gilbart, James Wilson, and possibly even Samuel Bailey — were unsound on the 'real bills' issue. Rothbard is quite right to suggest that some of these make uncomfortable allies for modern free bankers. However, his claim that White himself is fundamentally unsound — 'a variant of a banking-school inflationist' (p. 239) — is uncalled for. White's statement of the fallacy of the 'real bills' doctrine(s) (pp. 120–2) is clear evidence of the soundness of his position.

While on the subject of White's account of the controversies, Munn also comments on White's rather uncritical treatment of certain writers (p. 341). Dr Munn also points out that, 'White virtually ignores the writing of Scottish bankers. Hugh Watt, Scotland's most experienced banker, gets very little attention and Alexander Blair, the most senior banker, is ignored altogether. Neither of these men would have found themselves in complete sympathy with White's views . . .' (loc. cit.).

7. In Book 2, Chapter 2 of the *Wealth of Nations*, Smith gave a qualified support to free banking. He suggested that banks should be compelled to redeem their notes on demand, and that notes for less than a certain sum should be prohibited, but that banks should otherwise be left free.

8. Bentham's main concern in his *Defence of Usury* (1788) was to attack the usury laws, but in the process he also came out against other restrictions on banks. However, he did not develop these comments into a detailed argument for free banking.

9. Quoted in Meulen (1934, p. 113).

10. In fact, it is questionable whether the Act involved much liberalisation of the Bank's monopoly. As Joplin appears to have been the first to realise, the earlier Acts implicitly defined banking as

involving the issue of notes and this definition had to be construed strictly since the Acts were penal statutes. This meant that the six-partner rule did not apply to banks that refrained from issuing notes. This was never tested in the courts, however, and all the 1826 Act did, in this respect, was to clarify the matter.

11. Quoted in Smith (1936, p. 63).
12. Quoted in White (1984b, p. 61).
13. White (1984b, pp. 65–7).
14. See the *Digest* of evidence presented before the Bank Charter Committee of 1832.
15. See White (1984b, p. 66) and Halevy (1961, pp. 86–7). The quote is from White.
16. Quoted in White (1984b, p. 67).
17. This of course raises the question of why people who are fundamentally sympathetic to *laisser faire* in most trades should have rejected *laisser faire* in banking. Perhaps part of the mystery is resolved by Rothbard (1988, pp. 234–7) who presents evidence that a number of contemporary UK writers supported the currency principle in order to achieve an outcome they interpreted as fundamentally *laisser faire*. He states:

> the fervent desire of Richard Cobden, along with other Manchesterians and most other currency school writers, was to remove government or bank manipulation of money altogether and to leave its workings solely to the free-market forces of gold or silver. Whether or not Cobden's proposed solution of a state-run bank was the proper one, no one can deny the fervor of his *laisser-faire* views or his desire to apply them to the difficult and complex case of money and banking. (p. 237)

18. Quoted in White (1984b, p. 132).
19. I take the currency school position to be the advocacy of a monopoly note issue for the Bank of England with a legislated 100 per cent marginal reserve requirement. I take the banking school position to be the defence of the legislative status quo, albeit with a recommendation that the Bank should hold greater reserves. Given these definitions, both schools were fundamentally opposed to free banking. Note, however, that Rothbard (1988) implicitly defines the currency and banking schools quite differently, and it is this that leads him to talk of currency school writers who were sympathetic to free banking (see n. 17).
20. Quoted in Smith (1936, p. 69).
21. For more on Bagehot's views on free banking, see Chapter 2, note 23.
22. This account of early US banking history relies primarily on Sumner (1896), Smith (1936) and Hammond (1957).
23. An interesting question is why branching restrictions were able to persist so long. The answer, presumably, is that they persisted

because the small banks lobbied to keep them.
24. For a good discussion of political movements in the Jacksonian period see Blau (1947).
25. Quoted in Dunne, p. 2.
26. For the first condition see Rolnick and Weber (1984), p. 270; for second and fourth see Rolnick and Weber (1984), table one; and for the third see Rolnick and Weber (1984), p. 271.
27. Quoted in Rockoff (1974, p. 146).
28. Quoted in Rockoff (1974, p. 151).
29. Smith (1936, pp. 45–6). A curious and relatively neglected feature of US banking history is the importance of fraud as a cause of bank failure. This appears to be a persistent theme:

> Fraud has always been a major problem for banks because they deal in very large quantities of the most easily fenced of all commodities — money. In the United States over the period 1865–1931, fraud and violations of the law were cited by the Comptroller of the Currency as the cause most responsible for failures of national banks. Frauds also are responsible for the most costly losses to depositors and the insurance agencies. . . . The ratio of the number of citations for fraud to the total number of identified causes of failures ranges from 63% over the years 1914–1920 to 18% over the decade 1921–1929. For the period 1934–1958, the Federal Deposit Insurance Corporation reports that for 'approximately one-fourth of the banks, defalcation or losses attributable to financial irregularities by officers and employees appear to have been the primary cause of failure' . . . During 1959–1971, fraud and irregularities were responsible for 66% of the failures. (Benston et al 1986, pp. 2–3)

30. For example, Rolnick and Weber (1984, p. 288) find that 79 per cent of the failures they consider occurred during the relatively short periods (i.e. 7 years out of 22) when bond prices were falling.
31. A possible objection to this needs to be considered. King (1983, p. 147) disputes the argument that the bond deposit provision caused these failures and argues that, 'there are natural means for any bank to undo any pure portfolio restriction. Banks should simply have as owners or creditors individuals who would otherwise hold amounts of government debt.' This 'irrelevance theorem' is an important result, but it does not strictly apply here because of the shareholders' limited liability. Suppose that a portfolio restriction is imposed on a bank and it arranges a swap with someone who would otherwise have held the assets it is required to hold. Now suppose that there is a sufficiently large fall in the value of those assets. Had there been no restriction, the person who held the assets would have had to take the capital loss. With the restriction and the swap, however, bank shareholders would be able to take advantage of their limited liability by

declaring the bank bankrupt in order to pass the capital loss onto the bank's creditors. In the former case the bank would have continued in business, in the latter it would not. This justifies the claim in the text that the portfolio restriction and the capital loss can produce a different outcome in the presence of limits to the shareholders' liability.

32. Sumner (1896, pp. 415–6).
33. For more on Illinois' free banking experience, see Economopoulos (1988).
34. The case of Massachussetts is rather interesting. Although the 'free banking' law was passed in 1851, no free banks were set up under it until 1859. The reason appears to be that the banks would have had to back their note issues with the bonds of New England states or municipalities, and for most of the 1850s the prices of these were apparently well above par on account of their scarcity (see Rockoff 1974, p. 149). Free banks in Massachussetts were therefore 'priced out' of the market. In a sense, their problem was the opposite of that of free banks elsewhere — bond prices were too high, not too low.
35. For more on the Suffolk system, see Trivoli (1979).
36. This account of the New York Safety Fund is based on Smith (1936, p. 43) and King (1983).
37. Our discussion of the National Banking System is based on Sumner (1896), Smith (1936) and Timberlake (1984).
38. The passing of these Acts owed a great deal to the emergency atmosphere created by the Civil War rather than to any clearly established defects of the existing system. As Cagan (1963, p. 16) states, Secretary Chase:

> proposed a new, uniform currency backed by US bonds to replace state notes, appealing to the difficulties of Treasury finance complicated by the war as well as to the permanent advantages such a reform of the currency system would bring. When he first made the proposal, Congress would not even take it up for debate. But by 1863, when hopes for an early Union victory had dimmed and the mounting expenditures cast doubt on the Treasury's ability to finance such a large military effort, the proposal took on the character of a war measure. The opposition weakened, and the bill passed by a narrow majority.
>
> Had the southern representatives and senators been attending the Congress in Washington, their concern for states' rights would almost certainly have prevented the passage of the bill. The National Banking System can therefore be said to be a direct consequence of the Civil War.

39. In addition, the 1865 Act prohibited note issues in excess of 90 per cent of a bank's paid-in capital. It also imposed a 25 per cent specie

or greenback reserve requirement against note issues, though this latter restriction was abolished in 1874 (see Cagan 1963, pp. 18–9).

40. Another potentially dangerous feature of the National Banking System was that it made bank notes effectively indistinguishable since, in the last resort, the Treasury committed itself to redeem them at par. Had there been no other externally imposed restrictions on the note issue, banks would have had no incentive to restrict their issues, and a monetary explosion might have occurred of the kind discussed in note 15 of the last chapter. I should like to thank Catherine England for bringing this to my attention.

41. The reserve-centre banks also supported out-of-town banks during crises: 'Critics charged that New York banks protected themselves in times of crisis and shortchanged their correspondents. The opposite was, in fact, true, and central reserve-city banks' loans rose in these periods, providing assistance to the interior banks. Interest rates on these loans did rise, but that was what any sound institution, commercial or central bank, would do.' (Eugene White (1983, pp. 73–4))

42. Cannon (1901, pp. 103–4) had somewhat earlier arrived at a similar conclusion about the usefulness of clearing-house loan certificates. As he put it, when discussing the 1893 crisis:

> The only avenue of relief provided by the laws was the issue of additional national bank-notes, but . . . it was apparent that the national banks were bound hand and foot by indiscreet legislation, and were therefore unequal to the task of extending the relief so much needed, and which, under more favorable laws, might easily have been supplied. . . . The remedy that was applied affords one of the finest examples the country has ever seen of the ability of the people when left to themselves to devise impromptu measures for their own relief. The most potent factors in staying the force of the panic were the clearing-house loan certificates issued by the clearing-house associations throughout the country.

43. For good discussions of the political and legislative background to the Act, see Dunne (undated), Dewald (1972) and West (1977). Note that while Dewald tends to see the measures adopted as more or less inevitable, Dunne sees them more as a combination of legislative accidents.

Appendix to Chapter Five

The Controversy Over Scottish Free Banking

This appendix examines the renewed controversy on Scottish free banking in the wake of Lawrence White's book (1984b). This book was reviewed by Goodhart (1985, 1987b), Gorton (1985a), Munn (1985), Rothbard (1988), Sechrest (1988) and Cowen and Kroszner (1988b), and each of them raised questions about his interpretation of the Scottish free banking experience which are worthy of examination. These centre around three main issues:[1] the cyclical stability of the Scottish banking system and the role of the Bank of England in Scottish cycles; the development of 'non-market' institutions in the Scottish banking system; and the convertibility of Scottish bank notes.

We begin with the cyclical stability issue.

The Cyclical Stability of the Scottish Banks and the Role of the Bank of England

A key part of White's thesis concerns his claims regarding the stability of the Scottish banking system and the role of the Bank of England in promoting monetary disturbances. White refers to the 'relative mildness of Scottish cycles' (p. 44), but the only direct evidence he presents is a table for the period 1809–30 showing that Scottish banks had a lower failure rate than English ones — an annual average of 0.40 per cent as against 1.81 per cent. However, his choice of period is somewhat arbitrary, and Sechrest points out that one gets a somewhat

152

different picture if one looks at the period 1772–1830 as a whole. In that case, the relative failure rate of the Scottish banks is still lower than for English banks, but it is not significant at the 1 per cent level (Sechrest 1988, pp. 251–2). Even if one accepts that the Scottish failure rate was significantly lower, however, it is not clear what that means. As Rothbard (1988, p. 230) argues, 'why should lack of bank failure be a sign of superiority? On the contrary, a dearth of bank failure should rather be treated with suspicion, as witness the drop of bank failures in the United States since the advent of the FDIC. . . . Bank failures are a healthy weapon by which the market keeps bank credit inflation in check . . .'

This evidence clearly does not provide strong support for White's claim that the 'Scottish free banking system proved far hardier during periods of commercial distress than did its English counterpart' (p. 44). Nor, on the other hand, does it enable one to reject it. One must therefore presume that White's claim is a subjective evaluation based more on anecdotal evidence than hard statistical analysis. While it would obviously be nice to have harder evidence, one has to evaluate the issue on the basis of whatever one can find, and White's assessment does not seem unreasonable.

Related to this is the complex issue of the role of the Bank of England in Scottish fluctuations. White maintains that the cycle was caused by the Bank of England, but as Goodhart (1987b, p. 130) points out, he provides 'only limited empirical support' for this claim.[2] Once again we are reduced to subjective judgments, and once again White's assessment seems a reasonable one to me. The counterclaim is that free banking tended to exacerbate cycles and that the Bank of England was able to ameliorate them (Goodhart 1987b, p. 131). Goodhart goes on to say:

> I would argue that the position of Scottish banks *vis-à-vis* the Bank of England in these years was *not* significantly different from that of banks outside of London in England. The Scottish banks relied on London, and ultimately on the Bank, as a financial centre, just as did the English country banks. The Scottish banking system could be regarded as a satellite to the London centre, as the Canadian banks were to New York before 1914, and as the Swiss banks were to Paris before 1870. [his italic]

The significance of this was that the Canadian and Scottish satellite systems 'could relieve pressures on their reserves in their own area by drawing on New York and London, thereby transferring the reserve pressure to the centre' (1985, p. 62).

This raises several issues. To begin with, the view that Scottish free banking exacerbated cycles, and the Bank of England tended to dampen them, is itself only a questionable assessment of the historical experience — and one that I certainly would *not* share. Second, while it is difficult to deny that Scotland and Canada were effectively satellite systems operating on 'reserve centres' in London and New York, it seems to me that that is not the main issue. The key issues are surely the following:

- Did the monetary shocks tend to arise in the less regulated satellite systems and spread to the reserve centres, or the other way round? *and,*
- How well did the satellite systems respond to monetary shocks compared to the systems at the reserve centres?

My own reading of British and North American monetary history is that shocks tended to hit Scotland and Canada from the 'reserve centres' of London and New York, and not that shocks originated internally and were then transferred to the centres. My reading also suggests that the satellite systems were better at coping with shocks when they did occur. A very casual comparison of Canadian and American monetary history strongly suggests, and Kurt Schuler's work seems to confirm, that the Canadians were reasonably successful at avoiding the suspensions and widespread bank failures that repeatedly afflicted the US banking system, and we have already suggested that the Scottish banking system coped better with the shocks emanating from London than did its English counterpart. In short, the freer satellite systems were less likely to generate monetary shocks than the more regulated reserve centres, and they were apparently better at dealing with them as well.[3] I would suggest that this is exactly what we should have expected.[4]

Another version of the argument that the Scottish banking system was dependent on the English one is given by Rothbard. An obvious question is why the Scottish banks 'did not remain tied to specie and let their currency float against the Bank of England note' when the Bank was ordered to suspend specie payments in 1797 (White 1984b, p. 46, note 12). Rothbard suggests that the 'evident answer' is that 'Scottish banks were *not* free, that they were in no position to pay in specie, and that they pyramided credit on top of the Bank of England' (1988, p. 231). It seems to me, however, that this explanation is valid only if we suppose that the Scottish banks used gold as their medium of redemption, and the evidence suggests that they did not.[5] As Fetter (1965, p. 122) points out, 'there was a tradition, almost with the force of law, that banks should not be required to redeem their notes in coin. *Redemption in London drafts was the usual form of payment to noteholders* [my italic].' Drafts on London were thus the medium of redemption rather than gold, and there is therefore no reason to suppose — as White (loc. cit.) says, and Rothbard seems to suggest — that the Scottish banks' 'reserves were immobilized' by the suspension of the Bank of England. The Scottish banks were therefore perhaps less 'dependent' on London than Rothbard makes out.[6]

Private Interest and 'Non-market' Institutions

A major point of contention has been the claim that the forces of private self-interest would lead to the development of institutions (like the note exchange and a lender of last resort facility) with which the banking system could protect and police itself. A problem arises with White's analysis of the note exchange (1984b, pp. 20–1) which implies that the note exchange should be in the individual interests of all note issuers. This implies that all Scottish note-issuing banks should have joined the exchange willingly, but some in fact did not. White mentions this but fails to explain it, and he 'neglects the reign of terror exercised by the public banks in Edinburgh which forced the other banks to join the exchange' (Munn 1985, p. 341). Similarly, White ignores the self-assumed role of the Bank of Scotland's Alexander Blair as 'policeman of the system,'[7] as well as the Royal Bank's role as lender of last resort to the provincial banking companies (loc. cit.).

It seems to me that these criticisms would lead one to

reconsider parts of White's historical account, but the main point is that the Scottish experience does indicate quite clearly how unaided self-interest can lead to the development of useful institutions like the note exchange and the lender of last resort facility.[8] That the larger banks used their market power to 'encourage' the others to join the note exchange in no way contradicts its social usefulness. The situation faced by the smaller banks is comparable to that of any firm which is forced to come to terms with a successful innovation introduced by its competitors. In this context, it is worth noting a strong parallel between the development of the Scottish note exchange and the Suffolk system in New England — in both cases, it was used by the 'city banks' to check the note issues of provincial or country banks, and some of the latter banks were presumably reluctant to join it precisely because of that. It appears they only did so because the larger banks threatened to collect their notes and present them for redemption whether they joined the exchange or not. They would then have reckoned that since they would have to bear the costs of the note exchange, they might as well join it and get the benefits as well.

Convertibility of Scottish Notes

In their reviews both Rothbard (1988, pp. 232–3) and Sechrest (1988, pp. 248–50) stress the importance of another issue that White failed to discuss in any detail — the lack of full convertibility of Scottish notes during the free banking period. It is significant that Scottish notes were imperfectly convertible, even after the passage of the 1765 Act compelling the banks to make their notes redeemable on demand: as Checkland (1975, p. 185) noted, the 'Scottish system was one of continuous partial suspension of payments.'

Rothbard[9] and Sechrest appear to disapprove of this, but do not make their reasons clear. It seems to me, however, that this should be considered neither problematical nor unexpected. As we discussed earlier when dealing with option clauses, there are reasons to believe that the banks would want to modify a convertibility-on-demand note contract, and that the public would be willing to go along with them. If this is so, an agreement to relax the convertibility condition is mutually advantageous, and we would therefore expect to observe it. It is then hardly surprising that the law enforcing full convertibility on demand was largely a dead letter if the banks and the public had an incentive to connive to get round it. It is also interesting that Checkland notes the imperfect convertibility of Scottish notes and appears to approve of it: 'This legally impermissable limitation of convertibility, though never mentioned to public inquiries, contributed greatly to Scottish banking success. In this way, the banks limited the costs and dangers to which the system was, in theory, exposed.' (1975, p. 186)

Notes

1. There has, however, also been some controversy on the structure of the Scottish banking industry. Sechrest (1988, pp. 250–1) suggests that White's claims about the Scottish banking industry being unprivileged are exaggerated, since some banks enjoyed the privilege of limited liability. Munn (1985 pp. 341–2) comments on White's tendency to 'eulogise Scottish banking' and questions his claims that most banks were 'well-capitalised by a large number of shareholders' and that 'all but a few were extensively branched'. Cowen and Kroszner (1988b) also present evidence that calls into question 'the use of the Scottish system as a model of laissez-faire banking.' (p. 11)

2. Goodhart also argues that:

> . . . an economist must enquire why the Bank acted in this way, and should not treat such actions as 'exogenous', as White proposes (p. 111). One reason suggested, e.g. by Scrope (see p. 103), was that the Bank's actions were motivated by the profit motive. If so, then the problem lay rather in the Bank trying to act in some part as a competitive, profit-maximizing commercial bank in these years, and *not* as a central bank. . . . While it is unhappily true that in the first half of the nineteenth century several government-sponsored banks used their advantages to weaken outside competition . . . , this was owing more to a confusion between roles (profit-maximising commercial bank or non-competitive central bank) than to any inherent fault in central banking. (1987b, pp. 130–1, his emphasis)

Clearly, the bank's actions must be explained, but the main issue here is surely not central banking versus free banking — it is not clear what central banking even means in this context — but the way

these institutions used their privileges to put down their competition.
3. But as Professor Goodhart has pointed out to me in a recent letter, we also need to consider the cases of Sweden and Switzerland. He suggests that the case of Sweden is particularly persuasive from the free banking viewpoint because it is not possible to argue that Sweden was 'dependent on some alternative Central Bank for an assured source of extra high-powered money'. The case of Switzerland, on the other hand, is less supportive of the free banking case. He writes

> . . . until 1872, the Swiss banking system was also quasi-dependent on Paris as its effective Central Bank of last resort. Then, during the Franco-Prussian War the Swiss banks became cut-off from their French centre. The result was something of a debacle; without their usual source of additional high-powered money, the Swiss banks all simultaneously tried to retrench and brought about a severe financial crisis. As a result, the Swiss overwhelmingly agreed that they must have an independent central bank of their own. This does strike me as important additional evidence about the nature of the reliance of a quasi-dependent banking system on a centre of additional high-powered money.

4. See our earlier discussion on the stability of *laisser-faire* banking in Chapter 2.
5. This implies, incidentally, that it is the ratio of liquid assets drawable on London to notes rather than the gold–notes ratio that is the appropriate reserve ratio. This puts quite a different light on Rothbard's 'scandalous drop' (1988, p. 231) in reserve ratios in the early 19th century.
6. This still leaves the question of why the Scottish banks did not float. The answer, I would suggest, is that they used the paper pound as their medium of *account* and no individual bank had any incentive to change it. For more on this, see the discussion of the medium of account in Chapter 4.
7. Note that Blair was also a government minister, and this 'raises the question of the extent to which this self-policing was independent of government influence' (Munn, p. 341). There is, however, no apparent direct evidence of government interference.
8. Gorton (1985a, p. 274) is quite right to question the 'assumption' that 'non-market forms of organization were simply imposed by the government'. Our discussion of the note exchange clearly bears this out, but his claim that, 'Self-regulation by banks through the non-market institutions of the note exchange and the clearinghouse . . . seem hard to explain from Fama and White's point of view,' (p. 274) is questionable.
9. Rothbard (p. 232) implies that this enabled the banks to be

'outrageously inflationary', but implicitly defines this as the banks being able to 'keep their specie reserves at a minimum'. I do not understand this.

6

The Historical Experience of Central Banking

Even granted the market failures that we and many other economists had attributed to a strictly laissez-faire *policy in money and banking, the course of events encouraged the view that turning to government as an alternative was a cure that was worse than the disease . . . Government failure might be worse than market failure.*
(Milton Friedman and Anna Schwartz (1986)[1])

6.1 Introduction

This chapter examines the historical record of central banking. The objective is not to provide a detailed history, but to focus on the key historical issues and events that reveal the scope and limitations of central banking. As our earlier discussions indicated, the main justification for adopting central banking was to reduce instability, so it is primarily on these grounds that its historical experience should be judged. We shall try to form an assessment of the experience of central banking by focusing on the collapse of the gold standard, monetary policy and monetary regulation in the Great Depression, the adoption of the Keynesian philosophy of monetary policy, and the inflation of the past two decades. Before we get into these issues, we first set the stage by outlining the monetary regime as it stood at the turn of the century.

6.2 The Monetary Regime at the Turn of the Century

After the controversies of the early part of the century had died down, there was relatively little attempt in Britain to challenge either the institution of the Bank of England or the adherence to the gold standard. The English financial system appeared to be more stable than it had ever been before, and — though they still occurred — crises did not have the devastating impact they had had before. The system was flawed, but it seemed to work quite well in spite of its flaws, and it was widely felt that attempts to change it were likely, on the whole, to do more harm than good. As Sir Robert Giffen (1892, p. 464) put it:

> No change in a monetary standard, if it is a tolerably good one, ought to be proposed or considered unless upon grounds of overwhelming necessity. For a good money is so very difficult a thing to get, and Governments, when they meddle with money, are so apt to make blunders . . . These considerations apply especially to a country like England, where the standard is the foundation of a fabric of credit, whose extension and delicacy make the slightest jar apt to produce the most formidable effects . . . What impresses me is that, with our enormous liabilities and credits, with transactions of all kinds, the ramifications of which no man can follow out, we can never tell, when we touch that standard, what confusion and mischief we may be introducing.

This period also witnessed the gradual evolution of an almost universal international gold standard. Some countries (such as the USA) experienced major controversies towards the end of the century over silver or bimetallic standards, and these invariably ended with the defeat of the silver party, the demonetisation of silver, and the adoption of the gold standard. Paper standards were even less fashionable than silver, and no-one of any prominence supported them. It was widely recognised that they removed any guarantee against over-issue, and experiments with paper standards — inconvertible papers in colonial America, assignats in France, the Restriction in the UK, greenbacks in the US — seemed always to produce depreciation and monetary instability. By the turn of the century the ghosts of paper and silver currencies seemed well and truly exorcised, and the gold standard was more widely accepted than ever before.

Central banking was also gaining ground, and the governments of all the major countries had adopted it by the time the First World War broke out. The old controversies over free banking were almost completely forgotten, and even those of a *laisser-faire* disposition accepted the necessity for central banking, subject only to the constraint that the central bank maintain the convertibility of the currency into gold. Within that framework, the task of the central bank was the reasonably well-defined one of protecting the solvency of the banking system by managing the gold reserve in order to prevent or defuse liquidity crises. It would do this by following Bagehot's advice to protect the reserve in 'normal' times, but lend freely in a crisis. As we discussed in Chapter 2, this places a considerable burden on the bank to judge the market properly, so the bank's task was still difficult even if it was quite well-defined.

This monetary regime, based on the twin pillars of gold and central banking, seemed to work reasonably well until the catastrophe of the First World War blew it away, along with much else. Underneath the surface, however, there were two factors at work which were already undermining it, and which were to make it impossible to restore successfully after the war.

The first was a gradual increase in what was expected of the central bank. A new generation of economists was more ready to play with schemes for monetary reform, and less afraid of the potential 'confusion and mischief' they might cause. Economists like Irving Fisher and Knut Wicksell were wondering whether it might be possible to 'improve' on the gold standard and develop monetary policies to stabilise prices more effectively. Meanwhile, Georg Knapp won a large following in Germany with his doctrine that money was a creature of the state and its apparent implication that the state should be freed of all the constraints that the present monetary system imposed on it. Underneath all this, there was a drift away from *laisser-faire* liberalism towards a belief in a more active role for government. It was widely felt that the old liberalism had run out of steam, that its legislative programme — electoral reform, minimal government, and free trade — had been substantially achieved, and there was little else it could do. 'Progressives' were dissatisfied with this and demanded more, and state interventionism came back into fashion. These trends had already had a substantial impact by the time the war broke out, but they were to be decisive afterwards.

The other factor was the changing pattern of demand for gold. In the old days the demand for gold came mostly from private individuals who wanted to store it, or to have it coined, and governments and their central banks could still be considered, perhaps, as relatively marginal operators. This changed as economies became more sophisticated. Credit instruments gradually replaced gold as media of exchange — recall the case of Scotland, for instance — and the profitable investment opportunities provided by increasingly sophisticated capital markets encouraged the gradual replacement of gold as a store of value by bonds and equities. Gold reserves were increasingly centralised in central banks' vaults, and the central banks' demand for it became an ever-more important component of its overall demand. This was to lead to a gold market that was dominated by a very small number of central banks, and this in turn was to undermine the discipline which the gold standard imposed on them.

6.3 The Monetary Regime After the First World War

These tendencies probably still had a long way to go before they could work themselves out when the First World War broke out in 1914 and the major combatants abandoned convertibility. Governments became desperate as it dragged on, however, and some of them relied heavily on printing money to finance their war efforts. When those governments collapsed, many of their successors were too weak to resist the pressure to print money at an ever faster rate, and their inflations escalated rapidly. In this way, most of central and eastern Europe succumbed to hyper-inflations which produced massive economic and social dislocation, and eventually left their currencies worthless. The hyper-inflations only ended when the governments responsible for them managed to re-establish control over their finances and introduce new currencies whose values were pegged to gold or foreign currencies.

The other combatants also faced problems. In Britain, there was a severe recession in 1919–20 as the troops returned home and the munitions industry was wound down. The British authorities pursued a policy of deflation to force down the levels of domestic wages and prices and eventually enable a return to the gold standard at the old parity. Wages and prices moved down reasonably quickly at first, but some time after 1923 they began to 'stick', and a serious unemployment problem emerged. The policy of deflation was continued, nonetheless, and in 1925 Britain once again resumed convertibility at the old rate. This decision provoked a great deal of controversy, and it was obvious that the gold standard no longer enjoyed the near-universal support in Britain that it had enjoyed in the past.

The experience of the United States was very different. The Federal Reserve had been established to operate within the context of the international gold standard, but this had collapsed within a year of it starting operations. The Fed therefore found itself in the awkward position of being nominally subject to the discipline of the gold standard, but of being the only major player still in the game. The founders of the Fed had not anticipated this, and the Fed had no clear idea what to do with the large gold flows that entered the USA during the War. In the pre-Fed days, the gold inflows would have led to more or less automatic increases in money supply and higher prices. It seemed pointless to allow this to happen when there was no longer an international gold standard, so the Fed tried instead to 'sterilise' the inflows to reduce their effects on the domestic economy. It continued with this policy for much of the 1920s as well. This policy:

> was a conscious attempt, for perhaps the first time in monetary history, to use central-bank powers to promote internal economic stability as well as to preserve balance in international payments and to prevent and moderate strictly financial crises. In retrospect, we can see that this was a major step toward the assumption by government of explicit continuous responsibility for economic stability. As the decade wore on, the System took — and perhaps even more was given — credit for the generally stable conditions that

prevailed, and high hopes were placed in the potency of monetary policy . . . (Friedman and Schwartz 1963, p. 240)

The gold standard that was restored after the war was therefore a very different institution from that which had prevailed before the war broke out. The underlying reason for this was that the central banks were now sufficiently big players in the gold market that they effectively controlled it and destroyed any 'automatic' discipline it imposed. The central banks' bigger role reflected the reduced private demand for gold. This demand would have been reduced in part because the public had grown used to using paper during the war when they would previously have used gold, but some countries (such as Britain) also encouraged the public to economise on gold by adopting a gold-bullion standard in which the currency was convertible but there was no gold coinage.

The central banks' dominance of the gold market made them vulnerable to each others' policies, and the automatic adjustment mechanism of the classical gold standard was superseded by a game dominated by three players — the Federal Reserve, the Bank of England and the Bank of France — whose objectives were quite different and who were generally indifferent to the effects of their policies on each other. The principal offenders were the Federal Reserve and the Bank of France. The Fed continued to sterilise gold inflows during the 1920s to prevent inflation, but in the process it suppressed one of the adjustment mechanisms that would have helped restore equilibrium, and this put additional pressure on the countries which were losing gold to deflate their economies. France adopted a similar policy in 1926–8. These countries' central banks accumulated massive stockpiles of gold which made it more difficult for other central banks — the Bank of England in particular — to maintain convertibility. This in turn gave ammunition to the critics of the gold standard who argued that it was not worth the costs it imposed on the domestic economy. Overall, it is probably not too much of an exaggeration to say that the difference between the two gold standards was that the first one had forced central banks to submit to the discipline of the market, but the new one forced the market to submit to the dominant central banks.

6.4 The Keynesian Philosophy of Monetary Policy

This period saw a strong shift of opinion away from the old ideas of what a central bank should do towards the more ambitious view that it should adopt a monetary policy to stabilise the economy. A number of factors contributed to this. One was dissatisfaction with the gold standard, especially in the light of how it operated in the 1920s. Another was the growing influence of Knapp's views in the English-speaking world. Knapp's book *The State Theory of Money*[2] was translated into English in the early 1920s, and was soon seized on by the circle of economists around Keynes as providing the philosophical underpinnings for their views on British monetary policy. Keynes's approval of chartalism is obvious in the following passage from his *Treatise on Money*: 'the age of chartalist or State money was reached when the State claimed the right to declare what thing should answer as money . . . when it claimed the right not only to enforce the dictionary but also to write the dictionary. To-day all civilised money is, beyond the possibility of dispute, chartalist' (1930, p. 4).

In the 1920s Keynes and his followers had put forth a series of policy proposals — of which the main planks were opposition to the official policy on gold, and public works to help reduce unemployment — but their influence on policy in those years was somewhat limited. In part this was because of the resistance of what was left of the old view on economic policy, in part because the policies they recommended seemed to have no strong support in economic theory. Keynes was becoming respectable, though, and his views appeared to be vindicated by the Bank of England's forced abandonment of the gold standard in 1931 and Britain's subsequent rapid recovery after the adoption of Keynesian policies of deficit financing, public works, and devaluation. In this way Keynesianism established itself as the new orthodoxy in Britain, and it soon acquired a large following abroad as well.

At the same time, the Keynesians were gradually developing the theoretical underpinnings for their policy platform. As set out in *The General Theory of Employment, Interest and Money* (1936), the basic premise of the Keynesian system was that the 'capitalist system' was prone to produce large amounts of 'involuntary' unemployment in which workers could not find work even though they were able and willing to work at going wage rates. This amounted to an assertion that markets in some important sense failed, and the solution the Keynesians offered was for the government to intervene to 'manage aggregate demand' to stabilise employment. The role of monetary policy in this was to manipulate interest rates and the exchange rate in order to influence demand. Monetary policy was now one in a range of government policy instruments to be co-ordinated to stabilise the macroeconomy.

The new Keynesian view of monetary policy departed from traditional views of monetary policy in two significant respects:

(1) It placed a much greater burden on the monetary authority. Its principal objectives were no longer to stabilise the banking system and maintain convertibility, but to help stabilise the economy as a whole — a much more difficult task. Underlying this was the belief that the problem of macroeconomic instability could be solved simply by giving the authorities sufficient power and trusting them to do the right thing. This was taken for granted rather than defended in any great depth, however, and little attention was paid to the problems of how the authorities were to know what to do, or what mechanism existed to ensure that what they did was in the social interest. (2) The Keynesian philosophy of monetary policy saw little need for pre-commitment. The monetary authority could make statements if it felt that they would encourage the public to respond in the way it wanted, but it ought not to consider itself bound by them. Ethical arguments that the state should honour its promises were dismissed on the ground that such a commitment would hinder the state's freedom to achieve the 'higher good', and little thought was given to the time-consistency problems that might arise if the public did not believe the authorities' promises and reacted instead to what they thought they were up to.

As we shall see, these problems were to come home to roost later, when Keynesian policies were vigorously pursued in the early 1970s after the collapse of the Bretton Woods system. In the meantime, we return to our monetary history and resume it where we left it in the 1920s.

6.5 The Great Depression[3]

In the late 1920s there was considerable concern about the stock market boom and there were calls for the Fed to do something about it. The Fed responded by raising interest rates and adopting a much more deflationary policy in early 1928. These measures succeeded in curtailing the stock market boom — it broke in October 1929 — but they also pushed the economy into recession. The downturn changed into crisis a year later when bank failures in some of the agricultural states led to widespread attempts to convert deposits into currency — a deposit run. The failures spread, and they culminated in December 1930 with the failure of the prestigious Bank of the United States. This was a major shock to public confidence, but the crisis slowly subsided, and there were tentative signs of recovery. Unfortunately, the Federal Reserve then proceeded to reduce its credits further, and the pressure this put on banks' reserves helped produce a second and more severe panic in 1931.

The domestic crisis was also accompanied by a crisis abroad. In May 1931 the Austrian Kreditanstalt failed. This was the largest commercial bank in Austria and its failure sent shock-waves around the world. A number of German banks failed soon afterwards, and there were widespread attempts to withdraw funds from banks whose solvency was suspect. The pressure on the Bank of England's shaky reserve position at length became intolerable, and Britain was forced off the gold standard in September. Many other countries followed suit, and the international gold standard effectively collapsed.

The Fed began open market purchases in April 1932, but only in a half-hearted way and not for long, and the economy again began to show signs of recovery, only to be cut back again by a new banking crisis. The third crisis was the most severe of all. It began with a spate of bank failures in the Mid- and Far-West and spread across the nation. A number of state governments responded by declaring 'bank holidays' which closed banks down in an attempt to gain time. The crisis continued to intensify, nonetheless, and the Federal Reserve's response was to raise interest rates and blame the failure on bad management.[4] The crisis was a classic case of the kind of liquidity panic that the Fed had been established to deal with, but the Fed refused to acknowledge that it had any responsibility to respond to the crisis and it had no policy to satisfy the demand for liquidity that was destroying the banking system.[5] In fact, it appeared to have no policy at all:

> In the final two months prior to the banking holiday, there was nothing that could be called a System policy. The System was demoralized. Each Bank was operating on its own. All participated in the general atmosphere of panic that was spreading in the financial community and the community at large. The leadership which an independent central-banking system was supposed to give the market and the ability to withstand the pressures of politics and of profit alike and to act counter to the market as a whole, these — the justification for establishing a quasi-governmental institution with broad powers — were conspicuous by their absence. (Friedman and Schwartz 1963, p. 391)

The agony was only ended when President Roosevelt intervened to declare a national banking holiday in March 1933. Banks were allowed to re-open only after their books had been inspected and they had been given a clean bill of health. Some did not re-open at all. From an original figure of about 17,300 banks, fewer than 15,000 were licensed to re-open, and the rest were either liquidated or merged with other banks. The extent of the failure of the Federal Reserve System can be gauged from a counterfactual experiment carried out by Gorton (1986). He compares what happened with what would have happened under the National Banking System had the Fed never been established. His conclusions are startling: his model predicts that a panic would have broken out under the National Banking System in December 1929, and had this happened *'failure and loss percentages would have been an order of magnitude lower'* (p. 29, my italic).[6,7] This seems to confirm that Federal Reserve policies intensified the banking crisis very considerably.

The effects of this on economic activity were extremely severe. The banking collapse appears to have set in train a vicious deflationary spiral in which bank failures led to 'firesale losses', high real interest rates, the contraction of credit and generally lower economic activity; these factors, in turn, produced more bank failures and still lower economic activity (see Bernanke

1983 and Ely 1988). Real US net national product fell by more than a third in the period 1929–33, and the majority view among those who have examined the issue is that monetary policy was a major — if not *the* major — cause of the collapse in economic activity.[8]

The bank collapses led to a spate of renewed regulations. One such measure was the Banking Act of 1933 (the so-called Glass–Steagall Act: see Ch. 2, n. 15) which separated commercial and investment banking. Another was the suspension of gold convertibility, and then the return to gold at a depreciated rate of exchange two years later. This was accompanied by changes in the law to compel private agents to accept payment in the depreciated paper and surrender their monetary holdings of gold. A third was the establishment in 1934 of the Federal Deposit Insurance Corporation (FDIC) under the provisions of the 1933 Banking Act. These measures have been traditionally viewed as a public-spirited attempt by Congress to respond to the crisis created by the banking collapse, but recent work by Shughart (1988), Timberlake (1988) and others has cast considerable doubt on this explanation, and tended to emphasise instead the 'private' interests of the parties involved. Let us consider each of these measures in turn.

The separation of commercial and investment banking has sometimes been justified on the grounds of a potential conflict of interest when commercial banks underwrote the sale of securities, or on the grounds that the ownership of securities affiliates made banks more likely to fail.[9] However, Litan (1988, pp. 279–80) suggests that there was very little evidence of conflict-of-interest abuse in the years preceding the Act — or in other countries since, for that matter — while Eugene White (1986, pp. 40–1) presents evidence that banks with securities affiliates were less likely to fail than those without.[10] A more plausible explanation for the measure is that it served the private interests of the banks and brokerage firms. As Shughart (1988, p. 98) puts it, the Act was a: 'government-sponsored market-sharing agreement for the financial services industry. . . . Simply put, the Glass-Steagall Act erected barriers that prevented any direct competition between commercial and investment banking. Such an agreement on how a market is to be divided is a classic example of a dimension of collusion through which the members of a cartel can maximize their joint profits.' The devaluation of gold was one of a package of measures that was billed as emergency measures to deal with the crisis, but whose real effect was to raise revenue for the federal government. As Timberlake (1988, pp. 110–1) explains:

> In the presence of a Federal Reserve System that had so bungled, government policy was to intervene in the financial markets to ensure that its own inflow of revenues was secure. By this time, tax revenues were not manipulable. Seigniorage from gold and silver expropriation, however, provided at least a one-time bonanza. The government's 'profit' of $2.8 billion from the revaluation of gold was, by one pen-stroke, almost the equivalent of one year's ordinary tax revenues. That same federal government almost 100 years earlier, in 1835–37, had returned its fiscal surplus to the states. The government of 1934 legislated the revenue into existence and kept all of the proceeds for itself.
>
> The second source of government revenue, especially on account of the cyclical dearth of taxes, was the sale of US Treasury (and other government agency) securities. Almost all of the new laws encouraged or stimulated a demand for securities from all levels of government, and from government agencies. Commercial banks, Federal Reserve Banks, the RFC, the 12 regional banks of the Federal Home Loan Bank System, the Exchange Stabilization Fund — all were induced to purchase government securities by a number of legislative devices. That some of these purchases might have helped revive the private sector was largely irrelevant to government spokesmen, although they professed otherwise as part of their political rhetoric. As it was, most of the legislation that established government corporations, such as the RFC, simply bled off resources from the private sector that private institutions could have used more efficiently.

The third main plank in the reform package was the establishment of the FDIC. As previously mentioned, this was based on the questionable premise that bank runs were a cause of bank weakness rather than a symptom of it, and it created serious moral hazard problems. Congress apparently recognised the potential for moral hazard problems to arise, but it sought to tackle those problems by restricting the banks' permitted range of activities. It therefore gave the FDIC extensive regulatory powers and increased the powers of the Federal Reserve to oversee the loan and investment activities of member banks. In effect, Congress imposed its own definition of 'safe and sound banking' on the banking system and regulated the banks to discourage activities that did not fall within that definition.

Despite these measures rather than because of them, the economy recovered extremely well from its trough of 1933. In the period 1933–7 real net national product rose nearly 60 per cent and wholesale prices had sharply recovered. The economy then turned down again in 1937–8 after the Fed sharply increased reserve requirements, but economic growth recovered when the Fed reversed itself. (This indicates, incidentally, the extent to which the Fed was tinkering around with the economy with no clear idea of what it was doing.) The recovery from the Depression was somewhat more rapid in Europe. Britain reached its trough in 1932, as did the other countries that abandoned the gold standard at about the same time. Large public works programmes and a readiness to devalue the currency seemed to be effective, and by 1935 unemployment had been substantially reduced. The major countries then began to embark on rearmament programmes and unemployment fell further. By the eve of the Second World War the recovery was more or less complete.[11]

6.6 Monetary Policy in the Postwar Period

After the Second World War there was a determined attempt to re-establish a stable world monetary system and avoid some of the failures of the past. One of these was the instability of exchange rates in the 1930s. Once the gold standard had collapsed, many countries had engaged in a free-for-all of competitive devaluations in order to protect domestic unemployment and 'export job losses'. It was widely recognised that this had been ultimately self-defeating, and the Western Allies were determined to avoid a repeat of it. They therefore met at Bretton Woods in New Hampshire in 1944 and agreed on the blueprint for a new world monetary order. This was to be based on a fixed-exchange-rate system and a world central bank — known as the International Monetary Fund — which was to police the system and act as a kind of international lender of last resort. The exchange rate system was intended to be fixed, but occasional devaluations were to be allowed in cases of alleged extreme necessity. At around the same time, the Allies set up the General Agreement on Tariffs and Trade (GATT) as a forum in which they could agree to reduce tariffs over time and prevent the competitive and mutually destructive protection that had characterised the thirties.

A major problem with the new system was that there was a latent conflict between the discipline of the fixed exchange rate system and the prevailing Keynesian orthodoxy which laid great emphasis on each country's freedom to pursue whatever policies it wanted. The basic problem was that all countries on the fixed-exchange-rate system had to pursue the same under-lying monetary policies to enable them to maintain the fixed exchange rates. If any one country persisted in an 'easier' monetary policy than the rest, it would lose reserves abroad, and be forced in the end to devalue its currency or tighten its monetary policy. In the event, the USA adopted a more expansionary monetary policy than the majority of its trading partners. It began running down its reserves at an early stage, but the problem became acute only in the late 1960s when the Johnson administration tried to finance the Great Society social programmes and the Vietnam War without any major increases in taxation. These were paid for by borrowing — much of it from the banking system (or printing money, in other words). Countries like Germany and Japan found themselves accumulating reserves which they tried to sterilise to keep down inflation. This led them to revalue their currencies, but they continued to build up reserves nonetheless. Britain, on the other hand, had been pursuing a monetary policy even easier than that of the USA, and its weak reserve position forced it to devalue the pound in 1967.

It was steadily becoming apparent that the main Western countries were unwilling to co-ordinate their policies just to maintain the fixed-exchange-rate system, and so the system was bound to collapse. A last-ditch attempt was made in 1971 to shore it up by devaluing the dollar, but monetary policies were moving even further apart, and the fixed-exchange-rate system was abandoned shortly afterwards.

6.7 The Great Inflation

With the collapse of the fixed-exchange-rate system, one of the last restraints on domestic monetary expansion — the loss of foreign exchange reserves — was removed, and the way was cleared for each government to pursue its own independent monetary policy. This coincided with widespread dissatisfaction in a number of countries with their relatively poor economic performances. There was a general feeling that the Anglo-Saxon countries ought to be doing better, and that the solution lay in more expansionary policies. (The fact that Germany and Japan had achieved their impressive economic performances with distinctly un-Keynesian policies was generally overlooked.) Some countries (such as Britain and Italy, with France, the USA and Canada not far behind) now embarked on policies of rapid fiscal and monetary expansion. These policies seemed to work at first, but the initial output growth rates could not be maintained, and the faster rate of money creation started to feed through and increase inflation. Inflation rose to an annual rate of nearly 30 per cent in Britain, for instance, and to the mid-teens in the USA and Canada. Governments usually tried to respond to the ensuing crisis by imposing wage and price controls, but it soon became apparent that these did not work. Something more was required.

Since Keynesians had nothing more to offer, governments were forced to turn instead to the monetarists who had been arguing all along that the problem was caused by monetary growth and that the only solution was to curb that growth. This had to be done despite the likelihood that tightening monetary policy would cause a temporary recession. The recession was the price that had to be paid to break inflationary expectations and bring inflation down. Monetarism was accepted more quickly in theory than in practice, however, and the process of adopting monetarist policies was a slow and hesitating one. Britain, for example, only agreed to adopt monetary targets as the condition for a loan it desperately needed from the IMF in 1976, while monetarist policies were initially adopted in the

USA and France and then relaxed for a while by new administrations in 1977 and 1981. Canada, on the other hand, adopted monetary targets in 1975, but for five years the monetary targets of the Bank of Canada were so lax that they had relatively little impact on the inflation rate. But slow and hesitating as the process was, all the major Western economies eventually accepted the need for monetary discipline to control inflation, and by the mid-1980s all of them had managed to bring down their inflation rates very substantially.

The 'great inflation' of the 1970s and early 1980s had provided yet another reminder of how damaging inflation could be to the proper functioning of a decentralised economy. The redistributions it entailed had caused considerable social and political strain, while the price volatility it engendered had seriously impaired the ability of the market mechanism to reflect costs properly and co-ordinate economic activity. According to the monetarists, and to the new 'rational expectations' school of thought that arose in the 1970s, the monetary policy problem was not to be thought of as how to find the *right* monetary policy at any given time, but of how to design an appropriate set of rules to guide the monetary authority and enable the private sector to predict its actions. The public choice literature also stressed that the monetary authority had private interests of its own, and could not be treated as a *deus ex machina* that was concerned only with the social interest (see Acheson and Chant 1973). The problem was therefore not to design any old institutional structure that one thought might help stabilise the monetary system, but to design one that harnessed the self-interests of all the players involved to promote the social interest. In other words, the search was for an incentive-compatible institutional framework that would deliver a stable monetary system. Most economists continued to think in terms of placing an appropriate set of constraints on the monetary authority, but following the leads of Klein (1974) and Hayek (1976a, 1976b), a few began to wonder what would be wrong with a competitive monetary system that dispensed entirely with any monetary authority — and the free banking controversy was reopened once again.

6.8 Central Banks and Economic Instability

We can now form an assessment of the historical record of central banking. Several principal features stand out. Despite being established to stabilise the banking system, it is difficult to avoid the conclusion that central banking has had just the opposite effect. Its responsibility for the Great Depression is reasonably well established. Government intervention also seems to be responsible for repeated financial crises in the UK and the USA in the 19th century, for the current deposit insurance problems in the USA and Canada, and for other problems besides. Nor is there any evidence that central banking reduces output fluctuations. The evidence, if anything, suggests that it aggravates them instead.[12] In addition to this, the establishment of central banking has been responsible for historically unprecedented rates of inflation. This was only to be expected, however, because of the incentives central bank officials and politicians have to collude to undermine the value of the central bank's currency.

Overall, central banking has an abysmal record, and it is hard to improve on Milton Friedman's assessment:

> In almost every instance, major instability . . . has been produced or at the very least, greatly intensified by monetary instability. Monetary instability in its turn has generally arisen either from governmental intervention or from controversy about what governmental monetary policy should be. The failure of government to provide a stable monetary framework has thus been a major if not the major factor accounting for our really severe inflations and depressions. Perhaps the most remarkable feature of the record is the adaptability and flexibility that the private economy has so frequently shown under such extreme provocation. (1960, p. 9)[13]

Notes

1. Quoted from Friedman and Schwartz (1986, p. 39).
2. John Zube insists in a letter to me that Knapp 'should not be judged merely by the title of his major work'. He discussed private payments systems in various places. For instance, on p. 127 of the German edition, he wrote:

'Diese Kunden und die Bank bilden sozusagen eine private Zahlungsgemeinschaft; die öffentliche Zahlungsgemeinschaft ist der Staat' ('These customers and the bank make up a private system of payments, so to speak; the official system of payments is the State).

I would like to thank him for pointing this out to me.

3. This account of the Great Depression relies heavily on Friedman and Schwartz (1963) and, to a lesser extent, on Hamilton (1987).

4. In part, the failure of the Fed to support member-banks reflects a lack of incentive on its part to do so. As Kaufman (1987, pp. 17–18) notes, the earlier clearing-house associations had an incentive to provide more support to banks and did so.

5. As Litan (1988, p. 58) notes, the panic was intensified by the refusal of President-elect Roosevelt to refute rumours of an impending devaluation of gold. This of course only aggravated the banking crisis by encouraging people to demand gold from the banks to avoid prospective capital losses.

6. There is no obvious reason to suppose that Gorton's counterfactual experiment is invalidated by the 'Lucas critique' (1976) of econometric modelling. It therefore deserves to be taken seriously. One's faith in it is reinforced by the fact that he reports that the currency/deposit equation on which the experiment is based passes a stability test over the National Banking System era.

7. The Fed's failure can also be gauged from the fact that Congress felt obliged to establish *another* lender of last resort, the Reconstruction Finance Corporation (RFC). Despite the fact that it had 'no net leverage on the monetary system' (ie, it could not create base money), Timberlake (1988, p. 109) suggests that it performed a useful role lending to commercial banks against sound assets that the Fed would not accept as eligible. There would have been no need for such an institution, of course, had the Fed had a less restrictive lending policy, or if the banks had been permitted to issue the notes required to satisfy the public demand.

8. This is the view of writers of a 'monetarist' disposition (from Currie in 1934, through Friedman and Schwartz 1963, to Hamilton 1987), and 'Keynesian' attempts — of which Temin's (1976) is the best known — to ascribe the Depression to 'exogenous' shocks are not generally regarded as particularly plausible.

9. One should note, however, that the same Act also established the FDIC to protect depositors against losses in the event of failure. Given the FDIC, there was no need for additional measures to protect depositors against failure. This suggests that the real motive for the separation of commercial and investment banking was not to protect depositors, and this lends further weight to the private-interest argument.

10. In this context Shughart (1988, p. 97) maintains that there is no

reason to expect a bank with a securities affiliate to be more prone to fail. He writes:

> A profit-maximizing commercial bank undertakes investments in such a way that the *ex-ante* risk-adjusted rate of return on its asset portfolio is at a maximum. Such forces would induce the bank not to overinvest in any asset, including any securities it may have underwritten. The market value of equities can fall unexpectedly, but this is true of all other assets that the bank may hold. It is therefore disingenuous to accuse bankers of bad management after the fact when unanticipated events have caused the realized rate of return on a particular asset to be less than expected.

11. The 1930s also saw the last major Western economy — Canada — join the central banking club. My reading of the episode is that the Bank of Canada was not established because of any pressing economic reason, but because it was felt that a central bank was something that all major countries had (see Chisholm 1979, 1983 and Bordo and Redish 1988). It is interesting to note also that the Depression in Canada was comparable in magnitude to the Depression in the USA, but Canada did not have any bank failures at all. That presumably reflects not only the superiority of the branch banking system that had been allowed to develop in Canada, but also the fact that Canada was so well-integrated into the North American economy that it could not avoid the severity of the Depression when it hit the United States. For a discussion of the political forces at work behind the spread of central banking in the various British Dominions, see Plumptre (1938).

12. This assessment is based on the literature stemming from Barro's (1977b) work on the effects of money 'surprises' on employment and output. While this work does not conclusively confirm the predictions of the classical output model, it does indicate quite strongly that monetary shocks do influence output, and unless the central bank can engineer shocks to offset exogenous shocks — which is far-fetched, in my opinion — then this suggests that monetary policy tends to destabilise output. In any case, Romer (1986) finds no evidence to suggest that output was more stable during the postwar Keynesian period than it was earlier, and this seems to confirm one's casual observation that Keynesian attempts at counter-cyclical monetary policy have failed.

13. Strictly speaking, this is Friedman's assessment of US monetary policy before 1960. It seems to me, however, that it applies just as well to US monetary policy post 1960 and to the experience of other countries.

7

Reforming the Monetary System

The man of system . . . seems to imagine that he can arrange the different members of a great society with as much ease as the hand arranges the different pieces upon a chessboard. He does not consider that the pieces upon the chessboard have no other principle of motion besides that which the hand impresses upon them; but that, in the great chessboard of human society, every single piece has a principle of motion of its own, altogether different from that which the legislature might choose to impress upon it. If those two principles coincide and act in the same direction, the game of human society will go on easily and harmoniously, and is very likely to be happy and successful. If they are opposite or different, the game will go on miserably and the society must be at all times in the highest degree of disorder.

Adam Smith (1759)[1]

7.1 The Problem of Political Money

The focus of most recent proposals for monetary reform is how to establish some form of credible discipline on the money issuer. The objective is to find a set of rules which it could adopt — or which could be imposed on it — to provide the private sector with a stable monetary environment in which to go about its business. Probably the most popular proposal which is claimed to meet this requirement is a Friedman-type rule — a commitment to make a particular monetary aggregate grow at a predetermined rate — but other popular proposals involve stabilising prices or adopting a gold standard. These proposals obviously differ in many respects, but they all have in common a politicised and regulated money supply that leaves a number of basic problems unresolved. As White (1986b, pp. 3–4) points out, a 'generic feature' of these plans is that:

> all of them presuppose that the mind of man can design a government bureau which, once off the drawing board and staffed with real self-interested residents of the nation's capital, will function more or less as planned . . . Each designer must tacitly assume . . . that his plan represents a roughly stable political-economic equilibrium in the face of internal and external pressure for piecemeal modifications. The attempt to design a pressure-proof agency confronts at least three difficulties. (1) It must be possible to specify the bureau's routine tightly enough for its mandate to require little interpretation, since extensive interpretation could serve as a means of subverting the rule in the interests of the staff itself, the legislature, the executive branch, or a private constituency. (2) The operation of the rule must leave no interest group wanting and able to overturn it . . . (3) And it must be possible to establish a disciplinary mechanism which will effectively prevent departures from the legislated instructions . . . (my numbers)

Perhaps the most difficult of these requirements is the second one — to prevent vested interest groups subverting the rule once it is established. The threat of subversion is both internal and external.

The internal threat arises because there is no guarantee that the people controlling the central bank will promote the social interest. In the absence of any specific mechanism to encourage them to do so one must presume that their interests diverge from the social interest, and that central bank officials will put their own interests first. One way they would do that is by lobbying for more privileges. This is likely to be quite successful because legislators' lack of time and technical expertise makes them reliant on 'experts' such as central bank officials to guide them. A recent instance of this occurred with the US Depository Institutions Deregulation and Monetary Control Act of 1980. As Timberlake (1985, 1986) points out, in the discussions preceding the Act the Fed persistently lobbied for more powers and eventually obtained them — despite the purpose of the legislators which was to relax controls over the US monetary system. Central bank officials also tend to promote their own interests in the way they handle crises. One of their primary concerns is to avoid any controversy that might provoke political or legislative intervention to curtail their privileges or replace them. This often leads them to bail out insolvent institutions when that seems like an easier option — i.e. less risky to them — than closing one down. (The bailouts, of course, are always disguised as legitimate LOLR operations to deflect criticism.) The banks naturally anticipate this and take additional risks they would otherwise have shunned. In this way the central bank inadvertently subsidises excessive risk-taking and destabilises the banking system. In addition, central banks often prefer to pay for such operations by 'persuading' other banks to participate in the operation — as the Bank of England did in the Johnson–Matthey affair, for example — to avoid the awkward consequences of passing the costs of the operation back to their political masters. Rescue operations are thus paid for in a very arbitrary and presumably undesirable way. These examples illustrate, then, that central banks have a volition of their own and do not promote the social interest in the selfless way that is so often assumed.

Then there are the external threats. These come from politicians and interest groups seeking to use monetary policy for their own ends. As we have already seen, politicians often seek to raise revenue from the monetary system as an alternative to more explicit forms of taxation that might provoke a political backlash. Another is to redistribute income by manipulating interest rates or prices. The potential gains involved give the politicians and the groups they represent very strong incentives to interfere with monetary policy and, as we saw last chapter, the historical tendency is for constraints against intervention to break down under the pressure of these vested interests. Monetary policy becomes more or less inevitably politicised as a result. This means that it is left virtually defenceless against those groups that can capture political power and use it to further their own interests.

The essence of the problem is that there is a conflict between key private interests and the interests of society at large. This is the rock on which central banking schemes always seem to founder. They all approach the issue in a fundamentally mistaken way:

> All of us . . . have tended to follow the attitude: Well, now, what we have to do is to figure out the right thing. If only we can tell them what the right thing to do is, then there's no reason why able, well-meaning, well-intentioned people should not carry out those ideas. But then we discover, over and over again, that well-intentioned, able people have passed laws, or have established institutions — and lo and behold, they don't work the way able, well-intentioned people expected or believed they would work. And it isn't an accident that that happens. It happens for very systematic, explicit reasons. (Friedman 1977, p. 18)

The main reason, as we discussed already, is that these schemes all fail to harmonise individual incentives.

Apart from this, these proposals leave unresolved the problem of LOLR policy. The need for an LOLR remains because of the restrictions on the note issue, but the problem of finding an appropriate LOLR policy remains unsettled. As we saw in Chapter 2, the standard Bagehot prescriptions impose on the LOLR the burden of 'psychoanalysing' the market with no clear rule to enable it to distinguish between situations when it should protect its reserve and those when it should lend freely. In practice, that means it is forced to rely on its intuition and hope for the best — a sure recipe for eventual disaster.

In addition, some of these proposals have more specific drawbacks. One such proposal is for the establishment of a European central bank (as advocated by a recent editorial in *The Economist* 1988). The editorial continued: 'Once monetary policy had been rescued from national politics, governments would no longer be able to use their printing presses to finance reckless spending. The result would be lower inflation and greater financial stability.'[2] There is no reason at all to expect greater stability from a European central bank. Individual European governments might have less leverage over it than they have over their own central banks, but European governments as a group would still have considerable influence,[3] and it may also fall under the sway of the European Commission which desperately needs to find a new source of funding for the bankrupt Common Agricultural Policy. The problems of bureaucratic incentive, lender-of-last-resort policy, and the influence of politics on monetary policy, would all remain unresolved. Transferring them to a European central bank does not solve them, and creating another layer of central bank bureaucracy probably only aggravates them. The correct conclusion to draw from the failure of the individual European central banks is that central banking has failed, not that we should try again with a larger central bank. If a European central bank is established, it will fail for exactly the same reasons as its predecessors.

Another proposal is simply to persevere with monetary targeting, but as Laidler (1986) points out, the monetary growth rule has been seriously undermined by recent changes in the banking system. He writes:

> Only yesterday it seems, [the Friedman rule] . . . was by far the most popular device among supporters of constitutional constraints on monetary policy, but the fact of institutional change within the banking system . . . effectively undermines it. *To make a specific definition of 'money' part of any binding rule is to risk that rule's becoming irrelevant: and to fail to define it simply legitimises discretionary policy by permitting the authorities to do so on an ad hoc basis. There is no way out of this impasse.* (p. 309, my italic)

A third proposal is to re-establish a gold standard, but the central banks would be likely to dominate the market for gold as they did in the 1920s, and this would undermine the discipline it would provide. In addition, as Hayek (1984) says, 'To restore the gold standard would . . . require a return to beliefs that have been destroyed, and to do so would probably cause such fluctuations in the value of gold that the standard would break down before long' (p. 327, n. 7). There are therefore very serious problems with the existing monetary regime and any reforms that leave intact its basic feature of a politicised currency monopoly.

7.2 The Free Market Versus Central Planning

Free banking is a completely different sort of system in which problems like these simply do not arise. The fundamental difference is that free banking is a 'spontaneous social order' while central banking is an attempt to replace such an order with a centrally-controlled administration. The difference, in other words, is essentially that between a free market and a system of central planning. Two aspects of that difference are particularly worth pointing out. The first is that free banking is incentive compatible in a way that central banking regimes are not: that is, it provides a mechanism that aligns the private interests of the individuals operating within it. The mechanism it provides, of course, is simply the market. Central banking fails to promote the social interest, on the other hand, because it restricts the ability of private agents to look after themselves and introduces new agents into the monetary system — politicians and central bankers — whose interests are usually opposed to those of ordinary private agents. It suppresses the free market and fails to replace it with any alternative mechanism that could also perform its function.

Another major difference concerns the information requirements of central banking and free banking.[4] Central banking involves an attempt to make a particular group of individuals responsible for the well-being of the whole monetary system and this imposes a massive — indeed, superhuman — information burden on them. To fulfill their duties properly they must know how their decisions would affect millions of different people, and they simply do not — and cannot — have that sort of knowledge. Much of that information exists only as vague, perhaps unarticulated, ideas in people's minds, and does not exist in any external, objective sense at all. As Butos (1986, p. 851) has noted:

> In viewing the market process as a mechanism by which bits of information are transformed into market data, the tendency must be resisted to treat the knowledge problem as wholly a matter of somehow collecting dispersed knowledge, as if it were shells on a beach waiting to be picked up. Knowledge has no existence apart from the minds classifying it, and knowledge is significant only

because individuals attach usefulness to it. 'Objective' market data are surface-level manifestations of knowledge subjectively held by individuals. The content of such knowledge not only includes perceptions about existing market data and 'practical' knowledge, but also theories of causal relationships, anticipations of the future, and an unspecifiable body of inarticulated or tacit knowledge.

It is therefore not feasible to collect it centrally to process it. On the other side of the ledger, under free banking, markets would provide agents with whatever information they would need; it thus avoids unrealistic information requirements. Fundamentally, it starts from the premise that people are seldom endowed with the knowledge they need to operate efficiently, and one of the prime functions of markets is to provide them with it. As Brian Loasby (1976) put it:

> The argument for competition rests on the belief that people are likely to be wrong. . . . In the end, the case against an authoritarian system of resource allocation rests on the same principle as the case against an authoritarian structure in any discipline: part of the case . . . is that no person or body of persons is fit to be trusted with such power; the (other) part . . . is that no one person or group of persons can say for sure what new knowledge tomorrow will bring. Competition is a proper response to ignorance. (p. 192)

7.3 Depoliticising the Supply of Money

These considerations suggest to me that we have two basic options: to tinker with our current politicised monetary regimes to a greater or lesser extent, or to scrap them entirely and establish a form of free banking. This book has argued that free banking is superior in a number of important respects, and that the present regime is indefensible whether it is modified or not. Unfortunately this is still very much a minority view and the status quo has many articulate defenders. One of them is David Laidler who argues that:

> perhaps the current fashion among central banks for medium-term money growth targetting, unsatisfying though its intellectual basis undoubtedly is, is not so bad. It has, after all, proved possible to implement it without wholesale institutional reform, and it is

producing low and stable inflation. Though it would be pleasant to have more of a guarantee that inflation will continue to fall, and ultimately be eliminated, those of us who have lived through the past two decades should be grateful for small mercies. (1986, p. 312)

In a later paper he elaborates his position further and argues that, 'if politics is to provide the constraint upon monetary policy, responsibility for its conduct must be located where political power exists, and in the modern world that must mean with the government of the nation state' (1987, p. 18). It follows that, 'The political task in controlling monetary policy . . . is to deploy an already existing political opposition to inflation to *prevent it starting up*, instead of, as in the recent past, waiting for the experience of an accelerating inflation to mobilise this force' (loc. cit., my italics). He then proceeds to attack schemes for radical monetary reform:

> . . . an effective constitution is a figment of the economic theorist's imagination. Devices that seem satisfactory in the artificial safety of an economic model will not withstand the onslaught of politics in the real world. Monetary policy is an inherently political matter, and we will have a better chance of getting it right if we recognise that from the outset. . . .
> There has been a resurgence of interest among economists in the abstract design of monetary constitutions, and we have all gone back to military college to enjoy ourselves conducting simulated campaigns with a new array of high-tech weapons. While we have been doing so, we have not been paying attention to the conduct of monetary policy in the world around us. In Britain, money growth on any reasonable definition is now well into double digits, and in the United States it is almost there . . . Perhaps it's time for monetary economists to stop fighting imaginary battles in their classrooms, and to get back into their trenches. (loc. cit.)

This is the kind of argument to which the advocates of free banking need to respond. Laidler is surely right when he says that we should be 'grateful for small mercies' and that we cannot ignore the day-to-day conduct of monetary policy while we argue over ideal monetary constitutions. He is also right when he says that monetary policy is an inherently political matter, and that while we still have the problem of deciding on monetary policy we need to address ourselves to the source of political power and do our best to mobilise and maintain a sufficiently strong anti-inflationary coalition. Those, however, are not the points at issue. The key point — and a point that Laidler fails to address adequately — is the free bankers' claim that the only solution to the monetary policy problem is to abolish monetary policy entirely. This would eliminate the current need to appeal to the state to get monetary policy right. As for the politics, I see no obvious reason why it is impossible to dismantle the machinery of state intervention and then erect barriers against would-be interventionists to give the new monetary constitution a respectable chance of withstanding the 'onslaught of politics'. In any case, I think we have a duty to try and there is nothing better we can do. I would therefore reject Laidler's claim that an effective monetary constitution is a mere 'figment of the economic theorist's imagination' that has little practical relevance. It also seems to me that it is probably easier, in the long run, to maintain a depoliticised monetary system than it is to continue to play the political game: it is surely easier to erect barriers against intervention and defend them than try to maintain an effective anti-inflationary coalition that is almost certain to collapse in the end anyway. (We discuss this issue in more detail below. See also Dowd 1988e.) Without more radical reform, it is more or less inevitable that over time memories of inflation will dim, political forces will realign, and the current anti-inflationary coalition will gradually dissolve. We would then be defenceless against a renewed bout of inflation.

7.4 An Agenda for Reform

We come now to the problem of how to establish free banking from where we stand at present.[5] This is not a trivial issue. The trick is to dismantle controls over the monetary system without inadvertently destabilising it as we do so. We must bear in mind that the banking system is used to living under controls and that the automatic stabilising mechanisms of the market will not appear overnight. We must recognise, in fact, that in some ways the banking system has come to depend on the systems of regulation under which it lives, and we must beware of kicking out the props before we have given it the time it would need to prepare itself. Two particular instances of this come to mind. One of them concerns the relation between restrictions on the note issue and the LOLR function of the central bank. As we saw in Chapter 2, the 'need' for the LOLR arises in the first place because of restrictions on every bank's freedom to issue notes of its own — in response to demands to convert deposits into currency. It might therefore be unwise to scrap the LOLR function before we have allowed banks more freedom to issue their own notes. Freedom of the note issue should therefore precede the abolition of the central bank. The second instance concerns compulsory deposit insurance. As we also discussed, the abolition of deposit insurance would require that banks re-adjust their portfolios to reduce their risk-exposure, but this would take time. We should therefore avoid a sudden, unanticipated abolition of deposit insurance that might shake depositors' confidence and leave the banking system exposed to the danger of a major run. Deposit insurance must therefore be phased out to give the banks sufficient advance warning to prepare themselves.

The establishment of free banking would require reforms on a number of fronts: the deregulation of the monetary system, a redefinition of the MOA, the abolition of the central bank, and the reorganisation of government finances. It seems to me that we could start moving on all these fronts more or less simultaneously and complete the process within a relatively short time, say, in three or four years. Let us consider the deregulation issue first. The objective behind this would be to free financial intermediaries of all restrictions specifically relating to money and banks. Among reforms that would help to achieve this are the following:

- The amendment of legal tender laws to allow courts to enforce contracts made in any medium the parties to the contract freely choose.
- The abolition of restrictions on all banks' liabilities. Among other things, this would restore the right to free note issue, and banks would presumably begin to issue their own convertible notes.
- The repeal of the Glass–Steagall Act and the abolition of all restrictions on branch banking in the USA.

- The amendment of company law to remove any barriers against bank (or for that matter, any other) shareholders accepting extended liability.
- Where they still exist, the abolition of reserve requirements, interest rate ceilings, capital adequacy ratios and so on. Banks would learn from experience the appropriate reserve ratios to observe, the interest rates to charge and the gearing ratios to observe.
- The gradual withdrawal of compulsory deposit insurance in the USA and Canada. Banks and their customers would still be free to purchase deposit insurance if they wished, but the premiums and failure resolution procedures would be market-determined. As mentioned earlier, this reform would have to be phased in carefully to avoid exposing the banking system to a major run in the interim period.

As the process of deregulating the financial system gets under way, the authorities might usefully accompany it by extending the areas they declare as 'offshore' for regulatory purposes. In Britain, for instance, Scotland and perhaps the north of England could be declared offshore and regulations removed. Other countries might implement similar reforms or extend currently existing offshore areas. This would give offshore bankers the experience of unregulated banking before it is introduced generally, but it would also give bankers in the controlled sector an indication of how free banking operates and the practices they might imitate or avoid.

The second plank in the reform program would be to redefine the MOA along the lines we discussed in Chapter 4. Legislation would be passed to establish a commission that would announce a new commodity definition of the currently used MOA and a date when the new definition would take effect. From that date on, the pound, dollar or whatever would be a specified commodity-bundle instead of a particular inconvertible paper liability. Liabilities denominated in the MOA would then have to be redeemed with a medium which was valued in terms of that MOA. The legislation establishing the commission would also make arrangements for periodic revisions of the MOA and order the commission to choose commodity bundles whose value was the same as that of the MOA they were redefining.

This would avoid any jumps in the price level as new definitions take effect. (Note that there would be no restrictions against consenting private agents using *any other* MOAs they wished.)

We come now to the central bank itself and the reform of government finances. There are a number of issues here. The first problem is to keep some control over prices in the interim between the government announcing that it intends to establish free banking and the new definition of the MOA taking effect. We obviously want to avoid a major inflation in that period as regulations are relaxed and banks have greater freedom to expand their activities. Perhaps the best course of action is simply to order the central bank to keep prices as stable as possible. Hitting any price or money supply target is no easy task in a rapidly changing regulatory environment, of course, but it would only be an interim measure. It is also important to stress that the same sort of problem arises in a much more severe form if we keep the current regime, so one can hardly use it as an argument against free banking and in favour of the status quo. Indeed, the very difficulty of achieving such an apparently simple task only reinforces the need to establish a monetary system in which this kind of problem does not arise.

At about the same time we would prepare to transfer the central bank's debt management functions to the state. This would sever the link between government debt and the monetary system. Apart from protecting the banking system, this would also make the management of government debt more efficient. The present division of responsibility for debt management between the Treasury and the central bank often produces an unnecessary and wasteful rivalry between the two — the long history of feuding between the UK Treasury and the Bank of England particularly comes to mind. The carrying through of these measures would also require a certain amount of reorganisation in the Treasury itself. We would want to ensure that the Treasury could fulfill its functions efficiently without unnecessarily disturbing the banking system. I would suggest that the Treasury finance any borrowing by holding regular debt auctions in the same way, more or less, that many central banks do at present.

There is also the question of the government balances. We need to prevent the Treasury moving its balances around from one bank to another 'playing favourites' among them. This might enable the Treasury to cut its costs by getting better deals from the banks, but it would also undermine the independence of client banks by leaving them at the mercy of government fund managers. Perhaps this could be avoided by imposing a fixed formula to govern the allocation of the government balances among different banks and making sure that the observation of that rule is independently monitored. An obvious formula to use would be to allocate government balances in accordance with the banks' deposit market shares, perhaps with some minimum cut-off point to avoid excessively small balances. An alternative, and probably preferable, approach would be to privatise the management of government debt.

The next task would be to abolish or privatise what remains of the former central bank. At this stage the bank would no longer have any regulatory function, or any responsibility for managing the currency or government finances. What other functions it previously performed could be either privatised — such as providing a clearing system (as it does in the USA, for instance), organising financial markets and, perhaps, collecting information — or else they could be scrapped entirely — like the central bank's participation in international monetary organisations such as the IMF. There would be little point in keeping the bank operating as a unit once it had lost its principal functions, and there is no obvious alternative role it could fill. It would also be both costly and potentially dangerous to maintain a former central bank funded by the state with nothing much to do except agitate for the restoration of its former privileges. The best way to use its remaining assets would be to close it down and allow the market to redeploy them elsewhere.

Once these measures are completed, the final task would be to protect the free banking system from future intervention. We must assume that governments or other interested parties will try to manipulate the monetary system for their own purposes, and we cannot trust the unaided political process to keep them out. We therefore need to erect barriers to make it as difficult as possible for anyone to interfere with the monetary system, for *whatever* purpose.[6] Some people will, of course, immediately object that this cannot be done. It has never really been tried, however, and there is no logical reason why it could not work.

One might also point out that there are analogous cases of barriers against governmental interference that have worked reasonably well historically. An obvious example is the First Amendment to the United States Constitution. This provides that 'Congress that shall make *no* law . . . abridging the freedom of speech, or of the press' (my italic). Holzer (1981) argues persuasively that this amendment has managed to protect freedom of speech and press because of its unequivocal nature — even judges sympathetic to the government were forced to strike down attempts at interference because they were unable to get past the 'no law' provision. He writes (pp. 201–2):

> one fact is indisputable: whatever protection that speech/press has received is attributable solely to the express constitutional mandate that Congress make 'no law'. Without that provision, the government would long ago have successfully exerted its power over a multitude of speech/press areas — exactly as it has done over monetary affairs. The speech/press lesson for monetary affairs is clear: *Politically, the best way to attempt a total separation of government and money is through a constitutional amendment.* [He then adds (p. 202):] To accomplish its purpose, that amendment cannot be a halfway measure. Either the government can possess monetary power, or it cannot — and if it cannot, the constitutional amendment must sweep clean. *The few monetary powers delegated to Congress in the Constitution must be abolished, any reserved state monetary powers must be eliminated, and an express prohibition must be erected against any monetary role for government.* Strong medicine, perhaps, but the disease has very nearly killed the patient (his italics).

Countries with written constitutions might therefore consolidate free banking by passing 'free money' amendments that prohibit all government interference in the monetary system without exception. Countries like the UK, that have unwritten constitutions are less fortunate in this respect, but it is surely not beyond the wit of man to erect *some* barriers. Some barriers are better than none.

This completes our discussion of a reform package that could lead to the establishment of free banking. We turn now to its international ramifications and the problem of promoting support for it.

7.5 Free Banking in an International Context

We have concentrated our discussion so far on the domestic issues raised by free banking and said little about its international implications. These are not unimportant, but the key question for any country is whether it should go for free banking itself, and I would suggest that the answer should be affirmative regardless of whether other countries adopt it or not. What others do is not a matter of indifference, of course, because a free banking country would have to live with the events happening in the rest of the world — including the shocks generated by its systems of central banking — but there are no good reasons why a country ready to implement free banking should wait for the rest of the world to catch up. Indeed, the best way to promote free banking is to go ahead and adopt it. Internationally mobile banking operations from more regulated jurisdictions would be attracted to this country, and would increase the pressure on the remaining central banks to deregulate to stem the loss of business. The evolution of the euromarkets in the 1970s and 1980s shows how powerful these forces can be, but the process of financial deregulation still has a very long way to go.

In addition, the adoption of an MOA with a stable value would provide the rest of the world with an alternative standard to the current choice of a fiat money or gold, and one that would be considerably more reliable. This might encourage other countries to adopt similar standards, or to peg their currencies to the standard adopted by the free banking country. In the end, they might even choose to adopt free banking themselves. After all, practical success is probably the most persuasive argument of all.

7.6 Establishing Free Banking

No doubt many people will continue to argue that free banking is not worth bothering about because it is politically impossible. To the extent that this argument has any validity, it is valid only in the short run, and what is politically possible in the medium to long term is very much up to us. The supporters of free banking therefore have everything to play for. We need to persuade people that there is nothing fundamentally different about money to justify the peculiar kind of intervention that central banking represents. Free banking is simply the application of free trade to the business of issuing money, and it is desirable for much the same reasons that free trade in anything else is usually desirable, and for other good reasons besides. We also need to stress that there is no alternative route to monetary stability, and that unless we adopt it we shall face more banking crises and an eventual resurgence of inflation. To get free banking implemented, we must persuade progressive governments the world over that they should extend their programmes of deregulation and privatisation to the monetary system as well. In doing this we can also take heart from noting how much has already been achieved that was dismissed as politically impossible even a few years ago. This confirms that there is no fundamental reason why we cannot put free banking on the political agenda as well. Ten years ago it was still a major issue whether competition or central command was the superior way to allocate resources, but since then the opposition has crumbled and only the most reactionary socialists still refuse to accept the need for markets. That was always the fundamental issue, and now that people are generally ready to recognise the benefits of competition, our task is the comparatively straight-forward one of persuading them of the benefits of competition in money. There is a long way to go, and many vested interests to overcome, but Keynes was surely right when he argued that it is ideas rather than vested interests that ultimately count:

> I am sure that the power of vested interests is vastly exaggerated compared with the gradual encroachment of ideas. . . . But, soon or late, it is ideas, not vested interests, which are dangerous for good or evil. (1936, pp. 383–4)

Notes

1. Quoted from Smith (1759, Part 6, Chapter 2, penultimate paragraph).
2. *The Economist*, June 25th, 1988, p. 15. The editors go on to qualify their claim and say, 'Assuming, that is, that the central bank created to oversee the creation of the new money is well run. It might not be.' Exactly.
3. It is not necessarily an advantage to protect the independence of central banks, as the editors of *The Economist* propose. Independence certainly helps prevent political 'meddling', but it also gives the central bank officials considerable rein to do what they like. The right mix of these two evils is not immediately obvious. One advantage of free banking is that it avoids both evils by getting politicians and bureaucrats out of the monetary system. In this context it is worth noting that after a lifetime of studying Federal Reserve behaviour, Milton Friedman (1983) came to the conclusion that the Fed had *too much* independence and recommended greater Congressional supervision (i.e, greater political meddling).
4. A good discussion of the information requirements of central banking and free banking is Butos (1986).
5. One possible counter-argument that is sometimes made is that we are closer to free banking than we sometimes think because currencies compete with each other. There is some truth to that, but the degree of competition among currencies is still more limited than it would be under genuine free banking, and the extensive regulatory systems that exist today are quite incompatible with free banking.
6. A common view is that the state should have some 'residual monetary power' for use in emergencies like a major war. I would not accept that. Even in an emergency, there is nothing to stop a government raising taxes or issuing debt to finance additional expenditure. My reading of history suggests that governments thrive on emergencies, and that they need emergency monetary powers only because they are unwilling to reveal the true cost of their policies to voters and parliamentarians who would oppose them if they knew what was going on. In short, I am not convinced that there is a 'need' for emergency monetary powers.

Bibliography

Acheson, K. and Chant, J. (1973) 'Bureaucratic theory and the choice of central bank goals: the case of the Bank of Canada', *Journal of Money, Credit, and Banking*, 5, pp. 637–55.

Andréades, A. (1909) *History of the Bank of England*, P. S. King.

Andrew, A. P. (1908) 'Substitutes for cash in the panic of 1907', *Quarterly Journal of Economics*, pp. 497–516.

Anonymous (1833) *A Digest of the Evidence on the Bank Charter Taken Before the Committee of 1832*, James Ridgway.

Bagehot, W. (1848) 'The currency monopoly', *The Prospective Review*. Reprinted in Mrs. R. Barrington (ed.) *The Works and Life of Walter Bagehot*, Longman, Green and Co., vol. 8, pp. 146–87.

Bagehot, W. (1873) *Lombard Street: A Description of the Money Market*, H. S. King.
  Reprinted in N. St. John Stevas (ed.) (1978) *Collected Works of Walter Bagehot*, *The Economist*, vol. 9.

Barro, R. J. (1977a) 'Long-term contracting, sticky prices and monetary policy', *Journal of Monetary Economics*, 3, pp. 305–16.

Barro, R. J. (1977b) 'Unemployment and unanticipated money growth in the US', *American Economic Review*, 67, pp. 105–15.

Barro, R. J. (1979) 'Money and the price level under the gold standard', *Economic Journal*, 89, pp. 13–33.

Barro, R. J. (1985) 'Bank deregulation, accounting systems of exchange, and the unit of account: a comment on the McCallum Paper', *Carnegie–Rochester Conference Series on Public Policy*, 23, pp. 47–54.

Barro, R. J. and Gordon, D. B. (1983a) 'Rules, discretion and reputation in a model of monetary policy', *Journal of Monetary Economics*, 12, pp. 101–21.

Barro, R. J. and Gordon, D. B. (1983b) 'A positive theory of monetary policy in a natural rate model', *Journal of Political Economy*, 91, pp. 589–610.

Barth, J. R. and Regalia, M. A. (1988) 'The evolving role of regulation in the savings and loan industry', in C. England and T. Huertas (eds), *The Financial Services Revolution*, The Cato Institute, Ch. 6.

Benston, G. G. *et al.* (1986) *Perspectives on Safe and Sound Banking: Past, Present, and Future*, MIT Press.

Bentham, J. (1788) *Defence of Usury: Shewing the Impolicy of the Present Legal Restraints on the Terms of Pecuniary Bargains. In a Series of Letters to a Friend. To Which is Added, a Letter to Adam Smith, Esq; LL,D. On the Discouragements opposed by the above Restraints to the Progress of Inventive Industry*, Williams, Colles, White, Byrne, Lewis, Jones, and Moore.

Bernanke, B. S. (1983) 'Nonmonetary effects of the financial crisis in the propagation of the Great Depression', *American Economic Review*, 73, pp. 257–76.

Blau, J. L. (1947) 'Introduction: Jacksonian social thought' in Joseph L. Blau (ed.) *Social Theories of Jacksonian Democracy: Representative Writings of the Period 1825–1850*, Hafner Publishing Company.

Bordo, M. D. and Redish, A. (1988) 'Was the establishment of a Canadian central bank in 1935 necessary?', in C. England and T. Huertas (eds) *The Financial Services Revolution*, The Cato Institute, Ch. 4.

Brunner, K. (ed.) (1981) *The Great Depression Revisited*, Martinus Nijhoff Publishing.

Buchanan, J. M. (1962) 'Predictability: the criterion of monetary constitutions', in L. B. Yeager (ed.) *In Search of a Monetary Constitution*, Harvard University Press, Ch. 6.

Butos, W. N. (1986) 'The knowledge problem under alternative monetary regimes', *Cato Journal*, 5, pp. 849–71.

Cagan, P. (1963) 'The first fifty years of the national banking system — an historical analysis', in D. Carson (ed.) *Banking and Monetary Studies*, Irwin, Ch. 2.

Cameron, R. (1967) 'Scotland, 1750–1845', in R. Cameron *et al.* (1967) *Banking in the Early Stages of Industrialization*, Oxford University Press.

Cameron, R. (ed.) (1972) *Banking and Economic Development*, Oxford University Press.

Cameron, R. (ed.) *et al.* (1967) *Banking in the Early Stages of Industrialization*, Oxford University Press.

Cannon, J. G. (1901) *Clearing-Houses: Their History, Methods and Administration*, Smith, Elder & Co.

Capie, F. (1986) 'Conditions in which very rapid inflation has appeared', *Carnegie–Rochester Conference Series on Public Policy*, 24, pp. 115–68.

Chant, J. (1987) *Regulation of Financial Institutions — A Functional Analysis*, Bank of Canada Technical Report 45, January.

Chappell, D. and Dowd, K. (1988) 'Option clauses and banknote convertibility', School of Management and Economic Studies, Money and Finance Project, discussion paper 88.1, University of Sheffield.

Checkland, S. G. (1975) *Scottish Banking: A History*, Collins.

Chisholm, D. (1979) *Canadian Monetary Policy 1914–1934: The Enduring Glitter of the Gold Standard*, unpublished Ph.D. thesis, Cambridge University.

Chisholm, D. (1983) 'La Banque du Canada: était-elle necessaire?', *L'Actualité Economique*, 59, pp. 551–74.

Clapham, Sir J. (1945) *The Bank of England: A History*, Cambridge University Press, 2 vols.

Coase, R. H. (1960) 'The problem of social cost', *Journal of Law and Economics*, 3.

Conant, C. A. (1909) *A History of Modern Banks of Issue*, G. P. Putnam and Sons.

Congdon, T. (1981) 'Is the provision of a sound currency a necessary function of the state?' *National Westminster Bank Quarterly Review*, August, pp. 2–21.

Cowen, T. and Kroszner, R. (1987) 'The development of the new monetary economics', *Journal of Political Economy*, 95, pp. 567–90.

Cowen, T. and Kroszner, R. (1988a) *The Evolution of an Unregulated Payments System*, unpublished manuscript.

Cowen, T. and Kroszner, R. (1988b) 'Scottish banking before 1944: a model for laissez-faire?', *Journal of Money, Credit, and Banking*, forthcoming.

Currie, L. (1934) 'The failure of monetary policy to prevent the Depression of 1929–32' in *Journal of Political Economy*, vol. 42, April.

Dewald, W. G. (1972) 'The National Monetary Commission: a look back', *Journal of Money, Credit, and Banking*, 4, pp. 930–56.

Diamond, D. W. and Dybvig, P. H. (1983) 'Bank runs, deposit insurance, and liquidity', *Journal of Political Economy*, vol. 91, pp. 401–19.

Dowd, K. (1988a) 'How necessary is state deposit insurance?', manuscript, School of Management and Economic Studies, University of Sheffield, January.

Dowd, K. (1988b) 'Automatic stabilising mechanisms under free banking', *Cato Journal*, 7, pp. 643–59.

Dowd, K. (1988c) 'Some lessons from the recent Canadian Bank failures', forthcoming in G. G. Kaufman (ed.) *Research in Financial Services: Private and Public Policy*, JAI Press.

Dowd, K. (1988d) 'Option clauses and the stability of a *laisser faire* monetary system', *Journal of Financial Services Research*, 1, forthcoming.

Dowd, K. (1988e) *Private Money: The Path to Monetary Stability*, Hobart Paper No. 112, Institute of Economic Affairs.

Dunne, G. T. (undated) 'A Christmas present for the President: a short history of the creation of the federal reserve system', reprinted by the Federal Reserve Bank of St. Louis.

Originally printed in *Business Horizons*, 6 (1963), no. 4, 43–60.

Economist, The (1988) 'Lo! a central bank for Europe', 25 June, pp. 15–6.

Economopoulos, A. J. (1988) 'Illinois free banking experience', *Journal of Money, Credit, and Banking*, 20, pp. 249–64.

Ely, B. (1988) 'The big bust: the 1930–33 banking collapse — its causes, its lessons', in C. England and T. Huertas (eds) *The Financial*

BIBLIOGRAPHY

Services Revolution, The Cato Institute, Ch. 3.

England, C. (1988) 'Nonbank banks are not the problem: outmoded regulations are', in C. England and T. Huertas (eds) *The Financial Services Revolution*, The Cato Institute, Ch. 9.

England, C. and Huertas T. (1988) *The Financial Services Revolution*, The Cato Institute.

Faig, M. (1986) *Optimal Taxation of Money Balances*, unpublished Ph.D. dissertation, Stanford University.

Faig, M. (1988) 'Characterization of the optimal tax on money when it functions as a medium of exchange', *Journal of Monetary Economics*, 22, pp. 137–48.

Fama, E. F. (1980) 'Banking in the theory of finance', *Journal of Monetary Economics*, 6, pp. 39–57.

Fama, E. F. (1983) 'Financial intermediation and price level control', *Journal of Monetary Economics*, 12, pp. 7–28.

Fama, E. F. (1985) 'What's different about banks?', *Journal of Monetary Economics*, 15, pp. 29–39.

Fetter, F. W. (1965) *Development of British Monetary Orthodoxy 1797–1875*, Harvard University Press.

Fischer, S. (1977) 'Long-term contracting, sticky prices and monetary policy: a comment', *Journal of Monetary Economics*, 3, pp. 317–24.

Fischer, S. (1982) 'A framework for monetary and banking analysis', *Economic Journal Supplement*, pp. 1–16.

Fischer, S. (1986) 'Friedman versus Hayek on private money', *Journal of Monetary Economics*, 17, pp. 433–9.

Fisher, I. (1920) *The Purchasing Power of Money: Its Determination and Relation to Credit, Interest and Crises* (new edn), Macmillan.

Frankel, S. H. (1977) *Money: Two Philosophies: The Conflict of Trust and Authority*, Basil Blackwell.

Friedman, M. (1951) 'Commodity-Reserve Currency', *Journal of Political Economy*, 59, pp. 203–32.

Friedman, M. (1960) *A Program for Monetary Stability*, Fordham University Press (reprinted in 1983).

Friedman, M. (1968) 'The role of monetary policy', *American Economic Review*, 58, pp. 1–17.

Friedman, M. (1969) 'The optimum quantity of money', in M. Friedman *The Optimum Quantity of Money and Other Essays*, Macmillan.

Friedman, M. (1977) 'The monetarist controversy: a seminar discussion', Federal Reserve Bank of San Fransisco *Economic Review* Supplement, pp. 12–26.

Friedman, M. (1983) 'Monetary policy: theory and practice', *Journal of Money, Credit, and Banking*, 14, pp. 98–118.

Friedman, M. (1984) 'Monetary policy in the 1980s', in J. H. Moore (ed.) (1984) *To Prosperity: US Domestic Policy in the Mid-1980s*, Hoover Institution Press.

Friedman, M. (1986) 'The resource cost of irredeemable paper money', *Journal of Political Economy*, 94, pp. 642–7.

Friedman, M. and Schwartz, A. J. (1963) *A Monetary History of the United*

States, 1867–1960, Princeton University Press for the National Bureau of Economic Research.

Friedman, M. and Schwartz, A. J. (1986) 'Has government any role in money?', *Journal of Monetary Economics*, 17, pp. 37–62.

Garcia, G. (1988) 'The FSLIC is "broke" in more ways than one', in C. England and T. Huertas (eds) *The Financial Services Revolution*, The Cato Institute, Ch. 10.

Garrison, R. W., Short, E. D. and O'Driscoll, G. P. (1988) 'Financial stability and FDIC insurance', in England and Huertas (eds).

Giffen, Sir R. (1892) 'Fancy monetary standards', *Economic Journal*, vol. 2, pp. 239–55.

Girton, L. and Roper, D. (1981) 'Theory and implications of currency substitution', *Journal of Money, Credit, and Banking*, 13, pp. 14–30.

Glasner, D. (1987) *Competitive Banking and Monetary Reform*, (tentative title), manuscript, Manhattan Institute.

Goodhart, C. A. E. (1985) *The Evolution of Central Banks*, published by the Suntory–Toyota International Centre for Economics and Related Disciplines, London School of Economics.

Goodhart, C. A. E. (1987a) 'Why do banks need a central bank?', *Oxford Economics Papers*, 39, pp. 75–89.

Goodhart, C. A. E. (1987b) Review of L. H. White *Free Banking in Britain*, *Economica*, pp. 129–31.

Gorton, G. (1985a) 'Banking theory and free banking history', *Journal of Monetary Economics*, 16, pp. 267–76.

Gorton, G. (1985b) 'Clearinghouses and the origin of central banking in the US', *Journal of Economic History*, 45.

Gorton, G. (1985c) 'Bank suspension of convertibility', *Journal of Monetary Economics*, 15, pp. 177–93.

Gorton, G. (1986) 'Banking panics and business cycles', working paper 86–9, Federal Reserve Bank of Philadelphia, March.

Gorton, G. (1987) 'Incomplete markets and the endogeneity of central banking', Rodney L. White Center for Financial Research, No. 16, The Wharton School, University of Pennsylvania.

Gorton, G. and Haubrich, J. G. (1986) 'Bank deregulation, credit markets and the control of capital', forthcoming in the *Carnegie–Rochester Conference Series*.

Gorton, G. and Mullineaux, D. J. (1986) 'The joint production of confidence: endogenous regulation and 19th century commercial-bank clearinghouses', forthcoming in the *Journal of Money, Credit, and Banking*.

Graham, F. D. (1930) *Exchange, Prices and Production in Hyper-Inflation: Germany 1930–1923*, Princeton University Press.

Graham, W. (1886) *The One Pound Note*, James Thin.

Greenfield, R. L. and Yeager, L. B. (1983) 'A *laisser faire* approach to monetary stability', *Journal of Money, Credit, and Banking*, 15, pp. 302–15.

Gregory, Sir T. E. (1926) 'Central bank policy', *Manchester Statistical Society*, December.

Haberler, G. (1941) *Prosperity and Depression: A Theoretical Analysis of Cyclical Movements*, Economic Intelligence Service, League of Nations.

Halevy, E. (1961) *The Triumph of Reform (1830–1841)*, vol. 3 of *Halevy's History of the English People in the Nineteenth Century*, (translated by E. I. Watkin), Ernest Benn Limited.

Hall, R. E. (1981a) 'Explorations in the gold standard and related policies for stabilizing the dollar', manuscript, NBER, March.

Hall, R. E. (1981b) 'The government and the monetary unit', manuscript, NBER, November.

Hall, R. E. (1983) 'Optimal fiduciary monetary systems', *Journal of Monetary Economics*, 12, pp. 33–50.

Hamilton, A. (1790) 'Report on a national bank', in A. Hamilton *Papers on Public Credit, Commerce, and Finance*, reprinted (1934) in The American Heritage Series, Columbia University Press.

Hamilton, J. D. (1987) 'Monetary factors in the Great Depression', *Journal of Monetary Economics*, 19, pp. 145–69.

Hammond, B. (1957) *Banks and Politics in America*, Princeton University Press.

Hayek, F. A. (1943) 'A commodity-reserve currency', *Economic Journal*, pp. 176–84.

Hayek, F. A. (1960) *The Constitution of Liberty*, Routledge & Kegan Paul.

Hayek, F. A. (1976a) *Choice in Currency: A Way to Stop Inflation*, Occasional Paper 48, Institute for Economic Affairs.

Hayek, F. A. (1976b) *Denationalisation of Money: An Analysis of the Theory and Practice of Concurrent Currencies*, Hobart Paper, Institute of Economic Affairs.

Hayek, F. A. (1973, 1976c, 1979) *Law Legislation and Liberty*, Chicago University Press, 3 vols.

Hayek, F. A. (1984) in B. Siegel (ed.) *Money and Crisis: The Federal Reserve, the Economy, and Monetary Reform*, Ballinger Publishing.

Hendry, D. (1985) 'Monetary economic myth and econometric reality', *Oxford Review of Economic Policy*, 1, pp. 72–84.

Hercowitz, Z. (1981) 'Money and the dispersion of relative prices', *Journal of Political Economy*, 89, pp. 328–56.

Hetzel, R. L. (1986) 'A congressional mandate for monetary policy', *Cato Journal*, 5, Winter, pp. 797–820.

Holzer, H. M. (1981) *Government's Money Monopoly: Its Source and Scope, and How to Fight It*, Books in Focus.

Homer, S. (1963) *A History of Interest Rates*, Rutgers University Press.

Hoover, K. (1988) 'Money, prices and finance in the new monetary economics', *Oxford Economic Papers*, 40, pp. 150–67.

Hutton, G. (1960) *Inflation and Society*, Allen and Unwin.

Jevons, W. S. (1875) *Money and the Mechanism of Exchange*. Reprint (1920) (20th edn) Kegan Paul, Trench, Trubner and Company.

Jonung, L. (1985) 'The economics of private money: the experience of private notes in Sweden 1831–1902', paper prepared for the Monetary History Group.

Joplin, T. (1822) *An Essay on the General Principles and Present Practice of Banking, in England and Scotland* . . ., Edward Walker.

Kane, E. J. (1985) *The Gathering Crisis in Deposit Insurance*, MIT Press.

Kareken, J. H. and Wallace, N. (1978) 'Deposit insurance and bank regulation: a partial-equilibrium exposition', *Journal of Business*, 51, pp. 413–38.

Kaufman, G. G. (1987) 'The truth about bank runs', Staff Memorandum SM-87-3, Federal Reserve Bank of Chicago.

Kerr, A. W. (1918) *History of Banking in Scotland*, A. & C. Black.

Keynes, J. M. (1919) *Essays in Persuasion*.
Reprinted (1963) W. W. Norton and Company.

Keynes, J. M. (1923) *A Tract on Monetary Reform*, Macmillan.

Keynes, J. M. (1930) *A Treatise on Money*, Macmillan.
Reprint (1935).

Keynes, J. M. (1936) *The General Theory of Employment, Interest and Money*.
Reprinted (1977) in Royal Economic Society *The Collected Works of John Maynard Keynes*, vol. VII.

Kimbrough, K. P. (1986) 'The optimum quantity of money rule in the theory of public finance', *Journal of Monetary Economics*, 18, pp. 277–84.

King, R. G. (1983) 'On the economics of private money', *Journal of Monetary Economics*, 12, pp. 127–58.

Klein, B. (1974) 'The competitive supply of money', *Journal of Money, Credit and Banking*, 6, pp. 423–54.

Klein, B. (1978) 'Competing monies, European monetary union and the dollar', in M. Fratianni and T. Peeters (eds) *One Money for Europe*, Macmillan.

Knapp, G. F. (1905) *Die Staatliche Theorie des Geldes*.
Translated and printed in English by H. M. Lucas and J. Bonar (eds) (1924) *The State Theory of Money*.

Kydland, F. E. and Prescott E. C. (1977) 'Rules rather than discretion: the inconsistency of optimal plans', *Journal of Political Economy*, 85, pp. 473–91.
Reprinted in R. E. Lucas and T. J. Sargent (eds) (1981) *Rational Expectations and Econometric Practice*, University of Minnesota Press.

Laidler, D. (1975) 'Thomas Tooke on monetary reform' in *Essays on Money and Inflation*, University of Chicago Press.

Laidler, D. (1986) 'Money in crisis: a review essay', *Journal of Monetary Economics*, 17, pp. 305–13.

Laidler, D. (1987) 'The political control of inflation: a sceptical view', *Economic Affairs*, 7, February–March.

Lewis, M. K. and Davis, K. T. (1987) *Domestic and International Banking*, Philip Allan.

Litan, R. E. (1988) 'Reuniting investment and commercial banking', in

C. England and T. Huertas (eds) *The Financial Services Revolution*, The Cato Institute, Ch. 12.

Loasby, B. J. (1976) *Choice, Complexity and Ignorance*, Cambridge University Press.

Longfield, S. M. (1840) 'Banking and Currency', *Dublin University Magazine*, February.

Lucas, R. E., Jr. (1972) 'Expectations and the neutrality of money', *Journal of Economic Theory*, 4, pp. 103–24.

Lucas, R. E. (1976) 'Econometric policy evaluation: a critique' in K. Brunner and A. K. Meltzer (eds) *The Phillips Curve and the Labour Market*, Carnegie–Rochester Conference Series, vol. 1, North Holland.

Luckett, D. (1980) (2nd edn) *Money and Banking*, MacGraw-Hill.

MacLeod, H. D. (1896) 'A history of banking in Great Britain', in W. G. Sumner (ed.) (1896) *A History of Banking in All the Leading Nations*, reprinted by Augustus M. Kelley.

Martin, J. G. (1856) *Twenty-One Years in the Boston Stock Market*, Redding and Company.

McCallum, B. T. (1985) 'Bank deregulation, accounting systems of exchange and the unit of account: a critical review', *Carnegie–Rochester Conference Series on Public Policy*, 23, pp. 13–46.

McCulloch, J. R. (1831) *Historical Sketch of the Bank of England: With an Examination of the Question as to the Prolongation of the Exclusive Privileges of that Establishment*, Longman.

Menger, K. (1892) 'On the Origin of Money', *Economic Journal*, 2, pp. 239–55.

Meulen, H. (1934) *Free Banking: An Outline of a Policy of Individualism*, Macmillan.

Mill, J. (1821) *Elements of Political Economy*, Baldwin, Cradock and Joy.

Mints, L. W. (1945) *A History of Banking Theory in Great Britain and the United States*, University of Chicago Press.

Munn, C. W. (1981) *The Scottish Provincial Banking Companies 1747–1864*, John Donald Publishers.

Munn, C. W. (1985) 'Review' of L. H. White *Free Banking in Britain*, *Business History*, 27, pp. 341–3.

Nataf, P. C. (1987) *An Inquiry into the Free Banking Movement in Nineteenth Century France, With Particular Emphasis on Charles Coquelin's Writings*, unpublished manuscript.

Niehans, J. (1978) *The Theory of Money*, Johns Hopkins University Press.

Norman, G. W. (1837) *Remarks upon Some Prevalent Errors with Respect to Currency and Banking*, Pelham Richardson.

O'Driscoll, G. P. (1988) 'Deposit insurance in theory and practice', in C. England and T. Huertas (eds), Ch. 7.

Phelps, E. S. (1973) 'Inflation in the theory of public finance', *Swedish Journal of Economics*, 75, pp. 67–82.

Plumptre, A. F. W. (1938) 'The arguments for central banking in the

British dominions', in H. A. Innis (ed.) *Essays in Political Economy (in Honour of E. J. Urwick).*

Rockoff, H. (1974) 'The free banking era: a reexamination', *Journal of Money, Credit, and Banking*, 6, pp. 141–67.

Rockoff, H. (1986) 'Walter Bagehot and the theory of central banking', in F. Capie and G. E. Wood (eds) *Financial Crises and the World Banking System*, Macmillan.

Rolnick, A. J. and Weber, W. E. (1983) 'New evidence on the free banking era', *American Economic Review*, 1080–91.

Rolnick, A. J. and Weber, W. E. (1984) 'The causes of free bank failures: a detailed examination', *Journal of Monetary Economics*, 14, pp. 267–91.

Rolnick, A. J. and Weber, W. E. (1985) 'Banking instability and regulation in the US free banking era', *Federal Reserve Bank of Minneapolis Review*, Summer 1985, pp. 2–9.

Rolnick, A. J. and Weber, W. E. (1986) 'Inherent instability in banking: the free banking experience', *Cato Journal*, 5, pp. 877–90.

Romer, C. D. (1986) 'Is the stabilization of the postwar economy a figment of the data?', *American Economic Review*, 76, pp. 314–34.

Rothbard, M. N. (1987) 'The myth of free banking in Scotland', *Review of Austrian Economics*, 2, pp. 229–45.

Samuelson, P. A. (1969) 'Nonoptimality of money holding under *laisser faire*', *Canadian Journal of Economics*, pp. 303–8.

Sandberg, L. G. (1978) 'Banking and economic growth in Sweden before World War I', *Journal of Economic History*, 38, pp. 650–80.

Sargent, and Wallace, (1982) 'The real bills doctrine versus the quantity theory: a reconsideration' in *Journal of Political Economy*.

Schuler, K. (1985) *Hands Off! The History of Canadian Free Banking*, manuscript.

Schuler, K. (1988a) *Canadian Banking 1837–1867*, unpublished manuscript, University of Georgia.

Schuler, K. (1988b) *Evolution of Canadian Banking, 1867–1914*, unpublished manuscript, University of Georgia.

Schwartz, A. J. (1988) 'Bank runs and deposit insurance reform', *Cato Journal*, 7, pp. 589–94.

Scott, Sir W. (1981) *The Letters of Malachi Malagrowther*, William Blackwood.

Sechrest, L. J. (1988) 'White's free-banking thesis: a case of mistaken identity', *Review of Austrian Economics*, 2, pp. 247–57.

Selgin, G. A. (1985) 'The case for free banking: then and now', *Cato Institute Policy Analysis*, 60,

Selgin, G. A. (1987) 'Free Banking in China, 1800–1935', unpublished manuscript, George Mason University.

Selgin, G. A. (1988a) 'Accommodating changes in the relative demand for currency: free banking vs. central banking', *Cato Journal*, 7, pp. 621–41.

Selgin, G. A. (1988b) *The Theory of Free Banking: Money Supply under Competitive Note Issue*, Rowman and Littlefield.

Selgin, G. A. and White, L. H. (1987) 'The evolution of a free banking system', *Economic Inquiry*, 25, pp. 439–57.

Senate of Canada (1985) *Deposit Insurance*, Tenth Report of the Standing Senate Committee on Banking, Trade and Commerce, Ottawa, December.

Shortt, A. (undated) *Adam Shortt's History of Canadian Currency and Banking, 1600–1880*, Canadian Bankers' Association.

Shughart, W. F., II (1988) 'A public choice perspective of the 1933 Banking Act', in C. England and T. Huertas (eds), op. cit., Ch. 5.

Sinclair, Sir J. (1822) *Hints on Circulation . . . with an Account of the Paper Circulation of Scotland*, Archibald Constable.

Smith, A. (1759) *The Theory of Moral Sentiments*, Liberty Classics.

Smith, A. (1776) *An Inquiry into the Nature and Causes of the Wealth of Nations*, vol. 1, (edited by E. R. A. Seligman), J. M. Dent and Sons, Ltd, London, and E. P. Dutton, New York.

Smith, V. C. (1936) *The Rationale of Central Banking*, P. S. King.

Spencer, H. (1882) *Social Statics*, D. Appleton and Co.

Sumner, W. G. (1896) 'A history of banking in the United States', in W. G. Sumner (ed.) *A History of Banking in All the Leading Nations*, reprinted (1971) by Augustus M. Kelley.

Sylla, R. (1972) 'The United States 1863–1913', in Cameron (ed.) (1972) *Banking and Economic Development*, Oxford University Press.

Taylor, D. (1982a) 'Official intervention in the foreign exchange market, or, bet against the central bank', *Journal of Political Economy*, 90, pp. 356–68.

Taylor, D. (1982b) 'The mismanaged float: official intervention by the industrialized countries', in M. B. Connolly (ed.) *The International Monetary System: Choices for the Future*, Praeger, Ch. 3.

Temin, P. (1976) *Did Monetary Forces Cause the Great Depression?*, W. W. Norton.

Thornton, H. (1802) in F. A. Hayek (ed.) (1939) *An Inquiry into the Nature and Effects of the Paper Credit of Great Britain* (2nd edn), Allen & Unwin.

Timberlake, R. H., Jr. (1978) *The Origins of Central Banking in the United States*, Harvard University Press.

Timberlake, R. H., Jr. (1981) 'The significance of unaccounted currencies', *Journal of Economic History*, 41, pp. 853–66.

Timberlake, R. H., Jr. (1984) 'The Central Banking Role of Clearing-house Associations', *Journal of Money, Credit, and Banking*, 16, pp. 1–15.

Timberlake, R. H., Jr. (1985) 'Legislative construction of the Monetary Control Act of 1980', *American Economic Review Papers and Proceedings*, 75, pp. 97–102.

Timberlake, R. H., Jr. (1986) 'Institutional evolution of federal reserve hegemony', *Cato Journal*, 3, Winter, pp. 743–63.

Timberlake, R. H., Jr. (1987) 'Private production of scrip-money in the isolated community', *Journal of Money, Credit, and Banking*, 19, pp. 437–47.

Timberlake, R. H., Jr. (1988) 'New deal monetary legislation for the welfare of the government: comment on Shughart', C. England and T. Huertas (eds), pp. 107–11.

Trivoli, G. (1979) *The Suffolk Banking System: A Study of a Private Enterprise Clearing System*, Adam Smith Institute.

Trivoli, G. (1984) 'The government's money monopoly: externalities or natural monopoly?', *Kyklos*, 37, pp. 27–58.

Trivoli, G. (1986) 'Currency competition versus governmental money monopolies', *Cato Journal*, 5, pp. 927–42.

Vaubel, R. (1977) 'Free currency competition', *Weltwirtschaftliches Archiv*, pp. 435–59.

Viner, J. (1937) *Studies in the Theory of International Trade*, Harper Brothers.

Weber, E. J. (1988) 'Currency competition in Switzerland 1826–1850', *Kyklos*, 41, pp. 459–78.

Wesslau, O. E. (1887) *Rational Banking Versus Banking Monopoly*, (edited by Bancroft Cooke), Elliot Stock, London.

West, R. C. (1977) *Banking Reform and the Federal Reserve, 1863–1923*, Cornell University Press.

White, E. N. (1983) *The Regulation and Reform of the American Banking System, 1900–1929*, Princeton University Press.

White, E. N. (1986) 'Before the Glass–Steagall Act: an analysis of the investment banking activities of national banks', *Explorations in Economic History*, 23, pp. 33–55.

White, E. N. (1988) *Free Banking During the French Revolution*, unpublished manuscript, Rutgers University.

White, L. H. (1983) 'Competitive money, inside and out', *Cato Journal*, 3, pp. 281–99.

White, L. H. (1984a) 'Competitive payments systems and the unit of account', *American Economic Review*, 74, pp. 699–712.

White, L. H. (1984b) *Free Banking in Britain: Theory, Experience, and Debate, 1800–45*, Cambridge University Press.

White, L. H. (1986a) 'Depoliticising the supply of money', forthcoming in T. Willett (ed.) *Political Business Cycles and the Political Economy of Stagflation*, The Pacific Institute.

White, L. H. (1986b) 'Problems inherent in political money supply regimes: some historical and theoretical lessons', forthcoming in T. Willett, loc. cit.

White, L. H. (1986c) 'Accounting for non-interest-bearing currency: a critique of the "legal restrictions" theory of money', manuscript, New York University.

Wilson, J. (1847) *Capital, Currency, and Banking*, The Economist.

Woodward, S. (1988) 'A transaction cost analysis of banking activity and deposit insurance', *Cato Journal*, 7, pp. 683–99.

Yeager, L. B. (1983) 'Stable money and free-market currencies', *Cato Journal*, 3, pp. 305–26.

Yeager, L. B. (1985) 'Deregulation and monetary reform', *American Economic Review 75, Papers and Proceedings*, pp. 103–7.

Author Index

Acheson, K. and Chant, J., 175
Althorp, Lord, 127
Andréades, A., 146
Andrew, A.P., 145

Bagehot, 39–42, 52, 123, 130, 148, 182
Bailey, S., 128, 147
Barro, R.J., 74, 82, 89, 178
Barth, J.R., 51
Benston, G.G., 17, 25, 49, 51, 58, 60–61, 150
Bentham, J., 125, 148
Bernanke, B.S., 17, 170
Blair, A., 148, 156, 159
Blau, J.L., 149
Bordo, M.D., 117, 178
Buchanan, J.M., 98
Butos, W.N., 184, 195

Cagan, P., 144, 151
Cameron, R., 89, 125, 147
Cannon, J.G., 52, 151
Capie, F., 83
Chant, J., 50
Chappell, D., 31
Checkland, S.G., 89, 106, 157, 158
Chisholm, D., 117, 178
Cobden, R., 148
Clapham, Sir J., 146
Cowen, T., 50, 152, 157
Currie, L., 177

Davis, K.T., 104
Dewald, W.G., 151
Diamond, D.W., 17, 54–60

Dowd, K., 31, 52, 59, 105, 147
Dybvig, P.H., 17, 54–60
Dunne, G.T., 149, 151

Economopoulos, A.J., 136, 150
Ely, B., 35, 170
England, C., 151

Faig, M., 80, 83
Fama, E.F., 50, 106, 112, 158
Farrer, Lord, 111
Fetter, F.W., 14, 52, 106, 108, 128, 147, 155
Fischer, S., 15, 81, 82, 104
Fisher, I., 48, 66, 106, 162
Friedman, M., 3, 4, 5, 15, 71, 72, 77, 78, 88, 106, 115, 160, 164, 169, 176, 177, 178, 182, 195

Garrison, R.W., 59
Giffen, Sir R., 161
Goodhart, C.A.E., 10, 15, 19, 22, 23, 45, 46, 53, 152, 153, 154, 157, 158
Gordon, D.B., 74
Gorton, G., 10, 18–24, 49, 152, 158, 169, 177
Graham, F.D., 73
Graham, W., 95
Greenfield, R.L., 12, 109, 110, 112
Gregory, Sir T.E., 66, 81

Haberler, G., 83
Hake, A.E., 15
Halévy, E., 148
Hall, R.E., 72, 98, 106–7, 112

Hamilton, J.D., 131, 176–7
Hammond, B., 148
Haubrich, J.G., 24, 49
Hayek, F.A., 16, 48, 72, 111, 175, 183
Hendry, D.F., 82
Hercowitz, Z., 73
Holzer, H.M., 192
Homer, S., 138
Huertas, T., 57
Hutton, G., 80, 83

Indiana State Auditor, 136

Jackson, A., 134
Jevons, W.S., 14
Jonung, L., 91, 117
Joplin, T., 124, 147

Kane, E.J., 37, 49, 51–2, 61
Kareken, J.H., 59
Kaufman, G.G., 19, 25, 51–2, 57–8, 177
Kerr, A.W., 146
Keynes, J.M., 66, 78–9, 111, 166, 194
Kimbrough, K.P., 80
King, R.G., 15, 37, 91, 108, 149–50
Klein, B., 88, 175
Knapp, G.F., 111, 162, 166, 176
Kroszner, R., 50, 152, 157
Kydland, F.E., 73–4, 76

Laidler, D., 15, 65, 89, 104, 183, 185–7
Law, J., 62, 65
Lenin, V.I., 79
Lewis, M.K., 59
Litan, R.E., 51, 57, 170, 177
Liverpool, Lord, 126
Loasby, B., 185
Longfield, M., 45, 126
Loyd, S.J., 128
Lucas, R.E., 69
Luckett, D., 136

McCallum, B.T., 95, 105, 107
McCulloch, J.R., 126

MacLeod, H.D., 14, 147
Martin, J.G., 138
Menger, K., 112
Meulen, H., 15, 95, 120, 146, 147
Mill, James, 124
Mill, John Stuart, 14
Mints, L.W., 14, 147
Munn, C.W., 146–7, 152, 155, 157
Mushet, R., 65, 147

Nataf, P.C., 14, 117
Niehans, J., 84, 92
Norman, G.W., 126

O'Driscoll, G.P., 35, 59

Palmer, J.H., 128
Parnell, Sir H., 1, 44, 65, 125–7, 147
Plumptre, A.F.W., 178
Prescott, E.C., 73–4, 76

Redish, A., 117, 178
Regalia, M.A., 51
Rice, T.S., 128
Robinson, F.J., 126
Rockoff, H., 41, 136, 138, 148–9
Rolnick, A.J., 57, 136–7, 149–50
Romer, C.D., 178
Rothbard, M.N., 63, 65, 147–8, 152–6, 158
Russell, S., 104

Samuelson, P.A., 116
Sandberg, L.G., 117
Sargent, T.J., 64–5, 68–9, 81
Schuler, K., 51, 91, 117, 154
Scott, Sir W., 14
Schwartz, A.J., 4, 15, 50, 78, 160, 164, 169, 176, 177
Scrope, G. Poulett, 147, 157
Sechrest, L.J., 152–3, 156–7
Selgin, G.A., 50, 71, 106, 117
Seymour, H., 15
Short, E.D., 59
Shortt, A., 117
Shughart, W.F., 170–1, 177

Sinclair, Sir J., 147
Smith, A., 65, 124, 147, 179, 195
Smith, V.C., 14, 45, 53, 84, 103,
    117, 119, 130, 144, 146–8,
    150
Spencer, H., 130
Sumner, W.G., 133, 148–50
Sylla, R., 142

Taylor, D., 69
Temin, P., 177
Thornton, H., 62
Timberlake, R.H., 52, 142, 150,
    170–1, 177, 180
Tooke, T., 128
Trivoli, G., 150
Tucker, B., 15

Vaubel, R., 91–2
Viner, J., 14, 147

Wallace, N., 59, 64–5, 68–9, 81
Watt, H., 147
Weber, E.J., 117
Weber, W.E., 136–7, 148–9
Wesslau, O.E., 14, 15
West, R.C., 151
White, E.N., 117, 150, 170
White, L.H., 9, 14, 52–3, 61–2, 86,
    89, 91, 93–4, 102–3, 105,
    108, 112, 114, 123, 125,
    146–8, 152–3, 155, 157–8,
    180
Wicksell, K., 162
Wilson, J., 129–30, 147
Woodward, S., 60

Jeager, L.B., 12, 107, 109, 110, 112

Zube, J., 176

Subject Index

Act of 1826, 125, 147
Act of Union (1707), 120
Aldrich-Vreeland Act, 145
ANCAP, 72, 98, 102–3
Anti-bullionists, 63
Ayr Bank episode, 52, 122

Bagehot's Rules, 39–42, 52–3, 162, 182
Bank Charter Act (1844), 14, 33, 129–130
Bank 'Contagion', 23–4, 50, 136
Bank failure rates, 25, 152–3, 169
Bank Holding Company Act (1957), 51
Bank panics, 16–19, 46
  See also Bank runs
Bank runs, 10, 16, 19, 23–5, 34, 36, 39, 42, 55–8, 188
Bank War (US), 134
Banking school, 63, 65, 128
Bank deposit requirements, 135, 137–8, 141–3, 149–50
Branch-banking restrictions, 34–5, 50–1, 132, 142, 148
Bretton Woods, 4, 167, 172
'Bubble' explanation, 10, 17–18
Bullion Committee (1810), 62

Canada, Bank of, 175, 178
Canadian 'free banking', 22–3, 39, 47, 49, 91, 117, 154
Capital ratios, 20–1, 59–60, 189
Central bank discretion, 4, 164–5, 183, 195
Central banking, 2, 10, 117, 160–78, 184–5

Central banking trading losses, 69, 81
Charles II, 118
Chartalism, 111, 162, 166, 176–7
Chinese 'free banking', 117
Clearing-house Associations, 21, 144
Clearing-house loan certificates, 144, 150–1
Clearing System (Deposit), 20
Clearing System (Note), 44–6, 53, 122, 124–6, 131, 155–6
Coase Theorem, 103
Convertibility, 3, 6–8, 48, 61–5, 88, 95–6, 105, 120, 122, 154–7
  indirect, 107
Convertibility contract, 8, 28
  See also Option clauses
Counterfeiting, 12, 106, 108
Currency (convertible), 11, 85, 88, 90–1, 96
Currency (fiat), 9, 85, 88, 90, 160
Currency school, 64, 128, 129, 148

Deposit insurance, 11, 54–61, 188–9
  private, 58–9, 61
'Deposit run', 26–7, 35, 50
Depository Institutions, Deregulation and Monetary Control Act (1980), 180–1

Economies of scale, 6, 35, 90–1, 104
'Emergency currency', 20, 33, 144–5

See also Clearing-house loan
  certificates
England, Bank of, 12, 23, 38–9,
  47, 108, 118–20, 124–30,
  152–4, 160, 190
  privileges of, 118–19, 124–30
  suspension of, 119–20
European Central Bank, 182–3,
  195
Extended shareholder liability, 58,
  60, 118, 158, 189
Externalities: confidence, 11, 87–9
  information, 11, 19–23, 89
  macroeconomic, 11, 75–77
  transaction costs, 11, 86, 103–4

Failure resolution, 51–2
Federal Deposit Insurance
  Corporation (FDIC), 25, 37,
  57, 170–1, 177
Federal Reserve System, 13, 145,
  164, 168–72, 177
Federal Savings and Loan
  Insurance Corporation
  (FSLIC), 37, 49
First Amendment (to US
  Constitution), 192
First World War, 3, 13, 162–3
France, Bank of, 165
Fraud, 15, 149
'Free bank' failures (US), 38,
  135–41
Free banking, 1, 6, 9, 44, 61–5,
  124–5, 146–8, 175, 184–5,
  195
Free banking controversy:
  Britain, 2, 12, 14, 126–30, 147–8
  France, 2, 14
  USA, 2, 14
Free banking school (Britain),
  14–15, 61, 63–5, 125–30
Free trade, 2, 52
French 'free banking', 117

General Agreement on Tariffs and
  Trade, 173
Glass–Steagall Act, 51
  See also National Banking Act
  (1933)

Gold standard, 3, 13, 72, 160–6,
  180, 183
Great Depression, 13, 160, 168–72,
  176–8
Great Inflation, 160, 174–5
Great Society, 173

Hamilton, Alexander, 131

'Ideal' monetary system, 11,
  84–107
Illiquidity risk, 24–6
Information costs, 19
Incomplete information, 18–23,
  49–51, 82
Inflation, 3, 141, 163, 174–5, 186–7
Inflation – output trade-off, 4
Insolvency risk, 24
Interest ceilings, 20–1, 34–5, 189
Interest stabilization, 81
'Island story', 69–70, 72, 76

Keynesianism, 3–4, 13, 160,
  166–7, 173–5
Knapp, 176–7
  See also Chartalism
'Knowledge problem', 184–5

Laisser-faire, 2, 6, 10, 12, 116, 148,
  162–3
Laisser-faire banking system, *see*
  Laisser-faire monetary
  system
Laisser-faire monetary system, 1,
  31, 95, 106, 110, 116–17,
  157, 160
Legal tender, 12, 102–3, 110–12,
  188
Lender of last resort, 7, 23, 32,
  38–43, 52, 66, 71–2, 82, 134,
  155–6, 158, 181–2, 188
Liability insurance, 7, 36–8
  See also Deposit insurance,
  Safety fund
Liability insurance losses, 37
Lloyds, 59
'Lucas Critique', 71, 106

McFadden Act, 51
Medium of Account (MOA), 6, 9,
    11–12, 84–5, 92–103, 105,
    106–7, 109–11, 112, 114–15,
    158, 188–90, 193
Medium of Exchange (MOE), 6,
    11–12, 15, 17, 84–95, 98,
    100–2, 105, 107, 109–10, 163
Medium of Redemption (MOR),
    95–6, 98, 100, 104, 106–7,
    156
Monetarism, 174–5, 177
Monetary growth rules, 70–2,
    179–80, 183, 185–6
Monetary policy, 4–5, 11, 164,
    167, 172–6, 178
    politicised, 179–87
    as taxation, 11, 78–81
Monetary policy problem, 13,
    66–8, 167, 175, 187
Monetary third-party effects, 15
Money surprises, 178
'Moral suasion', 43

National Banking Act (1933), 35,
    51, 170, 177–8, 189
National Banking Acts (1863,
    1864), 141, 150
National banking system, 12,
    141–5, 150, 169
National Monetary Commission,
    145
Natural monopoly, 6, 11, 84–5,
    90–92, 104
North America, Bank of, 131
Note monopoly, 2–3, 11, 32–3, 39,
    47, 52–3, 66–83, 95–6
'Note run', 26–31, 33

One hundred per cent reserve
    banking, 25–6
Option clauses, 15, 18, 28–31, 50,
    119, 146
Over-issue, 10, 32, 43–8, 63–5,
    125–6

Pareto optimality, 64–5, 68–9, 113
Paterson, William, 118
'Policy activism', 3
Political Economy Club, 125
Price stabilisation rules, 72–3, 162,
    180
Public choice, 5, 175
'Public good' arguments, 41, 52–3,
    85

Rational expectations, 5, 175
'Real bills' doctrine, 11, 60–5, 147
Reconstruction Finance
    Corporation (RFC), 171, 177
Regulators' inability to control
    risk taking, 43–4
Regulatory explanation, 23–44
Reichsbank, 53
Reserve ratios, 20–1, 155, 158,
    172, 189
'Residual monetary power', 195
Resource costs, 15, 88–9
Restriction period, 8, 108
Royal Bank of Scotland, 52, 120–2

'Safe and sound banking', 42, 172
Safety fund, 37, 140, 150
Scotland, Bank of, 52, 120–2
Scottish 'free banking', 2, 12, 22–3,
    39, 47, 49, 91, 120–4, 152–8
Scottish One Pound Note, 14, 123
Second World War, 13, 172
Secondary markets, 19–22
'Separation of functions', 12,
    109–10
Six-Partner Rule, 118–19
Small note ban, 14, 119
Subordinated debt, 57, 60
Suffolk system, 21, 139–41, 150
Swedish 'free banking', 22–3, 39,
    47, 91, 117, 154, 157–8
Swiss 'free banking', 117, 158

Time consistency, 11, 73–5

Unemployment, 166–7, 172
Unit of account, 6, 9, 84, 92
United States, (First) Bank of the,
  131
(Second) Bank of the, 133–4
Civil War, 12, 33, 38, 57, 141,
  150

'free banking', 12, 39, 47,
  135–41, 148

Vietnam War, 173

William III, 119